MEXICAN CHICAGO

GABRIELA F. ARREDONDO

Mexican Chicago

RACE, IDENTITY, AND

NATION, 1916–39

UNIVERSITY OF ILLINOIS PRESS

URBANA AND CHICAGO

Library of Congress Cataloging-in-Publication Data
Arredondo, Gabriela F.
Mexican Chicago : race, identity, and nation, 1916–39 /
Gabriela F. Arredondo.
p.   cm. — (Statue of Liberty-Ellis Island Centennial series)
Includes bibliographical references and index.
ISBN-13 978-0-252-03269-1 (cloth : alk. paper)
ISBN-10 0-252-03269-1 (cloth : alk. paper)
ISBN-13 978-0-252-07497-4 (pbk. : alk. paper)
ISBN-10 0-252-07497-1 (pbk. : alk. paper)
1. Mexican Americans—Illinois—Chicago—Social conditions—
20th century. 2. Mexican Americans—Race identity—Illinois—
Chicago—History—20th century. 3. Mexican Americans—
Illinois—Chicago—Ethnic identity—History—20th century.
4. Immigrants—Illinois—Chicago—Social conditions—
20th century. 5. Chicago (Ill.)—Race relations—History—20th
century. 6. Chicago (Ill.)—Ethnic relations—History—20th
century.
I.Title.
F548.9.M5A77   2008
305.868'720773110904—dc22   2007015801

GABRIELA F. ARREDONDO

Mexican Chicago

RACE, IDENTITY, AND

NATION, 1916–39

UNIVERSITY OF ILLINOIS PRESS

URBANA AND CHICAGO

Library of Congress Cataloging-in-Publication Data
Arredondo, Gabriela F.
Mexican Chicago : race, identity, and nation, 1916–39 /
Gabriela F. Arredondo.
p.   cm. — (Statue of Liberty-Ellis Island Centennial series)
Includes bibliographical references and index.
ISBN-13 978-0-252-03269-1 (cloth : alk. paper)
ISBN-10 0-252-03269-1 (cloth : alk. paper)
ISBN-13 978-0-252-07497-4 (pbk. : alk. paper)
ISBN-10 0-252-07497-1 (pbk. : alk. paper)
1. Mexican Americans—Illinois—Chicago—Social conditions—
20th century. 2. Mexican Americans—Race identity—Illinois—
Chicago—History—20th century. 3. Mexican Americans—
Illinois—Chicago—Ethnic identity—History—20th century.
4. Immigrants—Illinois—Chicago—Social conditions—
20th century. 5. Chicago (Ill.)—Race relations—History—20th
century. 6. Chicago (Ill.)—Ethnic relations—History—20th
century.
I. Title.
F548.9.M5A77   2008
305.868'720773110904—dc22   2007015801

To Noé Tomás

As he grows up, may he come to appreciate
how much our lives are connected to
and enriched by those who went before us.

Contents

Acknowledgments

Much like child rearing, researching and writing a book truly takes a village. I must first acknowledge the many generous people who took the time to share their memories and experiences of Chicago "back then," especially Jesse Escalante and Agapita Flores. Even as their words helped bridge the years and bring alive an era long past, many served as a painful reminder of how much further we as a nation still have to travel in our quest to eliminate racism.

This project was born and guided through its infancy at the University of Chicago. During my graduate-school years there, I was fortunate to study with an inspiring group of outstanding scholars, including Kathleen Conzen, Thomas Holt, George Chauncey, and, from afar, George Sánchez. Kathy Conzen's incisive critiques, quiet encouragement, and patient friendship shaped this work in fundamental ways.

I was lucky to meet Vicki Ruiz even before I went to Chicago. Over the years, she has taught me what it means to be a true mentor: advising, challenging, and encouraging me all along the way. She has a gift for setting the bar very high and then guiding and inspiring her mentees to reach above and beyond it. In the process, she has remained a staunch advocate and has become an esteemed friend.

I owe a great debt to several other scholars who took me under their intellectual and political wings early on in my career: Bob Cherny, Bill Deverell, Neil Foley, David Gutiérrez, Bill Issel, Barbara Loomis, Nancy Mirabál, and David Roediger. Neil Foley and David Gutiérrez have remained constant sources of inspiration and advice, never fearing to ask hard questions or to challenge me to seek complex answers and always willing to debate politics or history for hours on end.

As this project matured and developed into a book, I benefited from the insights, comments, support, and good humor of many other superb colleagues and friends, including Barbara Berglund, Ned Blackhawk, Kathy Brosnan, Ernie Chávez, John Chávez, Yolanda Chávez-Leyva, Guillemo Delgado, Jonathan Fox, Ramón Gutiérrez, Jonathan Keyes, Geoff Klingsporn, Chad Heap, Susanne Jonas, Russ Kazal, Norma Klahn, Lydia Otero, Theresa Mah, Curtis Márez, Natalia Molina, Olga Nájera-Ramírez, Lorena Oropeza, Peggy Pascoe, Manuel Pastor, Steve Pitti, Sylvia Pedraza, Patricia Pessar, Eric Porter, Catherine Ramírez, Virginia Sánchez-Korrol, Gingy Scharff, Zaragosa Vargas, Carmen Whalen, Michael Willrich, and Pat Zavella.

Several brave and generous souls read drafts of chapters and offered thoughtful and extensive feedback that transformed this book in critical ways, including Fernando Alanís Enciso, Patricia Cooper, Matt Garciá, Bill George, David Gutiérrez, Beth Haas, Vicki Ruiz, Alexandra Stern, and Joe Trotter.

For the last several years, I have had the extraordinary pleasure of working among incredible colleagues in the Chicano Latino Research Center and the Latin American and Latina/o Studies Department at the University of California at Santa Cruz. This vital, dynamic, and inspiring community of scholars has provided the ideal environment in which to learn and grow. I am grateful also to my able and dedicated research assistants: Chris Kortright, Anica Montes-Acosta, Emma Estrada Lukin, Emma Smith, Michelle Stewart, and especially Adrián Flores, who has lived longest with this project. I also have had the pleasure of getting to know some excellent young scholars, including Maricela Chávez, Lilia Fernández, Michael Innis-Jiménez, Chelsey Juarez, Anne Martínez, Julia Mendoza, Christina Morales, Monica Perales, Gina Marie Pitti, Felicity Schaeffer-Grabiel, and Maureen Turnbull. I look forward to learning more from them and their exciting work in the future.

I am fortunate to count some amazing colleagues among my closest friends. Despite being scattered all over the country, they have enriched this project immensely: José Alamillo, Matt García, Michelle Molina, María Montoya, Doug Sackman, and Alex Stern.

The late Archie Motley at the Chicago Historical Society embodied the essence of the true archivist: incredibly knowledgeable, generous, intellectually curious, and always quick with a smile or a phone call to share one more thing he happened to run across. I am also greatly indebted to Scott Forsythe and the able staff at the National Archives and Records Administration, Great Lakes Region; Peter Alter at the Chicago Historical Society; Theresa Salazar of the Bancroft Library at the University of California at Berkeley; Margo Gutiérrez of the Benson Latin American Collection at the University of Texas at Austin; Les O'Rear at the Illinois Labor History Society; the staffs at the Special Collections of the Regenstein Library at the University of Chicago, the Special Collections at the University of Illinois at Chicago, the Illinois Historical Society in Springfield, the Illinois Regional Archives Depository in Springfield, and at the Wisconsin Historical Society in Madison. Thanks also to the archivists at the Archivo Histórico de la Secretaria de Relaciónes Exteriores and at the Archivo de Calles y Torreblanco in Mexico City. The staff at the Inter-Library Loan office in McHenry Library at the University of California at Santa Cruz worked diligently to track down obscure sources for me.

Joan Catapano at the University of Illinois Press has been a wonderful editor, guiding me deftly through the various stages and pitfalls of publication, always with good humor and patience. Vicki Ruiz, per usual, has gone beyond the call of duty as series editor, providing line-edited drafts of my entire manuscript—twice! To her and the anonymous readers for the University of Illinois Press, I am truly grateful for their comments.

This project benefited from generous financial assistance from many sources. A fellowship from the Committee on Institutional Cooperation largely made my graduate education possible. I am proud to have been part of a program so committed to the advancement of students of color. My research travels were funded also by a Mellon Travel Grant from the University of Chicago, a Committee on Research Grant from the University of California at Santa Cruz, a Faculty Research Grant from the Chicano Latino Research Center, and Divisional Research Awards from the Social Science Division at the University of California at Santa Cruz. Leave time granted by my department and a Pre-tenure Faculty Award from the Division of Social Sciences enabled me to focus on writing.

Without the encouragement, understanding, comfort, and advice of my family, I could not have undertaken or completed this project. Mis papás, Humberto Zamora Arredondo and Liza Flannery Arredondo, continue to teach me about dedication to education, civil rights, and ideals even in the face of often disheartening political times. I have always delighted in the joy my padrinos, Leopoldo and Lourdes Rosas, bring to life, and I am lucky to know such generous people. I am immensely proud of my hermanito, Nicolás, and my cuñada, Sarah, and their accomplishments. I look forward to the day when our lives don't keep us at opposite ends of the continent. Although they did not live to see the completion of this book, mis abuelitos, Hortencia Zamora Arredondo and Praxediz

Martínez Arredondo, animate every page. It is their strength in the face of extreme odds, their triumph over poverty and racial discrimination, and their dedication to family and education that kept me working and believing I could write this book.

My deepest appreciation is to Bill George. I am blessed to have found such an incredible person and am eternally thankful that he has chosen to spend his life with me. During the writing of this book, we welcomed Noé Tomás, our son, into this world. He brings us tremendous joy, and his smile every morning helps remind me what's truly important.

In the final stages of this project, I was diagnosed with cancer. After a year of chemotherapy, three surgeries, and eight weeks of intensive radiation and major burns, I'm happy to say that I'm recovering well and am hopeful for the future. This surely would not have been possible without the incredible support and truly humbling generosity of my family, friends, and colleagues. I am forever grateful. I look forward to guiding Noé as he grows up and to growing very old, with Bill at my side.

And finally, I'd like to thank Carolyn Helfman, my dedicated elementary-school teacher who sincerely believed this little Mexican girl really could learn English. ¡Si se puede!

¡Adelante!

Much abbreviated and earlier versions of chapters 2 and 5 were published elsewhere: "Navigating Ethno-Racial Currents: Mexicans in Chicago, 1916–1939," *Journal of Urban History* 30.3 (Spring 2004): 399–427; "Cartographies of Americanisms: Possibilities for Transnational Identities, Chicago, 1916–1939," in *Geographies of Latinidad: Mapping Latina/o Studies into the Twenty-First Century,* ed. Matt García and Angarad Valdívia (Durham, N.C.: Duke University Press, forthcoming).

Introduction

"You're not Mexican," taunted the children. "You can't be—you're not dark enough." "Yeah, we should know. Our gardener is Mexican." I have carried that painful schoolyard encounter with me ever since. Back then, I did not even have the language to react to such taunts. Since we had just moved to Texas from Mexico, I was still learning English. Even if I had known more English, however, I doubt I would have known how to react. At that young age, all I knew was that I had just moved from the only home I had ever known and was trying to navigate a foreign world in a new language. I knew I was Mexican and had never been told otherwise. Nor had I ever considered what it really meant to be Mexican—until I was out of Mexico.

Certainly I have not been alone in this. Indeed, if there is anything shared in the experiences of Mexican immigrants to the United States, it lies in the forced realization of one's place, one's identity, one's relation to others from Mexico, and how those elements are negotiated in the particular circumstances of the moment. This study is an exploration into these questions. What does it mean to be Mexican at various historical moments? How is that meaning constructed, and what are the consequences of "being Mexican"? Growing up, I gradually realized that that schoolyard encounter would be the first of many such battles to come. In learning to deal with their recurrence I have remained agonizingly fascinated with their existence, with how other Mexicans have grappled with these questions, and with what is revealed and can be learned about the greater society in which we live when examining their implications and consequences.

Over the years, I have come to understand some of the ignorance be-hind those children's words. And I have gained English and the knowledge necessary to explore and discuss questions of identity, race, class, ethnic-ity, and nation. I grew up a middle-class Mexican girl in Mexico and a middle-class Mexican woman in Texas. Needless to say, being Mexican, middle-class, and female in Mexico City and Texas in those years carried very different meanings and consequences. Mexico's history of racial ide-ology and practice is more gradated than that of the United States, and the country's legacy of European colonization and conquest has rendered much of the population highly variegated. Mexicans run the gamut from "white" to "brown" to "black."

It was only when we settled in the United States that I became the child of an interracial union (what was considered miscegenation in much of the United States when my parents married). My "Anglo" mother and "Mexican" father fell in love on the South Side of Chicago and moved shortly thereafter to Mexico City. After years of hearing countless tales of the Windy City, I leapt at the opportunity to live there myself and study it up-close. I went into the Ph.D. program in history at the University of Chicago, knowing that I wanted to write on Mexican Chicago.

In the broadest sense, this project is an examination of lived expe-riences and how people have understood and given meaning to them. My focus on race, identity, and nation is intended to problematize the historical constructions of Mexicanidad (or Mexicanness) and to inter-rogate narratives of Americanization while highlighting the gendered differences in social and cultural processes of racial definition. During the interwar period, systems of racial classification and the generation of meaning around race in Mexico and the United States varied notably; yet, both countries also held striking similarities.

In the early twentieth century, ideologies of racial democracy were powerful in the United States, Mexico, and Latin America more gener-ally. In the United States, widespread confidence in the merits of the "melting pot" fostered assimilationist practices that seemingly were color-blind.[1] Yet, equally strong segregationist sensibilities and restric-tive immigration laws helped to consolidate European ethnic groups as "white" while consigning Mexicans and Asians to racial otherness.[2] Like assimilationism in the United States, *mestizaje* in Mexico tried to func-tion as a color-blind means of unifying a diverse population. *Mestizaje,* however, was more pointedly about the project of nation building because of Mexico's postrevolutionary context. Throughout the 1920s and 1930s, *mestizo* nationalism touted racial hybridity even as it privileged Euro-pean whites and marginalized *indios*, blacks, and Asians.[3] *Mestizaje* also operated through ideas about modernity and backwardness that further informed the project of nation building.[4]

Both ideologies, however, functioned as national signifiers of future homogeneity predicated on original difference: assimilationism sought to create Americans, and *mestizaje* sought to create Mexicans. Both implied erasure of difference even as they exhibited similar anxieties about the dangers of race mixing.[5] Both rested on hierarchical notions of race despite their seeming advocacy of racial democracy or even racial neutrality.

Mexicans traversed this rough terrain and negotiated a myriad of situational identities. Like Mexicans in other parts of the United States during the early twentieth century, Mexicans in Chicago wrestled with the paradox of resisting essentialist racial hierarchies even as they lived and reinforced them in their everyday interactions. They learned the value of a certain kind of "whiteness" and its attendant imperatives of racialized exclusion. Filtered through their experiences in Mexico, many quickly understood how much more bifurcated divisions were between "white" and "black" in the United States. Coupled with their experiences in other parts of the country, they also internalized what the anthropologist Ronald Stutzman terms the real exclusion underlying the apparent inclusion.[6] That is, even the plasticity of Mexican racial positioning did not negate the real exclusions they experienced. The immigrant context of Chicago was critical to this process, as Mexicans dealt with Poles, Italians, Irish, Blacks, and others in their daily lives.[7] Nowhere were Mexicans the dominant group. Even when there were concentrations of Mexicans in a few city blocks, they mingled with neighbors from many other groups.[8] The ethno-racial dynamics of Chicago—namely, the presence of these groups and the strength of their individual group histories in the city—provided a distinct and fundamentally unique circumstance for Mexican settlement.

There are incredibly rich materials from contemporary sociologists, social workers, and others who worked among Mexican communities in Chicago. Many of these sources, however, reveal much more about the institutions and people who left the documents than about the Mexicans they wrote about. When read against the grain, however, these sources and a variety of other microscopic bits of evidence in archives, newspaper files, oral histories, case files, and manuscript collections reveal a much richer texture, and these people come alive.

In the southwestern United States, the constant influx of Mexican immigrants shaped and influenced the creation of social and cultural identities of older Mexican settlers. During this period, Mexicans in this area were divided between those who supported U.S. citizenship and cultural incorporation and those who worked toward the solidarity of all Mexican-origin people.[9] The situation in Chicago in the interwar years, however, shows at once how much this division depends on an older, settled community of Mexicans (which did not exist in Chicago until the late 1940s and 1950s) and also how much Mexican national political events and sensibilities were inseparable from such perspectives. Mexicans came to Chicago at a key moment in their history: during and after the revolutionary turmoil of the 1910s and 1920s.

Informed by the foundational theorizing of Michael Omi and Howard Winant on racial formation, I seek to portray what Martha Hodes calls "the workings of 'race,'" meaning the practices and processes that shape racial categorization and stratification.[10] At the same time, it is critical to acknowledge how multiply valenced the web of identification was in "becoming Mexican" in Chicago until World War II. That is, particular components surfaced in relation to social, material, and cultural conditions at specific moments in the experiences of Mexicans in the Windy City.[11] I endeavor to capture the interplay between the existence of differences within the Mexican population of Chicago's interwar years and the dynamics of their multiple social relations. This approach allows for acknowledging and understanding differential relationships among Mexicans while appreciating the broader dynamics mediating their social interactions.[12]

Identity remains a slippery subject. Nonetheless, I rely on Stuart Hall's view that "identities are the names we give to the different ways we are positioned by, and position ourselves within, the narrative of the past."[13] Through this project I strive to decipher how meaning is created in identity and takes on currency in everyday events, activities, and sentiments. I seek to provide insight into these larger questions in a particular site, at a specific historical moment: Chicago in the interwar period between 1916 and 1939.

Mexican women and men have lived in Chicago since at least the middle of World War I, yet scholars have only begun to study this history. The predominance of historical scholarship on Mexicans in the United States centers on the U.S. Southwest/Northern Mexico borderlands. Because those areas were once part of Mexico, the dynamics of ethno-racial contacts, notably Anglo-Mexican, already had long histories by the dawn of the twentieth century.[14] Thousands of Mexicans who came into Chicago during and immediately following the First World War, however, stepped into a new kind of ethnic and racial order, one very much under construction.

Perhaps the most remarkable early work on Mexicans in Chicago was the sociologist Paul S. Taylor's 1932 study (based on data gleaned from the late 1920s) of Chicago and the Calumet region.[15] Part of an eight-volume study covering much of the United States, volume 7 of *Mexican Labor* provides little analysis and offers instead snapshots of Mexican life ranging from labor to the movies, interspersed with interviews. After Taylor, there was a dearth of studies for the next forty years until the early 1970s. Writing in the spirit of Carey McWilliams, who had worked so diligently to bring the plight of the Mexican worker to a general audience, in 1976 Mark Reisler published *By the Sweat of Their Brow: Mexican Immigrant Labor in the United States, 1900–1940.*[16] Like Taylor, he studied Mexican workers in various parts of the United States and briefly covered the Chicago area.[17] Even thirty years later, this book remains current and informative.

With the 1970s came the emerging Chicano nationalist interest in the history of Mexicans in the United States. A few Chicano historians chose to focus on the Chicago area, known locally as Chicagoland. These scholars injected Mexicans into broader discussions of immigration history from which they had been absent. Early historians of Mexicans in the area tended to frame their work with the implicit assumption of eventual Mexican Americanization. By regarding Mexicans in the Midwest as "los desarraigados" (the uprooted), for instance, Gilbert Cárdenas explicitly tied his work into immigration historiography shaped by the much earlier work of Oscar Handlin.[18] Louise Año Nuevo Kerr's dissertation, "The Chicano Experience in Chicago, 1920–1970," has stood as the definitive history of Mexicans in Chicago for the last thirty years. Although never published as a book, it has had the influence of a monograph on at least two generations of scholars.

By the early 1990s, a handful of significant monographs emerged that focused on Mexicans in the Midwest. Dennis Valdes, Zaragosa Vargas, and Juan García examine Mexican immigration and the development of their communities from a regional perspective, to varying degrees touching on Mexican circumstances in Chicago.[19] However, Chicago is not their primary site of analysis. Their most significant contribution with regard to Chicago is in understanding the economic, labor, and migratory networks that drew and connected Mexicans to the greater Midwest.

Building on the work of later historians of Mexicans in the United States, such as Vicki L. Ruiz, George J. Sánchez, and David Gutiérrez, this project challenges static definitions of "American" and their under-lying assumptions of assimilation.[20] Ruiz's work on the cannery women of Monterey and her more recent work on Mexican women throughout the United States elegantly examines the lives of Mexican women and their experiences with varying forms of Americanism.[21] She has dem-onstrated how Mexican women understood and employed elements of Americanization in their life choices while interweaving other cultural elements and practices drawn from their connections to Mexico. Ruiz clarifies this process of women's selective participation and argues that Americanization is a gendered process, experienced differently by women and men. At heart, Ruiz's work provides a fuller recounting of "how women make meaning in their own lives and in the lives of others."[22]

In his work on Mexicans in Los Angeles, Sánchez illustrates that "be-coming American" is a dynamic process that does not occur on a linear trajectory, as previously expected. More importantly, he shatters long-standing beliefs that immigrant acculturation necessarily brought upward mobility. Gutiérrez challenges the dichotomy of "alien" and "citizen" to highlight the fundamental importance of ongoing cross-border migrations to the structuring of Mexican ethnic identities in the twentieth century. In doing so, he not only elucidates the distinctiveness of Mexican eth-nicity but also makes clear how inadequate ethnicity theories have been for explaining the Mexican experience in the United States. This project builds on Gutiérrez's work to examine the significance of citizenship, nationhood, and "alien-ness" in people's daily lives.

Ethnicity theories have structured much of the immigration histori-ography on Chicago, and there too they have been woefully inadequate for explaining the Mexican immigrant experience. The inadequacies of ethnicity models stem from their foundation in studies of European groups. Scholars generally discuss ethnic groups in Chicago as initially living in isolated neighborhoods who developed relatively tight-knit communities centered on cultural institutions like the family.[23] These groups experienced conflicts and divisions but ultimately worked their ways into American life, usually through combinations of mass cul-ture, the strength of ethnic allegiances (and ties to previously migrated groups), labor unionization, or electoral politics. Americanness was, in turn, defined by such markers as civic incorporation (and implied English-language acquisition and U.S. citizenship), growing labor power, rising home ownership, and increased level of education. Each of these elements operated as a means to measure the degree of progress various ethnic groups had made toward Americanization. Other historiographic works have shared the biases of ethnicity theories and contemporary expectations of Americanization in their examinations of cross-ethnic coalitions and union movements.[24] Lizabeth Cohen's *Making a New Deal*, for instance, paints Mexicans as simply one of many ethnic groups working toward multi-ethnic unions.

As they arrived in Chicago, Mexicans discovered a city within which several group identities and positions were being concurrently negotiated, alongside those of older immigrants. This was particularly true of the areas in which the majority of Mexicans settled: the Near West Side, Packingtown/Back-of-the-Yards, and South Chicago. Unlike Mexicans of the U.S. Southwest, Mexicans in Chicago did share many aspects of European immigrant experience. Like their Polish and Italian neighbors, for instance, Mexicans had left their homeland and lived in an extraordinary urban space. The majority were laborers, did not speak much English, and did not hold U.S. citizenship. Consequently, when they settled among similarly profiled Polish and Italian immigrants, it was not unreasonable to expect that they would share similar processes of assimilation, of "becoming American."

This monograph, however, contends that Mexicans in Chicago were not simply another ethnic group working to be assimilated into a city with a long history of incorporating newcomers. Rather, because of their experiences with racializing prejudice in their everyday lives through interactions with several groups, including Polish, Italian, Irish, and Black residents, and because of their own responses to such discrimination emerging from a revolutionary and postrevolutionary context, Mexicans in Chicago during this period became Mexican. That is, through myriad experiences in their daily lives, Mexicans fought the current of pejorative qualities ascribed to "being Mexican" by constructing their own Mexicanness to battle anti-Mexican prejudices. This process of racialization highlights the distinctiveness of their situation.

Chicago in the 1920s was a city in racial turmoil. Waves of recent eastern and southern European immigrants flowed into older, more settled groups and crashed on the crest of the Great Migration of southern Blacks from Mississippi, Alabama, and Arkansas. Mexicans arriving in Chicago were immediately swept into this tumult, as all these peoples worked through meanings of white and black that were at once destabilized by the turbulence and reinvigorated by nativist reactions to the upheaval. Indeed, much of this framing tied national identity to race in ways at once familiar yet also unrecognizable from their own experiences during and following the Mexican Revolution. Emerging from revolutionary strife and subsequent surges of Mexican nationalism (including the Cristero rebellions), these women and men wrestled with incongruous processes of racialization, nation-state formations, and their own iden-titification.

Mexican notions of racial categories were much more variegated than those in the United States. Mexico never had the one-drop rule (in which one drop of black blood made one black) and thus did not share in the United States' history of dichotomized white/black racial distinctions.[25] Particularly during and following the revolutionary years of the 1910s and 1920s, categorical gradations acknowledged racial mixtures through *mestizaje* and glorified the indigenous, the *indio,* while post-revolution-ary actors searched for ways to actualize an imagined *raza cosmica.*[26] In spite of these nuances, however, the fundamental racial rubric in Mexico during this era still preserved the most power and wealth for the whitest, the least for the darkest. After centuries of European imperialism and conquest, certainly Mexicans were familiar with the general contours of racial coding they encountered in Chicago, which in many ways explains their conflation of "European" and "white," something that other im-migrant groups seemed less inclined to do.[27]

Once in Chicago, Mexicans quickly learned that the critical deter-minant of one's place in the ethno-racial orders hinged on "being white." This did not mean simply being white in an essentialized form but rather included phenotypical interpolations of whiteness in terms of "looks," including skin color and hair color, style, and texture. This formulation was complicated by the fact that "being white" could cover the perfor-mance of whiteness through modes of dress, speech, or even classification by outsiders. Establishing their whiteness was critical to establishing "belonging."[28] Thus, they found themselves struggling alongside other immigrant groups with their own histories and trajectories of adjust-ment to claim their own place and identity in the ethno-racial orders of Chicago.[29]

As Mexicans navigated these currents in their daily lives, they also struggled with pressures by social workers, employers, politicians, so-cial scientists, and others to solidify an insular brand of Americanism in which "becoming American" involved requirements Mexicans could not or would not fulfill. Ranging from attainment of U.S. citizenship to English proficiency to eating specific foods, Americanization in Chicago also involved a continuing subtext of racialization that turned primarily on whiteness. As Mexicans discovered, full integration required a process of "whitening" that was read through markers like skin color, hair color, citizenship, dress, and language.

Over the course of the 1920s and 1930s, Mexicans increasingly dis-covered that they were not whitening on the model of their European neighbors. Efforts to mark their whiteness, elbowing their ethnic neighbors for position, only served to distinguish them from Blacks. Through the resolutions of repeated conflicts with European immigrants and growing discriminatory practices against them at the hands of those groups, Mexicans experienced separation and segregation that proved the inadequacies of melting-pot practices and that ultimately marked them as nonwhite racial others.

In the 1930s, the process of racialization took on new components for Mexicans. The infrastructure set up to combat the Depression increasingly segregated Mexicans from other groups. The strains of the economic Depression accelerated impulses toward discrimination from their ethnic neighbors. European ethnics gradually did assimilate on an insular model of Americanization, acquiring positions in significant structures that regulated the daily life of Mexicans, ranging from landlords and employers to police to courts. As these Europeans climbed the ethnic hierarchies, however, Mexicans remained peripheral. In addition, the hardship conditions of the early 1930s heightened competition for vastly reduced numbers of jobs and facilitated preferential treatment of European ethnics over Mexicans.

Understandably, the dynamism of Mexican life in Chicago during this period meant that they, like their ethnic neighbors, faced many sources of conflict and strong pressures to assimilate. Yet, given the context of forced deportations of Mexicans (first in the recession of 1921–22 and later in the 1930s) and federal repatriation programs to Mexico (two phases: 1929–33 and 1933–37), the *consequences* of such discord were much more severe for Mexicans than for European immigrant groups in Chicago. Such events, even fear of such reprisal, only fortified Mexican ambiguity toward the permanency of their lives in Chicago. Few Mexicans made a commitment to persisting in Chicago, and the relative ease of traveling back and forth to Mexico helped to strengthen this view. More importantly, however, whatever impulses Mexicans did have toward staying were increasingly stymied by growing levels of intolerance and discrimination against them in Chicago.

Consequently, unlike their European neighbors during this period and contrary to current immigration historiography, this work argues that most Mexicans chose to participate in activities from parades to unions in an effort to fortify themselves against rising anti-Mexican bigotry. In fact, Mexicans gained little incentive or opportunity for empowerment typically used by European ethnics. They hardly participated in electoral politics, nor did they seek U.S. citizenship to further their civic incorporation. Mexicans instead were concerned primarily with unifying themselves against the growing prejudice they experienced. Parades, festivals, celebrations, and sports teams became some of the tools of survival wielded against intensifying anti-Mexican sentiments.

By turning inward in attempts to unify and thereby strengthen their position in Chicago, Mexicans also highlighted the tremendous differences among themselves. Furthermore, efforts at unity revealed internal wounds created by those external conflicts fought in daily life. The inability of Mexicans to fuse those rifts further attested to the damage wrought by pressures to incorporate along expected trajectories. The growing demands for proof of U.S. citizenship in many facets of daily life, from employment to relief aid, further minimized opportunities for them. Ultimately, the repatriation of Mexicans—and more significantly, the threat of forcible deportation—combined with their ambivalence toward the permanency of their stays in Chicago, crushing any aspirations they may have held of belonging.

In spite of internal striations, their inward turn to unify against discrimination did give rise to a fragile sense of Mexicanidad, a sense of Mexican nationalism with a Chicago flavor. Unlike the "Mexican Americans" of the Southwest, this Mexicanidad was tied much more to postrevolutionary events in Mexico than to claiming space within their cities. Ironically, it was the circumstances of Chicago that fostered this sensibility and fed its vitality. Nowhere in Chicago did Mexicans have the cultural or demographic concentration to make significant inroads into Chicago's ethnic orders. Indeed, theirs was not an ethnic identity designed to rise into Chicago's Americanized ethnic social orders. Rather, Mexicanidad was about carving a space for their own survival. Emerging from the context of nationalist Mexico, their nascent "common peoplehood" was an identity forged in response to the rise of anti-Mexican sentiments with tools drawn from a collectively imagined Mexico. In a way, these Mexicans constructed an essentialized strategic identity that spoke to the realities of racial formation and exclusion despite instances of apparent inclusion. As Ann Stoler argues, "[A] notion of essence does not necessarily rest on immovable parts but on the strategic inclusion of different attributes, of a changing constellation of features and a changing weighing of them," a process similar to what Thomas C. Holt describes as "race marking."[30]

By the end of the 1930s, "Mexican" in Chicago meant not only not-assimilable but also not-American and "alien." The outbreak of war in Europe in 1939, its effects on their Polish and Italian neighbors, along with the eventual involvement of Mexico and the United States once again reconfigured the social and political landscape that Mexicans traveled. Participation in the war effort by those on "este lado" (this side of the U.S.–Mexico border) and the establishment of "guest worker" arrangements with Mexico (also known as the Bracero Programs) recast the possibilities for Mexican Americanization. The end of Mexico's nationalist period in 1940, with the departure of Lázaro Cárdenas and the growing power of Mexican civic and civil rights groups in the United States, further shifted the conditions of Mexican life in Chicago.

This book captures a significant moment in the histories of Mexicans in the United States specifically and in the histories of migrants more generally. Fundamentally multivalent, this project focuses on Mexican experiences while underscoring the significance of other ethnic groups with whom Mexicans interacted on a daily basis. It highlights Mexican perspectives of everyday interactions with these groups and with each other while studying the relationship of everyday experiences to the processes of racial, ethnic, and national identity formation as Mexicans in Chicago "became Mexican."

Overview of Chapters

Chapter 1 surveys the Mexican and Texan contexts from which Chicago's Mexicans emerged by following various paths taken in their migrations to Chicago. Young men and, surprisingly, young women out for an adventure were interlaced throughout these waves of Mexican migration to Chicago. The chapter chronicles the later years of the Mexican Revolution and the subsequent nationalist projects through the accounts and experiences of Mexicans who settled in Chicago. In paying close attention to the words of Mexicans themselves, the work makes clear that these people were not simply refugees from the violence and unrest. In choosing to come north, these Mexicans took advantage of economic, social, and personal opportunities that continued a process of modernization and urbanization already under way in Mexico.

Chapter 2 captures the scene in Chicago during the interwar period by mapping the tumultuous mix of peoples among whom Mexicans settled. Mexicans lived and worked with Poles, Italians, and African Americans along with groups of older immigrants like earlier waves of Poles and Irish. Mexicans' everyday experiences with these groups fundamentally shaped their possibilities, opportunities, and perceptions of life in Chicago. The chapter focuses on several sites in the daily lives of Mexican men and women where they experienced racializing incidents that shaped their settlement in and adjustment to Chicago. It moves through five zones of contact: 1) settlement and housing, 2) work and labor relations, 3) police relations, 4) heterosocial relations, and 5) commercial relations.

Each provides a critical thread in the evolving tapestry of Mexican racial positioning in Chicago before World War II. Taken together, they reveal how ethno-racial dynamics in Chicago were much more complex than contemporaries and historians have suggested.

Chapter 3 frames the expected trajectory of "assimilation" Mexicans faced from social workers, social scientists, and politicians and draws the contours of the insular brand of Americanism forming in Chicago and in the United States as a whole. Over the course of this period, it became increasingly clear that Mexicans were not assimilating on the trajectory set by their European neighbors. The "Mexican Problem" turned on the various consequences of disenfranchisement and the extent to which Mexicans did not see U.S. citizenship as a tool for empowerment. Concurrently, rising anti-Mexican prejudice continued to infuse "being Mexican" with pejorative connotations even as Mexicans refused to change flags.

The chapter explores several possible factors shaping this indifference to taking out U.S. citizenship papers, focusing particularly on the explanations of Mexicans themselves. Like some of their ethnic neighbors, Mexicans expected that their stay in Chicago would be temporary. The relative geographic proximity of Mexico, however, made this expectation somewhat realistic. Perhaps more significantly, their experiences with growing prejudices against them convinced many Mexicans that their "looks" singled them out as other. Many saw changing their citizenship as futile, since, as they said, their looks would not be changed by their nationality. Thus the core issues for Mexicans centered on a process of racialization that marked their looks in pejorative terms, singling them out as other and reinforcing their own sense of being alien.

The continued intergroup conflicts and growing prejudice against them served to stratify Mexican populations still further. Chapter 4 examines these internal striations, the divisions that erupted from the conflicted relationships Mexicans had with Americanism, with each other, and with their varied attempts to adapt. The chapter explores the gendered terrains of life in Chicago, specifically highlighting several aspects of social relations between Mexican women and men. It addresses the diversity of the Mexican population in Chicago and clarifies the elements that divided the population. Shifting gender norms and rising mass culture further demarcated the Mexican population along lines of generation, language, and looks.

Emanating through the fractious diversities of the Mexican population that emerge in this chapter were ever-louder calls for Mexicans to unify against growing discrimination. This attempt to shift people's energy into solidifying "the Mexican community" only served to exacerbate already evident differences of class, origin, gender, education, language, race, opportunity, and means. Heightened awareness of the diversity of the Mexican populations in Chicago complicated their calls for unity against discrimination, particularly as individuals experienced differing levels of prejudice. Many women spoke of liking their situation in Chicago better than that they had known in Mexico, while many men missed their lives in Mexico and bemoaned the "freedom" of women in the United States. Their situations were complicated by the presence of a wide variety of Latin Americans (ranging from Colombians to Cubans) living and working amidst the Mexicans of Chicago. A move familiar in the histories of Mexicans in the U.S. Southwest was to claim Spanishness. In the context of Chicago, however, adopting such an identity was more problematic in the face of a visible population of Spaniards.

As in Mexico, Mexicans deployed the tools of postrevolutionary nationalism to fashion a collectively imagined historical past in an effort to unify the incredibly heterogeneous population. In Chicago, however, Mexicans also wielded these tools to combat rising discrimination. Chapter 5 opens with a discussion of *lo mexicano* in Mexico and its gendered-male components, working through nationalist ideologies of *indigenismo* and *mestizaje* and the ways they contributed to visions of the patriarchal national subject. With this groundwork laid, it follows key players in Mexico on their visits to Chicago. The chapter focuses on the experiences of Mexicans in Chicago and how various actors contributed to expressions of *lo mexicano*, but in a Chicago context. What results from these expressions is an identity that Mexicans related to but that was distinct from *lo mexicano* as constructed in Mexico.

In Chicago, this Mexicanidad emerged as a fragile but proud identity that wove together elements of postrevolutionary Mexican nationalism and nostalgic conservative histories of "México Lindo" (Beautiful Mexico) with the acknowledgment of ever-present anti-Mexican biases.[31] It took the negative racialized connotations that "Mexican" increasingly carried in Chicago and turned them on their head by celebrating Mexican identity. Mexicans strategically embraced a somewhat essentialized identity in their search for survival. Played out in Chicago against a Latin American backdrop, Mexicanidad laid the groundwork for explaining and sharing common experiences and commonly expressed goals.

By 1939, Mexicans emerged with a tenuous though tangible sense of Mexicanidad that accepted its element of "foreignness," no longer attempting to "become American" on the contemporary model of assimilation. The outbreak of war in Europe in 1939 shifted the attentions of many of Chicago's Euro-ethnics, and the push to Americanize immigrants lost steam. The growing force of the labor unions coupled with the surging demands for wartime labor shattered their fragile group cohesion. The Bracero Programs once again opened the spigots to new waves of Mexican migrations to Chicago. The influx of new Mexicans surely must have begun to delineate the "old-timers" from the new arrivals, while calls to participate in the war effort again opened new possibilities for Mexicans to identify with and define their participation in Americanism.

1   Al Norte

Economic and social unrest in Mexico, coupled with economic opportunities and relative prosperity in the United States, fueled the desires of Mexican men and women to leave Mexico and go *al norte* during the 1910s and 1920s. Mexicans who came to Chicago represented a mix of working- and middle-class laborers, merchants, and small landowners and farmers. In spite of often frustratingly fragmentary evidence, it becomes apparent that most of these Mexicans were ambivalent at best about the permanence of their settlement in Chicago. Indeed, for the majority of migrants, the decision to go *al norte* often did not mean coming directly to Chicago. That many ended up in Chicago, however, reveals tangible links between Chicago and more common destinations in the U.S. Southwest.

This chapter focuses on three factors that are critical to understanding the attitudes and experiences of Mexicans in Chicago during the interwar period. The chapter opens with a sampling of the people that left Mexico and ended up in Chicago. This background illuminates some of their reasons for migrating, highlights the significance of the years of revolution in Mexico, and ultimately helps to explain their outlooks toward and expectations for their lives in Chicago. The discussion then focuses on the predominant paths of migration these people followed to Chicago. Understanding the migration and the its demography clarifies the gendered and ethno-racial nature of the migrants' experiences in Chicago that are discussed in later chapters. These encounters fundamentally shaped their dispositions and opportunities once in Chicago and fashioned many of their living and working patterns.

The standard narrative of Mexican migration to the Midwest begins near the end of World War I, as steel, meatpacking, agriculture, and railroad industries recruited workers for their expanding enterprises and to fill war-time labor shortages.[1] That the great majority of these jobs were slated for men provides one indicator of how seemingly gender-neutral information is in fact very gendered, in this case, gendered-male. Women's migration into the area was slight, though it did increase dramatically over the course of the 1920s. Throughout the interwar period, however, the numbers of women remained significantly smaller than those of men. An estimated twenty to twenty-five thousand Mexicans lived in Chicago by 1930, and women comprised only an estimated one-quarter of these.[2]

In 1913, the Mexican consul in Chicago lodged an official complaint with the mayor of Chicago, Carter Harrison II, about a popular film show-ing throughout the city.[3] Huge posters for the film, *A Trip through Bar-barous Mexico*, were plastered all over the windows of the theaters. The lobby cards were emblazoned with the national colors of Mexico and were reportedly attracting large crowds at the windows and into the theaters. The consul contended that the film was not an accurate portrayal of Mex-ico but rather "a public offense to my country [Mexico]" that damaged the country's image. He insisted that the posters, "in which the name of Mexico is denigrated," be covered or removed. Ultimately the word "bar-barous" was painted over in the largest posters, but it remained in the smaller lobby cards.[4]

The film likely was based on a scathing exposé of Porfirio Díaz's Mexico by the noted muckracking journalist John Kenneth Turner.[5] Dis-guised as a salesman, Turner traveled throughout Mexico documenting the abuses of the dictator's rule including the atrocious conditions en-dured by henequen (sisal) and rubber-plantation workers, the enslave-ment of workers and political dissidents, and even the hanging of Yaqui Indians in Sonora. *Barbarous Mexico: An Indictment of a Cruel and Corrupt System* was published in 1911 and ultimately served its purpose of countering the pro-Díaz media reports in the United States.

For the consul, however, the real damage of the film was its continu-ing portrayal of the "barbarity" of Mexico even as the revolution already had displaced the dictator. Díaz went into exile in 1911 and by 1913 was dead. As the film opened in theaters in Chicago, the Díaz loyalist Victoriano Huerta had just overthrown Francisco Madero's reformist government. Perhaps the consul objected to Huerta being painted with the same journalistic brush as Díaz, despite their similarities.

Mexico was not the barbarous, uncivilized place many Chicagoans imagined, even during these revolutionary years. The *ejidatario* of the 1910s and 1920s was not the *peón* of the prerevolutionary period.[6] Through land redistribution, the establishment of rural schools, the completion of the national railroad system, and the expansion of electrification projects, Mexicans in the rural countryside increasingly became educated and grew ever more aware of modern conveniences and new recreational activities.[7] The number of automobiles in Mexico, for instance, mushroomed in the latter half of the 1920s and grew throughout the 1930s; the first commercial radio station in Mexico began broadcasting in 1923. By 1925, the Department of Education under President Plutarco Calles established its own radio station, which broadcast to the newly built rural schools throughout the country. During the presidency of Alvaro Obregón (and later under Calles), José Vasconcelos served as secretary of education, becoming "the patron of the rural school" by sending hundreds of teachers to Mexican villages to teach reading, writing, arithmetic, and Mexican history.[8] Through education, the Secretaría de Educación Pública sought to spread the nationalist project into the rural countrysides, converting the diverse populations into one national Mexico.[9] The state-trained teachers served as agents between the government and the local rural communities.[10]

In many ways, the social, economic, and cultural revolutionary context and the opportunities presented in *el norte* were inextricable for those Mexicans who came to Chicago. Both fashioned the migration to Chicago in a number of important ways. The revolution shaped early waves of migrants directly through the demands of military service and economic displacement. Indirectly, the turmoil of the revolution and the subsequent efforts to build a national Mexico sensitized these Mexicans to the rhetoric of Mexican nationalism. Like the agricultural workers in California studied by the historian Devra Weber, these early migrants to Chicago were "molded in the crucible of displacement and proletarianization in Mexico and the United States."[11] Like the California cotton workers, understanding Chicago's laborers "as transnational workers clarifies their responses" to the circumstances they faced.[12]

The revolution exploded with Francisco Madero's overthrow of the longtime dictator Porfírio Díaz in 1910.[13] Madero's faith in the power of democracy, however, was destroyed as he discovered that he had unleashed a succession of power struggles. As the revolutionary tides grew more radical and power shifted to Pancho Villa and Emiliano Zapata, Madero and his vice president, Pino Suárez, were murdered in 1913. For a time, Victoriano Huerta, the former commander of the military under Díaz, took over the presidency and tried to counter the revolutionary drives. Facing opposition and armed uprising from the south (Zapata) and the north (Villa) of Mexico and unable to attract men to the federal army, Huerta resorted to forced conscription. Several of his successors, including Venustiano Carranza and Alvaro Obregón, also resorted to this method, providing a strong motive for migration.

Many of the men who ended up in Chicago in the 1920s came from a mix of backgrounds but reported similar experiences with serving in the army of one of the various revolutionary factions in Mexico.[14] A few, like Ignacio Elizalde, served in the military and ultimately were discharged. Elizalde fought five years with Villa and two with Obregón. He claimed that his discharge from the military came after he got a bullet in his leg "in the battle where Obregón lost his arm," the Battle of Celaya in April 1915. After working at customs houses in several towns along the Rio Grande, he came to Chicago in the early 1920s "to make money."[15] For Elizalde, as with many like him, the revolutionary context of forced military service and economic disruption reinforced migration toward economic opportunity in the United States as he set off in search of a good job.

I. M. Valle was also drafted to fight in the revolution, though he chose a more common alternative by defecting from the army. He was from Jalisco and fought in the army with Carranza and then Obregón and liked neither the army nor the fighting. "I quit," he said. "I ran away." Valle's escape from service in the revolution mirrored that of many Mexican men who migrated to the United States during this period.[16] Presumably he had heard of the tremendous job opportunities in the United States, for Valle headed north to Texas, where he labored on the railroads as a track worker for several years. After working his way to Chicago on the rails, he was employed for a year at Dewey Zinc Works, during which time he saved enough money to open his modest music shop in downtown Chicago.[17] For Valle, like Elizalde, the experiences of fighting in the revolution influenced his decision not to stay in Mexico but rather to head north in search of employment.

Unlike Valle, who came from a small rural town in the central plateau of Mexico, the clerk at the Mexican drugstore in South Chicago was from the urban capital of Mexico, Mexico City. This clerk had been in engineering school when he was forced to fight in the revolution. He admitted that he, too, deserted the Mexican military. "He had served two years in the revolutions, with General Amaro, which he said was not nice, and he did not like it." Like Valle and Elizalde, this clerk also chose to leave Mexico. The particulars of his circumstances are not revealed in his fragmentary account, but it does suggest that he represented a class of men who migrated to the United States with more education than the majority of track laborers and more experience with urban contexts than those from the rural central plateau.[18] In this case as well, the revolutionary context shaped his migration. Escaping military service, the clerk worked first in San Antonio and then moved on to Detroit, ending up finally in Chicago.[19]

Occasionally the revolution's stimulus to emigration took more direct economic form. When Obregón came into power in 1920, for instance, his troops in Monterrey received reports that the owner of a small tortilla plant did not support Obregón. The soldiers repeatedly tried to burn down the building. The owner insisted the reports were "misinformation given by I do not know whom." Nevertheless, he decided to sell the plant and moved his family, including his wife, his mother, his brother's widow, and her four children, to San Antonio, Texas. There he worked in the freight house of the "Kitty," the Missouri, Kansas, and Texas Railroad. One of his brothers went up to Chicago to work and wrote to him in San Antonio that Chicago needed a tortilla factory. So he moved his extended

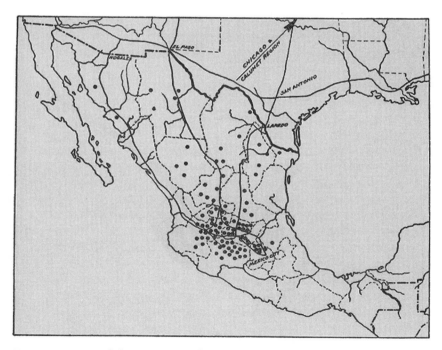

Fig. 1.1: Origins of the Mexican Colony, Chicago and the Calumet Region, 1919–30. One dot = 1 percent. From Taylor, Mexican Labor, *43.*

family, including now children of his own, to Chicago, where he and his brother went into business together.[20] The experiences of this Mexican businessman are similar to those of the middling and propertied peoples displaced by the revolution and reflect once again the mobility made possible by privilege. After all, in most areas, the poorest peasants were the least able to head north for work.[21] This owner of a tortilla factory lost all his property, but he was also able to take advantage of the new opportunities created by the steady demand for labor in the United States. His confidence in being able to find work in the United States was fueled by the growing ease of rail travel, a mobility that in turn facilitated his ability to seek employment and socio-economic stability.

Like the tortilla-plant owner, a family in Guanajuato also lost all their property in the revolution.[22] Just as Obregón took office, they too left their home and traveled to Texas. After working in a hotel for six months, the husband obtained work on the railroads and took his family to Chicago. By 1925, they had lived in Chicago for over four years in a railroad boxcar camp in South Chicago, notably a more working-class existence than that of the former tortilla-plant owner.[23]

Originally, one of the primary goals of the revolutionaries was to disentangle the Catholic church from the national state. Consequently, public espousal of anticlericalism dominated the governments of Mexico from 1917 until the Cristero uprisings in the late 1920s. The Catholic church, with its large landholdings and its stranglehold on local power, was perceived to be the single most important impediment to social change. Several articles in the Mexican Constitution attempted to secularize many aspects of Mexican life, from marriage to education to land reform, but little formal action was taken initially to enforce these provisions.

In 1924, however, Plutarco Calles decided to enforce the anticlerical provisions in the Constitution that his predecessor Obregón had ignored, thus inflaming still-smoldering conflicts with the Catholic church. In February 1926, Mexico's archbishop spoke publicly against the Constitution, professing that Roman Catholics could not accept such an anticlerical document.[24] Calles retaliated by closing church-run schools, monasteries, and convents. Then he deported foreign priests and nuns. Father James Tort, a Spaniard and later founder of Our Lady of Guadalupe church in South Chicago, was forcibly driven from Mexico during this period, along with several Cordi Marian sisters.[25] News of the new waves of conflict reached Chicago and was disseminated there in the Spanish-language press.[26]

In late July 1926, Mexico's archbishop declared a strike of all clergy, which further enraged Calles. For three years, the Cristeros, organized primarily by Catholic leaders in Michoacán, Jalisco, and Zacatecas, fought pitched guerrilla battles throughout the countryside. Government troops destroyed churches and killed priests, while Cristeros murdered government-paid schoolteachers and dynamited trains. Notably, the majority of Mexicans coming to Chicago between 1926 and 1929 were from areas affected by this strife, the central and western states of Guanajuato, Michoacán, and Jalisco.[27]

Hostilities peaked in July 1928, when a militant religious zealot, inspired by the Cristero teachings, assassinated the president-elect (and former president) Alvaro Obregón. Calles happily filled the resultant power vacuum with Emilio Portes Gil.[28] During his interim presidency, Gil along with Calles and Father John Burke (a Catholic leader from the United States) helped to settle the Cristero Wars, solidifying the anticlericalism that dominated during the 1930s.[29]

Just as the Cristero strife reached a resolution, at least formally, the Great Depression hit and further crushed already-weakened economic and social structures in Mexico. The government of Pascual Ortíz Rubio, serving from 1930–32, depleted the country's treasury with attempts to shore up the collapsing economy. Rubio's regime fired government workers and cut wages, while major employers and industries throughout the country cut their workforces, slowing or stopping production altogether. During his brief term and that of Abelardo Rodríguez, which immediately followed, the Mexican government continued to stray from the earlier nationalist project of social and economic reform.[30] Lázaro Cárdenas, however, solidified the nationalist project and the revolutionary reforms that had been derailed most effectively during the violence and strife of the late 1920s and early 1930s.[31] Cárdenas had supported Calles, but once in office, Cárdenas proceeded to solidify his position by removing many of Calles's appointments and by restructuring institutions that had bolstered Calles's power. He reformed the military, deported prominent Calles supporters, and eventually exiled Calles to the United States in 1936. Cárdenas took up the cause of agrarian reform, redistributing land to communal *ejidos* throughout the country and ultimately nationalizing many industries.[32] By 1940, the *ejido* system had significantly reduced, though certainly did not close, the "gap in the quality of life between rural and urban Mexico."[33]

Most of the Mexicans who remained in Chicago during the Great Depression, however, were effectively cut off from these reforms during the 1930s and could not appreciate the extent to which the lives of average Mexicans changed during this period. Greater political and economic stability fueled a population increase in Mexico, helping to counter the decrease of the revolutionary years. From a total population of just over fourteen million in 1920, Mexico grew to a total population of around twenty million by 1940.[34]

Chicago's Mexicans, however, were not immune to the ongoing effects of the revolutionary ideologies unleashed in Mexico during the period of their own migrations in the late 1910s and 1920s. In a sense, Mexicans who came to Chicago in the 1920s left Mexico midstream in the nationalist project, leaving at least a decade before a national Mexico emerged. The revolutionary context made Mexicans throughout the country aware of issues of national Mexican identity, raising questions around ethnic Mexicanness and racial *indio* or *mestizo* identities, while feeding the migrations *al norte*.[35]

Revolutionary displacements coupled with economic opportunities in the north during the 1920s, direct recruitment of workers by industry, and favorable legislative practices in the United States all fueled the migrations of Mexicans out of Mexico.[36] The Cristero unrest of the mid to late 1920s further contributed to the economic and social displacements already shaping the streams of Mexican migrations to the United States.[37] Like the revolutionary turmoil of years past, the Cristero strife merely underscored the desires of Mexicans in Chicago to "wait out" the unrest.

The continued turmoil of and frustrations with political and economic unrest in Mexico dovetailed with work opportunities in the United States, particularly between 1916 and 1929, inducing many Mexicans to travel *al norte*.[38] The majority of Mexicans leaving Mexico during this period traveled to and from the states of the U.S. Southwest, including Texas, Arizona, and California.[39] But a small though significant stream of Mexicans migrated to various parts of the Midwest, on routes that roughly paralleled the railroad lines.[40] The massive migrations of Mexicans into the United States during the revolutionary period in part reflected the mobility and opportunities afforded by the railroads.[41] Mexican railroads linked with the rails in Texas and the U.S. Southwest, which were, in turn, connected to multiple railways leading to Chicago. The railroad offered not only mobility but also employment to many Mexican men. As the historian Jeff Garcilazo has pointed out, many sought jobs on the rails because they paid more than similar work in Mexico and they allowed for seasonal transnational migration back home.[42] Through track work and rail-related jobs, the first significant numbers of Mexicans worked their way to Chicago. Mexican men could be found in Chicago as early as 1910, working for a variety of railroad companies. The local divisions of the Santa Fe, Rock Island, and Burlington Railroads, for example, reported at least 1,120 Mexicans employed in maintenance-of-way work.[43]

The rails also provided the means by which other large employers attracted and transported growing numbers of Mexican workers. Commercial beet-sugar farmers in the upper Midwest, for instance, recruited hundreds of Mexicans to areas in Michigan, Wisconsin, and Minnesota, particularly during and after the First World War.[44] By 1916, faced with restricted immigration of European workers and wartime labor shortages, the railroad companies recruited over two hundred male Mexican workers directly from revolution-torn Mexico to work on the railroads in Chicago.[45] Shortly thereafter, Chicago's steel and meatpacking industries also began recruiting male workers directly from Mexico, thus forming the first significant colony of Mexican workers within Chicago itself.[46] An estimated 68 percent of the men recruited to work in these big three industries—railroads, steel, and meatpacking—were from the Mexican states most affected by the Cristero Wars: the western-central states of Guanajuato, Jalisco, and Michoacán.[47]

By the mid-1920s, however, Mexican migration to Chicago was primarily indirect, as Mexican men and increasingly more women traveled along railroad lines from Mexico to Laredo and San Antonio through Kansas City to Chicago.[48] Others followed agricultural jobs, spending their summers in the beet fields of Michigan, Minnesota, or Wisconsin and returning to Chicago for the winter. Once in Chicago, many of these workers found local employment in the mills, the rail yards, or the packinghouses.[49]

Aside from the small groups recruited directly from Mexico (primarily before 1920), most Mexicans came to Chicago via frequently circuitous routes, paths structured by job opportunities and networks of kinship and friendship. Even the agricultural workers who wintered in Chicago had come to the city indirectly. That Chicago was not the place the people intended to go when they set out on their journeys significantly factored into their attitudes toward the permanency of their lives in Chicago. The majority regarded their stays in Chicago as temporary, expecting eventually to return "back home." The ease of rail travel and the geographic proximity of "home" fed these expectations as Mexicans flowed in and out of the city, bringing news of friends and relatives and of the political situations in Mexico.

The experiences of individual migrants clarify the human dimension of these patterns, illuminating kinship and friendship networks while underscoring elements of chain migration. Ladislao Durán came to the United States from Guadalajara in November 1918 "because he was out of a job and needed work." After working for the railroads in Brownsville, Texas, he returned to Mexico in September 1919 to get his family. He and his family then lived in a boxcar in Kansas City while he worked as a track laborer. In April 1920, the Chicago, Milwaukee, and St. Paul Railroad transferred the Duráns to Mannheim, Illinois. Ladislao's track work brought the family to Chicago. Once in Chicago, the Duráns found a place to live by talking with other Mexicans they met in the railroad yards.[50]

The railroad played a similar role for José Martínez. After entering Texas in 1905, he worked clearing mesquite near Laredo, then further north picking cotton.[51] A few years later, he and his new wife, María, went further north to Fort Worth, where he worked in a packinghouse. José began to have physical problems that he attributed to working indoors in the dampness, so he registered with an employment agency in Fort Worth. Soon thereafter he was sent to Illinois to work on the tracks for the Rock Island Railroad. Working for the Rock Island eventually brought him and María to Chicago.[52]

By June 1923, semiskilled rail workers like Juan Manuel Gómez had made their way to Chicago. Gómez had been a machinist for the Mexican National Railroad in Durango when he entered the United States at Eagle Pass, Texas, in early October 1922. Eight months later he was in Chicago, having worked his way along the rails.[53]

Agriculture generally, and beet-sugar companies in particular, brought others indirectly to Chicago. More so than other industries in the area, beet-sugar companies tended to recruit whole families, which meant that a few women joined the primarily male migrations. It also resulted in egregious child-labor practices.[54] Throughout the upper Midwest and the Dakotas, beet-sugar companies encouraged their workers to winter in urban areas in the United States. The benefits of this strategy were apparent: their workers would remain on this side of the border, reducing the difficulties of returning to the fields and the costs of traveling to the fields the next season, all while freeing the companies from having to house their workers in the winter. Thus, after beet season ended in November, companies provided these workers with information—in English and Spanish—on railroad fares to major cities in the United States, including Chicago.[55] From the perspective of the workers, getting to Chicago was easy because so many rail lines went there. The trip also cost less than traveling farther from the fields, and the city provided them the hope at least of remaining employed year round. Of the beet workers coming into Chicago at the end of November 1924, many reportedly had been in the United States for several years, having "worked for a time in the cotton fields of the south, and for the past three seasons in the Michigan beet fields."[56] Throughout the 1920s, beet workers arrived in Chicago in November with only fifty to seventy-five dollars to get them and their families through the winter. Too often this meager amount proved inadequate, as many found that "work [was] scarce in the winter."[57] The winter conditions also proved difficult since their "supply of clothing, bedding, and furniture [was] very meager."[58]

But families realized that the beet-sugar companies were willing to pay more dollars per acre if the families remained in *el norte* over the winters. Manuel Ramírez and his family, for instance, were offered two wages: either eighteen dollars per acre plus transportation from San Antonio to Michigan and back; or twenty-three dollars per acre and no transportation paid.[59] After failing to earn any profit plying his trade in Mexico as a candy maker, Manuel decided to try his fortune in the beet fields. "Other families had gone to Michigan and had come back with a small profit," so he reasoned that "he too might be as lucky."[60]

Kinship networks and chain migrations increasingly structured Mexican migration to Chicago during the 1920s. Pedro Mendoza and Juan Juariga provide a typical example. Pedro and Juan, born in Tepatitlán, Morelos, grew up together. Both men married women from their village; Pedro married Juan's sister. Early in 1923, Juan and Pedro were hired by the beet-sugar company that recruited from their village and sent them to work in Beals, Montana. After seven months, Juan sent their combined earnings to his sister, Pedro's wife, in Tepatitlán to pay for her and the children to take the train to Chicago. In the meantime, Pedro set out for Chicago as well—on foot, walking from Beals to Chicago, a distance of over 1,400 miles. Juan continued to work in the beet fields and later in St. Paul on the railroad, saving his earnings for the families to get settled in Chicago. Eventually, Pedro, Juan, and their wives and children were reunited in Chicago.[61]

Often employment opportunities within Chicago also were structured by kinship networks. As the superintendent of the Marshall Field mattress factory noted, "[I]f he wants another worker he tells some Mexican there [at the factory], and the employee always produces next day some brother or cousin or sister who wants a job."[62] To this employer and many of his contemporaries, Mexicans were essentially interchangeable.[63] Mexicans themselves took advantage of this prevalent sentiment in enterprising ways that frequently revealed *apparent* kinship networks. That is, many Mexicans referred to compatriots as their brothers or cousins to help each other gain access to jobs, housing, or other opportunities. Employers understood this practice as true kinship when in reality many were fictive kin or, more aptly, pragmatic kin.

In many of the factories, workers were assigned numbers when they hired on. Whenever they logged in or out, they used their numbers for identification. If workers decided to go to Mexico for a visit or to work a different job, some would lend or lease their assigned numbers to other Mexicans who wanted the work. Occasionally they sold their numbers outright. Thus, Mexicans often gave "the names under which they [were] employed, and not their own names."[64] In South Chicago, where this practice was first noted, "foremen [did] not seem to be aware of this practice. Perhaps all Mexicans look alike to them."[65]

More than revolutionary upheaval and economic displacement were at work, however, in the migration of Mexicans to Chicago. After living in the United States for twenty-six years (and at least ten of those in Chicago), a Mexican named Pedro was asked why he left Mexico. "Adventurando" (seeking adventure), he replied.[66] Frequently, men who described themselves as adventurers and out to see the world also noted their desires to separate themselves from the control of their fathers. This suggests that one explanation for the gendered-male migration to Chicago may be wrapped up in standards of masculinity and the needs of young men coming of age.

Salvador Zavala, for example, was born and raised in the state of Guanajuato and had five brothers. One was in Mexico City in 1924, working as the superintendent of the railway station. Two others were in Chicago. When asked why he had come to Chicago, Salvador explained that "his father had sent him here to bring back his brother . . . [who] had been up here for three years. . . . [H]is father thought that was long enough."[67] Apparently, Salvador remained in Chicago because his older brother was unwilling to return to Mexico with him. Salvador did want to return to Mexico, but he planned to stay in Chicago for another year. He clarified that the brothers were staying in Chicago because "here there is no father." Clearly, the Zavala brothers were eager to be far from the control of their father and sought to exert control over their own lives. For them, Chicago was incidental to their adventure, for the principal goal was to be far away from Guanajuato. Work opportunities certainly drew these single men to Chicago, and their wages were primarily to fund their lives away from home. Their father owned property in Guanajuato and, as reported by his sons, was wealthy. When asked about what work his father did, Salvador answered, "[H]e doesn't work. He has money." Then he added, "He doesn't work with his hands, but with his head," clarifying that his father bought and sold corn.[68] In Mexico, Salvador had still been in school, but in Chicago he worked washing floors at Swift and Company, meatpackers in the Stockyards neighborhood. His brother worked there as well, moving "quarter sections of meat from one tank to another." Claudio Zavala, likely one of Salvador's brothers in Chicago, died in 1927, allegedly resisting arrest on disorderly conduct charges in South Chicago. The officers, Patrolman Jeremiah O'Connell and Patrolman Vincent Lewandowski, shot him dead while trying to arrest him.[69] By 1930, Salvador apparently had still not managed to convince his other brother to move back to Mexico, for in April of that year, Angel registered with the Mexican consulate in Chicago.[70] By then, he was thirty years old and married. That he registered with the Mexican consulate, however, indicates that he had not changed his citizenship, still planned to return home eventually, and consequently remained uncommitted to staying in Chicago.

Like the Zavala brothers, a certain Mr. Gutiérrez left school in Morelia, Michoacán, "to see the world . . . [he] only intended to spend a few months up here." His father did not want him to leave home, but Gutiérrez left anyway. He worked his way to Chicago, arriving in 1920, three years after he left Michoacán. "After a while," he explained, "he stopped writing to his family . . . [and] ha[d] not heard from them directly for four years." He implied, however, that news of his welfare and of his family had passed through others traveling back and forth, speaking to the power of the human networks shaping Mexican migrations to and from Chicago. Like the Zavala brothers, however, he too planned to return home to Mexico and thus remained ambivalent about his long-term residence in Chicago.[71]

Adventure as a motivating factor is usually ignored in dominant explanatory paradigms of economic displacement because of revolutionary upheavals and attendant land seizures and redistributions. This attitude suggests that a potentially significant element of the Mexican population in Mexico used the revolutionary unrest as an opportunity. That these adventurers set out on escapades to explore and experience life in the United States during these years suggests a mobility not born out of desperation. These motivations also underscore the happenstance of these men ending up in Chicago in their wanderings. The overwhelming maleness of this segment of the migration to Chicago also contributed to the perceived threat such concentrations of single men posed to Chicago's civic order.[72] In addition, this element of mobility was notably an option reserved for men. Women, if they traveled alone at all, were required by the Mexican government to carry letters from a male family member (usually the head of house, whether her husband, father, or brother) affirming that her travel was "approved" by the family.[73]

This restriction on women's mobility helped to ensure the importance of family migration in structuring their movements. Fortunata X, for instance, left Mexico at the age of eighteen to live and work in Texas.[74] Through information she gave in her "first papers" (declaration of intention to become a U.S. citizen), Fortunata reveals much about her life. By 1923 she had moved from Hidalgo, Texas, to Lockhart, Texas, where she married Marco Ramos, a Texan by birth, on November 10. The couple stayed in Lockhart at least until January 1926, when Fortunata gave birth to their first child, Julia. Only two years later, the couple had moved to Chicago, where they had their second child, another daughter named Eloisa, in March 1928. She was followed in close succession by Juanita, born February 8, 1930; José, born September 18, 1931; Elvira, born March 13, 1934; and Adolfo, born June 15, 1936—all were born in Chicago. By the end of the 1930s, Fortunata and her family, including Marco, were still living in Chicago. She was unemployed, a laborer, and by April 1940 she had filed to become a U.S. citizen. On July 2, 1940, she succeeded in becoming a U.S. citizen like her husband and her six children. There were not, however, many women like Fortunata. The majority of Mexican migrants to Chicago were male. In 1924 there were an estimated twenty men to every one Mexican woman.[75] A study conducted that same year surveyed two thousand Mexican men in an attempt to more systematically determine the composition of the Mexican population, and it concluded that only eighty-five of those had their families with them.[76] Even as more women arrived over the course of the 1920s and more men came with their families, Chicago's Mexican population was still overwhelmingly male.

The 1920 U.S. census counted 1,141 Mexicans in Chicago. By 1930, the Mexican population, as counted by the federal census, had grown to nearly twenty-one thousand.[77] Over the course of only ten years, from 1920 to 1930, federal statistics indicate that there had been an increase in the net Mexican population by a factor of seventeen (1,700 percent).[78] Even with the extremely conservative numbers of the federal census, the Mexican population of Chicago by 1930 comprised around 1 percent of the three million or so residents.[79]

The unreliability of census figures for certain populations is well known, but even in the interwar period, contemporaries were aware of inaccuracies. As the Mexican consul, Luis Lupián, explained in an interview with Manuel Gamio in 1926, "[T]he census is very incomplete" for two main reasons. First, Mexicans were disinclined to answer any questions at all. He clarified that he believed their reluctance was "out of . . . fear that it will bring certain responsibilities."[80] The second reason the consul cited was purely logistical. As Lupián noted, "[T]hey are disseminated throughout the city and it is impossible to locate them all."[81] Many Mexicans feared the consequences of being located and the repercussions of being caught "without papers."[82] The real threats and possibilities of being deported during the interwar period kept many Mexicans "underground"—avoiding contact with "official" people as much as possible, even shying away from the offices of the consulate of Mexico.[83]

As a result of the Depression, repatriations, and deportations, at least one-quarter of the population of Mexicans in Chicago in 1930 had left by 1939. To explain this reduction, previous scholarship has pointed to the reduced proportion of single men during the 1930s as evidence that many young single men left Chicago. Contemporaries suggested that families, lacking similar mobility, bore the brunt of the economic and social problems. Of the 1,340 Mexican households surveyed by the 1935 Works Progress Administration (WPA) study, 63 percent were complete nuclear families, and only 13 percent had no children.[84] Single Mexican men who stayed in Chicago were hit even harder than those with families in Chicago during the early years of the Great Depression. As one observer noted, those few jobs that Mexicans could secure were given to men with families.[85] Men working in Chicago with wives and children in Mexico quickly found themselves unable to find work during these Depression years. Consequently, along with men who were indeed single, they were often among the first groups to take advantage of initial voluntary repatriation incentives.[86]

Mexican consulate records indicate, however, that many of the young single men were not as young as previous scholarship and contemporaries depicted. The majority of those single men who registered with the consulate were in their late twenties and thirties (see table 1.1).[87] Moreover, consulate records also reveal that more single men remained in Chicago during the Depression years than previously thought.[88] A sampling of those single male Mexican nationals registering with the Mexican consulate in Chicago reveals that they comprised over one-third of the Mexican population in Chicago. For example, from January 1929 to December 1930, years covering the months before, during, and immediately after the economic crash, 195 men registered with the consul's office. Of these, 120 were married; seventy-five were single, over a third of the registering population.

Judging from the emphasis of previous scholarship on the decline of the single-male Mexican population during the worst years of the De-

Table 1.1: Mexican Nationals, Single Men Registered at Mexican Consulate

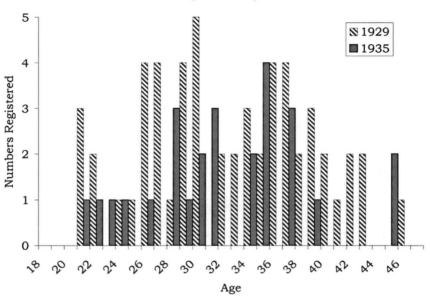

Data compiled from Departamento de Asuntos Comerciales y de Proteccion: Matriculas, Chicago, 1929, 1935. Archivo Histórico de la Secretaria de Relaciónes Exteriores,
Mexico City.

pression, one would expect that the proportion of single men would have
decreased. However, consulate records indicate preliminary evidence to
the contrary. Of the fifty-nine men registered in 1935, thirty-two were
married and twenty-seven single, suggesting that the proportion of single
men still in Chicago remained over one-third.[89] Ramiro Estrada, for instance, lived and worked in Chicago from 1923, and by March 1933 he
remained unmarried and was living just north of the Loop.[90]

Many of those Mexican men who had indeed been single (as opposed
to those who were alone in Chicago but had wives and children in Mexico)
in the 1920s were married by the mid-1930s, with their wives and children living in Chicago. Given persistent unequal sex ratios within the
Mexican population, intermarriage with women of other ethnic groups
was not uncommon. Some, however, married Mexican women they met
in Chicago. Juan Gómez, the machinist mentioned earlier, met and married his future wife, Carmen, in Chicago. The couple was married in June
1931, two years after Carmen had entered the United States from Celaya,
Mexico. In May 1932, their daughter, Rose Mary, was born, and their son
Flavio was born in 1935. Others went back to Mexico to find a wife, often

under the name of ___Ramiro Estrada___

Fig. 1.2: Ramíro Estrada, Chicago 1930. Petition for Naturalization No. 11491, National Archives and Records Administration.

marrying women from their hometowns. Gonzalo Sánchez Velázquez, for example, spent nearly ten years living and working in the United States before returning to his hometown of Muzquiz in the Mexican state of Coahuila to marry Josefa in June 1929. Two weeks later, he returned to the United States with Josefa. By 1930, the couple had a daughter and lived in Chicago in Back-of-the-Yards.[91] In 1920, twenty-eight-year-old Librado Ramírez (fig. 1.3) married Margarita, a young woman from his hometown of Penjamo, Mexico, thirteen years his junior.[92] Evidently he had been working in the United States for nearly ten years before marrying and somehow managed to remain in contact with others from his hometown living in this country. The couple married in San Antonio, Texas, and moved to Chicago the following year.

Though no contemporary studies assessed the growth of the Mexican female population in Chicago during this period, several sources indirectly evidenced such growth. Births and places of birth recorded at the Mexican consulate in Chicago reveal more than migratory patterns of families. They also confirm the kinship ties that shaped these migratory patterns and give evidence of the growing proportion of Mexican women.[93]

The siblings Margarita, Xavier, and Dora Gutiérrez, for example, traveled from Guadalajara in the west-central Mexican state of Jalisco. Later they were joined by their mother, Elena Salcedo de Gutiérrez, in Chicago. Elena's husband died in 1925, and by 1931 she lived in Chicago with three of her adult children (her other three, Clemencia, Alfonso,

certify that the photograph affixed to the duplica

(The seal of the court will be impressed so as to cover a portion of the photograph)

Fig. 1.3: Librado Ramírez, Chicago 1938. Petition for Naturalization No. 230047, National Archives and Records Administration.

certify that the photograph affixed to the duplica

Fig. 1.4: Elena Salcedo de Gutiérrez, Chicago, ca. 1939. Petition for Naturalization No. 200010, National Archives and Records Administration.

and Nina, remained in Mexico) working as a housekeeper. At the age of sixty, Doña Elena filed to change her citizenship, and on November 28, 1940, she became a U.S. citizen.[94]

Consulate birth records also hint at extended family networks in Mexican migration to the area (see table 1.2). The families of Consuelo Medina and Davíd Tapia, for instance, registered together at the Mexican consulate in Chicago in August 1929. Consuelo and Davíd were cousins, born within a month of each other in Irapuato, Michoacán. Consuelo's father, Luz

Table 1.2 Births Recorded with Mexican Consulate, Chicago, May 1929–May 1930

Child's Name	Sex	Birthdate	Birth Place
	May 1929		
MadeJesus Hernández S.	F	May 1928	Chicago
Alfonso Bravo Villar	M	Feb. 1929	Chicago
	June 1929		
Gonzalo Díaz Ortíz	M	Aug. 1927	Chicago
David Díaz Ortíz	M	Nov. 1928	Chicago
Ignacio González García	M	Nov. 1928	S.A.T.[1]
Apolonia González García	F	Feb. 1924	Indiana Harbor
MadeJesus Montes de León	F	July 1924	Chicago
Guadalupe Montes de León	F	June 1926	Chicago
	August 1929		
Consuelo Ortíz López	F	June 1925	Texas
Andres Ortíz López	M	June 1926	Chicago
Armando Ortíz López	M	May 1929	Chicago
Miguel Ortíz López	M	Aug. 1923	Chicago
Viviano Ortíz López	M	Dec. 1926/7[2]	Chicago
Consuelo Medina Salgado	F	Jan. 1923	Irapuato
Pablo Medina Salgado	M	Jan. 1925	Chicago
María del Pilar Medina Salgado	F	Oct. 1926	Chicago
David Tapia Medina	M	Dec. 1922	Irapuato
	September 1929		
Eugenio Bañuelos Castañeda	M	Dec. 1928	South Chicago
	October 1929		
Gilberto Palafox Contreras	M	July 1929	Toledo, Ohio
	January 1930		
Ricarda Torres Martínez	F	Feb. 1929	Chicago
Isabel Rivera Sánchez	F	Nov. 1920	Melano, Tex.
María de los Angeles Rivera Sánchez	F	Dec. 1919	Evansville, Tex.
Guadalupe Rivera Sánchez	F	Dec. 1927	Goodberry, Mich.
	February 1930		
José Luís Ortíz Lara	M	June 1929	Chicago
	April 1930		
Andres Sánchez Romo	M	Jan. 1930	Chicago
Eduardo Acosta Tejada	M	June 1929	Chicago
Amador Contreras Bravo	M	Dec. 1915	Albuquerque, N.M.
Dolores López Alcaraz	M	Aug. 1918	Wichita, Kans.
Manuela López Alcaraz	F	Dec. 1919	Wichita, Kans.
José López Alcaraz	M	Oct. 1921	Wichita, Kans.
Isabel López Alcaraz	F	July 1927	Rockdale, Ill.

Table 1.2 (cont.)

Child's Name	Sex	Birthdate	Birth Place
May 1930			
Cruz Andrade Chávez	M	June 1913	Cherryville, Kans.
Manuel Aguirre Hernández	M	Nov. 1929	Chicago
Esperanza Aguirre Hernández	F	Dec. 1927	Chicago
Antonio Silva Castillo	M	May 1930	Chicago

1. No indication in records of what S.A.T. means.
2. Year as noted in records.
Data Compiled from information in "Registro de Nacimientos en Chicago," Archivo Histórico de la Secretaria de Relaciónes Exteriores, Mexico City, 1929, IV-271-69.

Medina, was the brother of Davíd's mother, Guadalupe Medina. Though it is unclear whether both families traveled or even arrived together in Chicago, they clearly had reunited, as they signed the registry together.[95]

Between May 1929 and May 1930, there were thirty-five births recorded with the Mexican consulate in Chicago.[96] Of those, eighteen had been born in Chicago. Mari de Jesus and her younger sister, Guadalupe, were both born in Chicago in the mid-1920s. Miguel Ortiz López was born in Chicago in August 1923, early in the development of Mexican settlements in the area. By June 1925 when his sister Consuelo was born, his family had moved to Texas. Miguel's family evidently returned to Chicago within the next year, as his brother Andrés was born in June 1926 in Chicago. The López family stayed in the city for at least the next three years, during which they had two more little boys, Viviano and Armando.[97] This high birth rate and the increase in young Chicago-born children of Mexicans further evidenced the growing presence of a female population in the 1930s. A 1935 WPA study, for instance, noted that 52 percent of the seven thousand people in this survey were under sixteen years old.[98]

Various migration paths also added to the numbers of Mexican women in Chicago. Once established, kinship networks, indirect labor migrations, and the agricultural practice of hiring whole families and encouraging them to winter in Chicago all added to the Mexican female population in Chicago. By the end of 1919, Cristina X, born in Zacatecas, Mexico, had met Guadalupe Iniguez; in July 1920 she gave birth to their son, Antonio, in Toledo, Ohio. Two months later(!) they married. By September 1922, Guadalupe had arrived in Chicago, while Cristina returned to Mexico (presumably with Antonio, though the records do not state). On December 18, 1926, just in time for Christmas, Cristina entered the United States again at Laredo. Three years later, she gave birth to their second son,

Guadalupe, in Chicago, followed by Ignacio in July 1932. Only four years later, she died in Chicago on April 29, 1936, leaving her husband with three young children and a fourth from his first marriage.[99] Very likely, he received help and support from his younger brother, Antonio, and his wife, Margarita Mendoza, and their five children. Obviously the families were close because they lived together in the same house on Roosevelt Road when Guadalupe and Antonio applied for U.S. citizenship in 1936.[100]

Manuel Ramírez, his wife Josefina, and their children rode with about a hundred other Mexicans on a train from San Antonio to Detroit, then

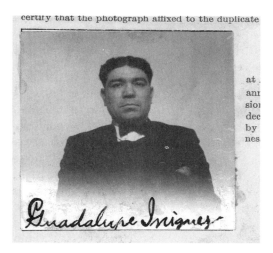

Fig. 1.5: Guadalupe Iniguez, Chicago, 1936. Petition for Naturalization No. 178708, National Archives and Records Administration.

Fig. 1.6: Antonio Iniguez, Chicago, 1936. Petition for Naturalization No. 179724, National Archives and Records Administration.

on a lake boat to a dock in northern Michigan. After another train and bus ride, the family arrived at their summer employment destination. At the end of the beet-picking season, the Ramírez family decided, as did many other beet-worker families, to winter in Chicago.[101] "They had heard of the cold winters," they explained, but they decided that "if other Mexicans endured them, they could too."[102]

In paying such close attention to the words and accounts of Mexicans themselves, it becomes clear that these people were not simply refugees from the revolutionary violence and unrest. The choice to come north for many Mexicans meant taking advantage of opportunities. Groups of male workers came directly to Chicago, recruited by industries to fill wartime labor shortages. Others followed more indirect routes shaped by work opportunities that drew them and their families ever northward. Still others came into Chicago from agricultural fields throughout the Midwest in the hopes of finding wintertime employment. As word of opportunities in the mills, the stockyards, the rails, and the hotels of the Loop spread, migrations increased. Initial migrants were joined by extended family members and by others from their hometowns. Young men and occasionally young women out for an adventure were interlaced throughout these waves of Mexican migration to Chicago. The variety of reasons for migrating, the nature of migration experiences, and the diversity of migrants themselves were central to shaping Mexican lives in and their perceptions of Chicago.

2 Mexican Chicago

Summer's heat scorched residents of Chicago on Sunday, July 27, 1919, and hundreds, white and black, sought relief at the beaches along Lake Michigan.[1] Between the Twenty-sixth Street beach (for blacks only) and the Twenty-ninth Street beach (for whites only) on the South Side, seventeen-year-old Eugene Williams, "a colored boy," floated across the liquid line separating blacks from whites.[2] In crossing into white territory, he became the target of "a mob of white men and boys" who threw stones at him, ultimately drowning him.[3] This incident ignited already-seething tensions and resulted in many days of rioting, murder, fires, and violence in several areas of Chicago. After nearly a week of race riots, as contemporaries termed these events, at least thirty-eight men were dead, hundreds had been injured, and many others were left homeless.[4]

By all official accounts, from the *Chicago Tribune,* the *Chicago Defender,* and the coroner's inquest report to the reports of the Chicago Commission on Race Relations and testimony of participants, the violence was between whites and blacks.[5] Yet, in the thick of the riots, at 5:00 PM on Tuesday, July 30, a "white mob" attacked two Mexicans, José Blanco and Elizondo González, near Forty-third and Ashland.[6] González was gravely wounded, but Blanco managed to strike his attackers and stabbed Joseph Schoff. Schoff later died of blood poisoning from the knife wounds on August 11. As described in the inquest report, Blanco had been outraged that the "deceased mist[oo]k the said José Blanco, a Mexican, for a negro, and during the said quarrel . . . Blanco inflicted the death wound."[7] The all-white-male jury was split on what actions the state should pursue. Three (E. N. Ware, O. W. McMichael, and Roy C. Woods) recommended he be released from police custody, while the other three (R. Keen Ryan, J. P. Brushingham, and Wm. J. Dillon) voted he be held on charges of manslaughter. The case went to the state's attorney and was in the process of being submitted to a grand jury when the Mexican vice consul stepped in and secured Blanco's release.[8]

No mention was made of Elizondo González's murder except in the records of the Mexican consulate, and it is likely that José Blanco would have been erased similarly had he not stabbed Schoff. Indeed, the official body count of thirty-eight, twenty-three "colored" and fifteen white, does not even include González. That González and Blanco were mistaken for Blacks by white rioters highlights how unfixed these categories of white and black really were in the lived experiences of Mexicans in Chicago in 1919. Their outrage at the mistake not only reveals their own recognition of the discriminatory consequences of being Black in Chicago but also speaks to racial ideologies coming out of revolutionary Mexico. It is notable that these incidents overwhelmingly involved males fighting each other, which raises further questions of how gender, specifically masculinity, factors into racializing experiences.

Building on the insights of the historian Thomas C. Holt, this work looks to ordinary daily life as the nexus for the creation of racist practices.[9] In particular, this chapter focuses on several sites in the daily lives of Mexican men and women where they experienced racializing incidents that shaped their settlement in and adjustment to Chicago. It moves through five sites of interaction: 1) settlement and housing; 2) work and labor relations; 3) police relations; 4) heterosocial relations; and 5) commercial contacts. Each provides a critical thread in the evolving tapestry of Mexican racial positioning in Chicago before World War II. Taken together, they prove that ethno-racial dynamics in Chicago were much more complex than contemporaries and historians have suggested.[10]

By examining such lived experiences, it is evident that Mexican contact with European immigrant groups and Blacks was central to their experiences and critical to the formation of Mexican ethno-racial understandings of themselves and their place in the ethno-racial orders of Chicago. That much of the interaction was expressed in male-male conflicts suggests that the seemingly gender-neutral process of raceing and the imbuing of pejorative meaning to "being Mexican" in fact played out in gendered-male terms.[11]

Settlement and Housing

Mexican residential and work patterns placed them squarely in the midst of several different groups.[12] Nowhere in Chicago were Mexicans the majority, and there existed no predominantly Mexican neighborhood.[13] Mexican settlement was always interwoven with residents of other ethnic and racial groups. Nevertheless, there were certainly areas of Mexican concentration where signs of their daily lives were clearly visible.

Mexican settlement concentrated in three general districts: the Near West Side, Back-of-the-Yards/Packingtown, and South Chicago.[14] Major settlement houses served the Near West Side and Packingtown: Jane Addams's Hull-House and Mary McDowell's University of Chicago Settlement House. Protestant churches ran smaller settlements in these areas, including Firman House (Congregationalist) on the Near West Side.[15] Only South Chicago did not have a major settlement house, but it did have a couple of smaller ones that occasionally helped Mexicans: the Congregationalist-run Bird Memorial and the Methodist-run Friendship Center.[16] Settlement houses were significant magnets for recent immigrants of all sorts, for they offered many programs to help orient newcomers and to aid their lives in Chicago. Services ranged from providing English classes and employment assistance to organizing social clubs and child care.[17] Several offered a variety of classes and supported Mexican efforts to create classes of their own. Hull-House, in particular, encouraged arts and crafts among its clients and became well-known for its kilns and the pottery produced by Mexicans of the area.[18] When Mary McDowell died in 1938, local Spanish-language newspapers hailed her for her work with Mexicans. "The loss of Miss McDowell," wrote the editors, "was a great loss to the Mexican people of Chicago. The Mexican will remember for some time to come the noble deeds of this great American woman."[19]

Each of these areas also housed various religious centers and houses of worship that organized classes, celebrations, and social clubs. As the historians Anne Martínez and Malachy McCarthy have shown, religion was central to Mexican migration and settlement. Martínez eloquently argues that religion was "the most significant factor influencing relations between the United States and Mexico from 1910–1929" and clarifies how events in various international theaters, up to and including the Cristero Wars, bore significantly on Mexican experiences in Chicago.[20] McCarthy focuses on the struggles of the Protestant and Catholic churches and their work among Mexicans in Chicago during this era.

Fig. 2.1: *Index Map of Mexican Colonies of Chicago and the Calument Region, 1928. From Taylor,* Mexican Labor, *56–57.*

Like settlement houses, religious organizations were integral to Mexican settlement and adjustment experiences. In fact, Hull-House reportedly loaned chairs to an early Mexican Catholic church that met in a storefront on the Near West Side at 818 West Polk Street.[21] This group later joined St. Francis Parish, headed by St. Francis church at Twelfth and Newberry. While the church itself was Italian, Reverend D. Saldívar, a Spanish Claretian, held masses and meetings in Spanish for the Mexicans. The Pentecostal church on Bunker Street was "the only church . . . entirely composed of and financed by Mexicans," according to Anita Edgar Jones, who studied Mexicans in Chicago for her 1928 doctoral dissertation.[22] Interestingly, five members of this congregation traveled to the Near West Side from South Chicago, suggesting some interconnectedness between people living in different areas of Mexican settlement. Mexicans also participated in Protestant churches in Back-of-the-Yards. Perhaps most prominent were the Lutherans, who held services in Spanish at the Lutheran church at Forty-third and South Mozart. Like the priest at St. Francis, Padre Fernández was a Spaniard by birth. In Packingtown there were eleven Catholic churches in the late 1920s, yet none had a Spanish-speaking priest.[23] Like the Pentecostals who traveled to the Near West Side from South Chicago, those who wanted a Spanish-speaking priest in Packingtown traveled to the Near West Side to St. Francis. St. Rose Church at Forty-eighth and Ashland reportedly held a few Mexican funerals during this era, and the Church of María Incoronata (also Italian) established a small Mexican Catholic mission in 1924.[24]

Notably, South Chicago had the first chapel designed explicitly to serve the needs of Catholic Mexicans. First established in 1924 and relocated to its current location in 1928, Our Lady of Guadalupe church blossomed under the guidance of the Claretians, the Cordi-Marian sisters, and Father James Tort, who, like several of the other area religious leaders, was a Spaniard who became a U.S. citizen.[25] The church's financial support came from Catholic sponsors. Even Illinois Steel contributed funds after conflicts arose between Catholic Poles, Slovaks, and Mexicans because of Mexican exclusion from local Polish and Slovakian parishes.[26]

Like many of Chicago's immigrant groups of the early twentieth century, Mexicans settled in areas largely, though not exclusively, determined by employment (see fig. 2.1). Mexicans living in Back-of-the-Yards worked primarily in the nearby meatpacking plants (including Armour and Swift). Settlers in South Chicago labored principally in the steel plants lining the shores of Lake Michigan (including branches of Wisconsin Steel and Illinois Steel). But other factors also helped to structure where Mexicans lived in Chicago, elements like the proximity of settlement houses with their many outreach programs, interactions with other immigrant groups like the Poles, Italians, and Irish, and the availability of and access to affordable housing. During the interwar period, Mexicans' everyday experiences with their immigrant neighbors influenced every one of these factors and fundamentally shaped their lives in Chicago. Whether they came as recruits of industry or as indirect migrants, Mexicans tended to live in close proximity to major employers. Those living in the Near West Side, for instance, worked for railroad companies or in the various factories along Roosevelt Road.

The areas where Mexicans lived were dominated by dilapidated housing. Mexicans often lived in cramped and poor conditions, and the vast majority were renters, not property owners. Being very poor, Mexicans frequently lived in the worst of the housing, in the rear of buildings and in dark basements.[27] The Quintero family, eleven children and two adults, were typical. They lived at 759 Bunker Street, "one of the worst of the streets running east from Halstead [sic]" on which many Italians lived.[28] The Quinteros lived in two dark rooms, one of which had a window. The family had arrived in Chicago with the father, working on the Rock Island Railroad. The father died in early November 1924, and the two sons, the mother, and one daughter worked to support the whole family. When their father died, however, the two sons were out of work, so their case worker from United Charities tried to get them jobs at Armour Packing. The eldest, twenty-one-year-old Delfino, was trying to get work on the railroad, "in the depot, because one made more money there, but if not in the depot, then on the tracks." Two of the younger children suffered from rickets, reportedly because of the inadequacies of their housing situation.[29] In another representative example, all five Durán children and their parents lived in two rooms, "one of which was an unlighted closet . . . [where] the children slept."[30] Clearly, Mexicans tended to live "in the poorest houses in the neighborhood . . . nearly always . . . in the rear houses, in the basement, or the most undesirable part of the buildings."[31]

The largest area of Mexican settlement, the Near West Side, lay just across the South Branch of the Chicago River, west of the Loop.[32] Housing conditions in the Near West Side tended to be the worst in Chicago due in part to the neighborhood's history as one of the first areas of immigrant settlement in the city.[33] Beginning in the 1850s, waves of German, Bohemian, and Irish immigrants flowed through the area, followed by Eastern European Jews, Greeks, Poles, and Italians.[34] When Mexicans began to arrive, they settled primarily among the latter groups.

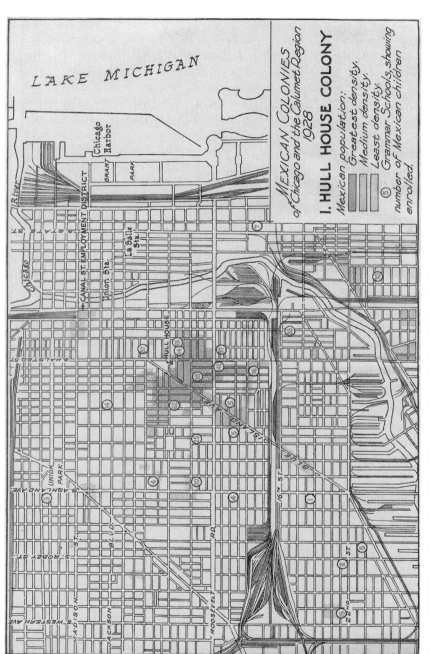

Fig. 2.2: *Hull-House Area, Near West Side, 1928. From Taylor, Mexican Labor, 56–57.*

The highest density of Mexicans was found along Halsted Avenue, between Harrison and Taylor Streets near Hull-House. Throughout the decade the population expanded as more Mexicans came into Chicago, and by the mid-1920s, settlement scattered west to Ashland and north to Madison. Estimates of the Mexican population immediately around Hull-House in 1928 ran upwards of 2,500. Of these, 672 were elementary school–aged children, which suggests that by the end of the 1920s the single-male population was becoming more integrated with women and children.[35]

Mexican settlement on the Near West Side of Chicago appeared to be less compact, however, than in South Chicago or in Packingtown/Back-of-the-Yards. This was due in large part to the decentralization of employment opportunities in the area. Unlike other neighborhoods in which they lived, there was no single dominant employer in the area. Instead, Mexicans worked in "candy [including the Cracker Jack factory and the Curtiss Candy Company], radio factories, and other small plants."[36] Others worked at the Illinois Central freight house, in radio factories on Roosevelt Road, or at the various hotels in the Loop, including the Drake Hotel, Stevens Hotel, and the Blackstone Hotel. Most of these employers hired Mexican men and women.[37]

By the mid-1920s, the Mexican population was interwoven throughout the greater West Side of Chicago. It extended west from the river to the Santa Fe tracks and included the area immediately around Hull-House, the settlements in Brighton Park and Corwith, and an area between Eighteenth and Twenty-second near Western Avenue. Sizable groups of Mexican men had been living in these areas, reportedly since around 1916, when they arrived to work on the railroads. Gradually displacing earlier Polish and Jewish immigrants, these men lived primarily in boarding houses near the Santa Fe tracks and the Illinois Central railroad tracks. As the population grew and other employers moved in, Mexican settlement expanded into Brighton Park.[38] In 1928, the Mexican population in Brighton Park (around Kedzie and Thirty-ninth Street) was estimated to number between seven and eight hundred individuals who worked nearby in the Santa Fe Railroad yards, the McCormick Works factory, and the Crane Manufacturing Company.[39] All three employers hired only men, which presumably factored into shaping the heavily male concentration of workers in the area.[40]

Thirty-eighth Street served as the major commercial center for the area, and walking down this street in the mid-1920s was vivid testimony to area patterns described above. Several Mexican commercial establishments clustered on Thirty-eighth Street. There were at least three poolrooms: one at 3334 Thirty-eighth; another at the corner of Thirty-eighth and Albany; a third at Thirty-eighth and Spaulding. Here more than twenty Mexican men played pool inside, though the poolroom had no name on its window. Next door, a tailor shop owned by F. G. Mena, a Mexican, replaced a Jewish grocery store in 1925. Mena had tried to open his shop in a nearby building where he lived with his wife and daughter, but his Jewish landlady "had been unwilling."[41] Further down Thirty-eighth Street (at 3327), a Mrs. McAvoy, one of the few Irish still living in the Brighton Park area, rented the back of her building to the Rodriguez family, consisting of Mr. and Mrs. Rodriguez and one child. Like so many Mexicans in the area, the Rodriguezes also had six boarders, while Mrs. McAvoy permitted Mr. Rodriguez to run a school in the vacant store downstairs.[42] He taught adult English classes in the day for fellow Mexicans; in the evenings, he taught children Spanish.

Just down the street from Mrs. McAvoy's building and around the corner from the Crane Manufacturing Company, a Mexican, Manuel Santa Cruz, operated a grocery store (at 3357 West Thirty-eighth Street) where many of the neighborhood Mexicans shopped. He had competition from two other Mexican grocers—one in the same block at 3353 Thirty-eighth Street and another on the corner of Thirty-eighth and Homan. On the window of the latter, a crayon drawing of an automobile announced that the store sold "chorizo Mexicano" and provided home delivery of groceries.[43]

Across the Santa Fe railroad tracks, Thirty-eighth Street turned into a residential area of sorts, that is, an area of several Mexican boxcar camps where Mexican track workers and their families lived in railroad boxcars left sitting on sidetracks or on open ground next to the tracks.[44] In many ways, these living conditions were worse than the dilapidated shacks other Mexicans lived in on the Near West Side, for railroad boxcars had no windows and were made entirely of steel and iron. In the hot humid summers of Chicago, the metal absorbed the heat, and the cars turned into large ovens. Even summer evenings in Chicago rarely cooled down to a temperature that would have made sleeping inside comfortable, as the metal retained and radiated much of the day's heat. Conversely, in the harsh cold and snowy winters of Chicago, the boxcars converted into freezers. Children living in them learned early on not to touch the walls for fear of being burned or having their fingertips freeze, depending on the season.[45] Nevertheless, there were scattered signs of domesticity. One contemporary observer recounted in 1925, "Outside . . . were a number of chickens. Ten Mexican boys, 4–14 years old were playing . . . with a soccer football."[46]

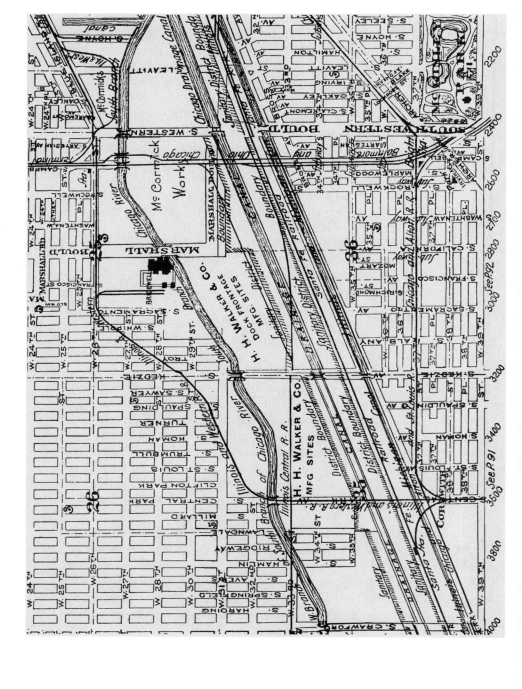

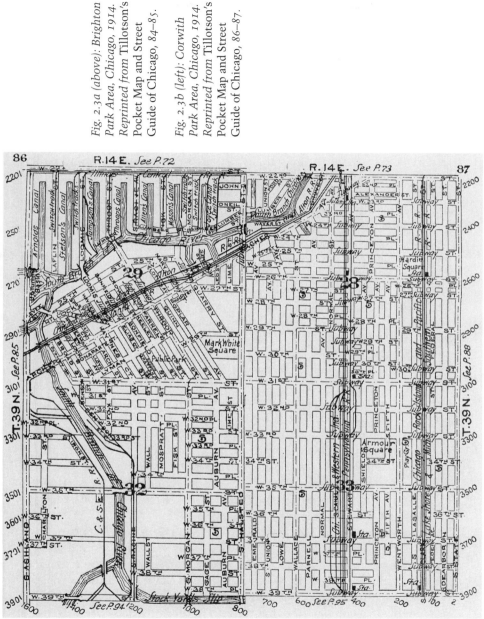

Fig. 2.3a (above): Brighton Park Area, Chicago, 1914. Reprinted from Tillotson's Pocket Map and Street Guide of Chicago, 84–85.

Fig. 2.3b (left): Corwith Park Area, Chicago, 1914. Reprinted from Tillotson's Pocket Map and Street Guide of Chicago, 86–87.

Yet another cluster of Mexicans lived further south in the north-ernmost reaches of the Armour Square area, along Alexander Street.[47] Bounded on the west by a subway station at West Twenty-third Street and Stewart and on the east by Wentworth Avenue, this drab little street was made up of two-story frame buildings. A group of Mexicans lived in the basements of these buildings or on the second floor in the rear apartments.[48] The street also had a couple of small factories, one store, and the Mission of María Incarnata, near the old Italian Catholic church. A Mexican pool hall was located nearby at Twenty-second Street and Princeton in a dirty room with a broken-glass storefront. When visited in early 1925, a sign in the window advertised beds for rent, and two Mexican men played pool at the one available dingy table in the largely unfurnished room.[49] Pool halls generally operated as more than enter-tainment venues. Like the one on Twenty-second Street, many offered beds for rent, usually short-term, and provided occasional meals to their tenants. Most proprietors also would receive mail for patrons who either had no permanent address or who left the area for work stints outside Chicago. This practice helped to strengthen informal social networks already at work in the pool halls, as men (primarily) would meet there and exchange tips on employment, housing, travel, and so on.

Spanish-language newspapers also helped to disseminate this and other kinds of information. *México* (renamed *El Nacional* in 1930) ap-peared to be the longest-lived and most widely circulated in Chicago. Established in 1924, this local paper operated under the same editor, Sam Fraga, until its demise in 1935. As the Mexican population grew during the 1920s, other newspapers emerged and folded, including *La Raza*, which lasted until about 1933. Several others appeared during the early to mid-1930s, including *El Indicador* (1933), *La Defensa* (1936–37), *La Lucha* (1934), but each was short-lived largely due to the economic hard-ships of the Great Depression. Nevertheless, as a whole, these organs provided information on issues of local interest, including housing and employment. They also informed their readers of neighborhood events, celebrations, and gatherings.

Like other areas of Mexican settlement in Chicago, Mexicans in Back-of-the-Yards/Packingtown could be found clustered around their employers and around the local settlement house. Of the three major areas of Mexican settlement, this neighborhood had the smallest number of Mexican commercial establishments. At their peak, they numbered sixteen in 1928, compared with forty-four in the Hull-House/Near West area and forty-two in South Chicago.[50] The majority were pool halls,

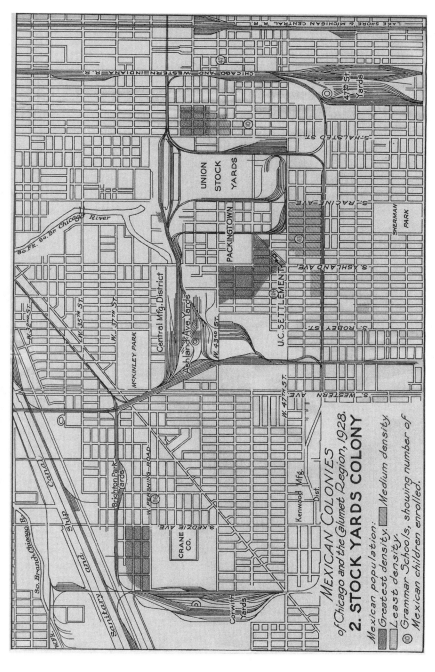

Fig. 2.4: *Back-of-the-Yards Area, Chicago, 1928. From Taylor, Mexican Labor, 56–67.*

restaurants, or grocery stores; a few operated as combination pool halls, restaurants, and barbershops.[51]

Three significant groups of Mexican concentration emerged in the area. The first, estimated in 1928 to number around a thousand, was immediately around the Mary McDowell Settlement House at Forty-fourth and Gross.[52] A smaller group lived directly southeast, and a third cluster was situated directly east of the Yards.

Wherever Mexicans settled and lived in Chicago, they found that their presence catalyzed feelings of ill will among their neighbors. As one Mexican man recounted, "[T]he Italians don't like us but I don't see why."[53] An Italian woman later clarified, "'We don't like to have the Mexicans moving in.'"[54] Another man, a Mexican clerk in a men's clothing store in South Chicago, commented, "[We deal] directly with other immigrant groups; these really do receive [us] with very ill will; especially the Poles."[55] Only three months later, this same man reportedly was falsely imprisoned and received death threats for investigating (in his capacity as a roving reporter for *México*) the case of two Mexicans who were shot in South Chicago.[56] On the Near West Side, Mrs. Quintero noted that her sons "have trouble with the Polish boys."[57]

Conflict, competition, and sometimes violence characterized these primarily male-to-male interactions. In 1927, on the Near West Side, for instance, a group of Polish men assaulted and killed a Mexican man near Fourteenth and Halsted. The man was killed but not robbed, reportedly to drive Mexicans out of the neighborhood.[58] Mexicans who settled on the east side of the Yards in Packingtown were forced to move to the west side because of conflicts with the Irish.[59] Even when Mexicans were allowed to rent on the west side of the Yards, property owners tried to concentrate them into a few blocks. As one contemporary explained, "'[T]he Irish won't rent houses to the Mexicans outside of the area indicated on your map.'"[60] This density of Mexican settlement itself created other kinds of conflicts with the Irish. Miss Garvey, an Irishwoman living on Alexander Street, expressed her outrage over a number of reported cases of Mexican women and men living together unmarried. Garvey had come to Chicago as a child from Ireland and was a devout Catholic working at the mission of María Incarnata. She explained that one of these outrageous couples lived next door to her. "A couple, both of whom had buried their firsts, had met in Texas and were living together here." She called first on the woman, then on the man, and "impressed their mortal sin upon them and told them how to get married. But they haven't done it."[61]

Because the Irish tended to control the real estate in Back-of-the-Yards, Mexicans and Poles in this area were forced into similar rental conditions, creating situations that frequently erupted into violence.[62] "The first Mexicans to move into Gross Street had their windows smashed by Poles."[63] In other cases the inadequacies of housing facilities meant that Mexicans and Poles had to share public shower facilities in Davis Square, one of two public parks in the area.[64] When the Mexicans went to use these showers, they reportedly had to go in groups to avoid trouble from the Poles.[65] Mexicans shared these experiences with other newly arrived immigrant groups as they sought to establish themselves.[66] As the newest population, Mexicans bore the brunt of their neighbors' intolerance. As became obvious for José Blanco and Elizondo González, however, the fluidity of their racial positioning only reinforced the ugly tenor of this discrimination.

Prejudice also awaited Mexicans as they moved into the rental market. Mexicans "depreciate property values," an Irish policeman in 1928 explained.[67] In the Brighton Park area of the Near West Side, a Jewish realtor maintained that "since the Mexicans have come in the real estate values have declined to almost nothing. But the rental value of the buildings go up."[68] In other words, as Mexicans moved into the rental market, they were charged higher rents than other immigrant groups. He went on to describe one flat in Back-of-the-Yards "that [had] rented for $38 . . . now rented to Mexicans for $52."[69] A landlord told of an instance of light-skinned, fair-haired Mexicans trying to "pass" for Irish to secure a less expensive rent. One Mexican "with sandy hair and the appearance of an Irishman," accompanied by his son, negotiated an apartment rental at a modest twenty-five dollars per month.[70] Approvingly, his son remarked, "¡Qué Bueno!" Hearing this, the landlord asked, "Are you Mexicans?" and immediately raised the rent to thirty-five dollars. This example reveals the awareness of the Mexican men to the racial coding of "looks," specifically that they tried to trade on their light skins and hair coloring. Clearly, "passing" for a more acceptable type of tenant involved more than simply looking the part, and "being Mexican" meant having to pay higher rents than others of Chicago's immigrant residents.[71]

Like those in Back-of-the-Yards, the first Mexican workers to settle in South Chicago were recruited by industry to break the packinghouse and steel strikes of 1919.[72] Employed principally in the area steel mills, these Mexican men worked and lived alongside Poles, Slovaks, and Blacks. As in other areas of Chicago, new in-migrations of Mexicans continued to settle near the principal employers in the area, Wisconsin Steel Works, Illinois Steel Company, Riverside Iron Works, and General Chemical. As in the Near West areas, the majority of Mexicans in South Chicago during the 1920s were male, for the major employers in the area hired only men.[73]

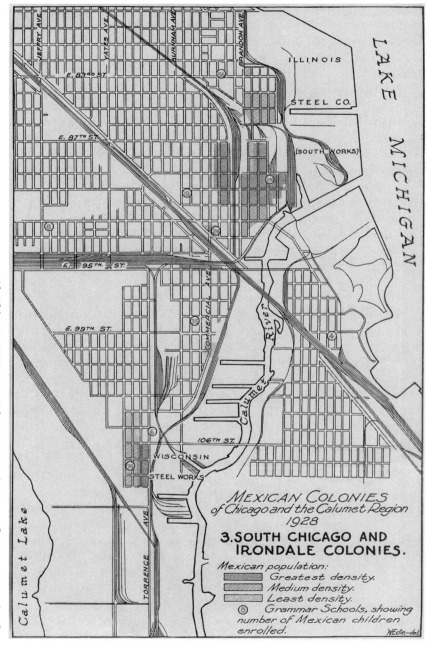

Fig. 2.5: South Chicago Area, 1928. From Taylor, Mexican Labor, 56–57.

The Mexicans who settled in South Chicago lived "chiefly [o]n the streets immediately west of the mills—the Strand, Green Bay, [and] Mackinaw Avenue[s]."[74] Clusters of Mexican men lived in the area around Eighty-ninth and Green Bay, close to the Illinois Steel plant, and around 106th and Torrance, near the Wisconsin Steel plant.[75] As the number of Mexicans increased, however, they expanded their area of settlement. By 1926, there were an estimated four to six thousand Mexicans living in South Chicago.[76]

South Chicago lacked the large settlement houses of the other two areas for organized activities, but several smaller institutions catered to the needs of local immigrant groups. Some were served by Neighborhood House on Buffalo Avenue, the Friendship Center on Houston, or the South Chicago Community Center on Brandon Avenue, located in Bird Memorial church (formerly First Congregational church).[77] Initially, the newly opened YMCA appeared to welcome Mexicans, even housing one as a resident. Soon, however, other boarders and locals complained, and he was evicted. Thereafter, Mexicans, like Blacks, were barred from using the YMCA. It was for whites only, and Mexicans were not deemed white.[78]

The central business district for Mexican commercial establishments in South Chicago extended along Eighty-ninth and Commercial Streets. Walking along this corridor in 1925, an investigator found on the corner of Green Bay and Eighty-ninth a Mexican poolroom and restaurant. On its window, the establishment advertised that it sold tobacco and fruit, with services that included a barber and rooms to rent. Across the street (at 8904 Green Bay) was another Mexican poolroom-restaurant named El Cantor del Gordo. A possible insight into the proprietor's former occupation on the radio in Mexico is revealed in the name of his restaurant—The Announcer of the Big Prize Lottery. Apparently it operated as a barbershop as well, for there was a barber chair on one side of the room. Shortly thereafter, however, this poolroom-restaurant-barbershop had failed, suggestive of the kind of turnover Mexican establishments underwent during the 1920s.[79] By 1928 a new establishment was in the same location, a restaurant called El Gato Negro (The Black Cat).[80] Nearby (9048 Green Bay), the Chapultepec Restaurant and poolroom advertised "hot tamales y cuartos" (hot tamales and rooms to rent). Three years later, in 1928, the establishment had moved around the block to 3231 Ninety-first Street.[81]

Like Corwith Yards on the Near West Side, South Chicago was characterized by a large number of boxcar colonies. Some of the largest of the boxcar colonies in Chicago lay on the east side of the C&WI (Chicago and Wisconsin) Railroad tracks between Eighty-second and Eighty-third Streets in South Chicago. In 1925, thirteen of the twenty dilapidated box-cars resting on the sidetracks appeared to be occupied by Mexican families. Each boxcar had an iron pipe chimney and a short flight of wooden steps up to the doorway. "Some cars [had] little porches built to them . . . a few cars [had] little chicken yards, [others had] a number of . . . potted plants."[82] An estimated thirty workmen and thirteen families lived in the boxcar camp.[83]

Unique to South Chicago of all the areas of Mexican settlement was Galindo's drugstore, Botica Galindo, located at 9014 Buffalo Avenue. Centrally located on a busy street with a carline running on it, the store had several rooms, one of which was "fitted up as a doctor's office and used by Dr. Serna."[84] The drugstore sold a variety of U.S. and Mexican patent medicines, drugs, remedies, bug powder, and several newspapers. It sold *México, El Universal* (published in Mexico City), a couple of Texas papers (very likely *La Prensa* from San Antonio), a smattering of "bullfighters papers," and a paper by an unnamed "local radical labor organization."[85] This drugstore also sold paperbound books from Mexico, a selection of pottery figures, and a few Mexican groceries. Reportedly, Galindo purchased most of his Mexican groceries through a dealer in San Antonio. Among the grocery items were Tamalina, *piloncillo, metates,* and *molcajetes.*[86]

Galindo's drugstore advertised in *México* and drew customers from all over the Chicago area.[87] Indeed, Mexican settlements, though somewhat scattered, were not isolated from each other, at least during the 1920s. Migratory patterns of railway workers and agricultural workers along with the back-and-forth migration of Mexicans to and from Mexico until about 1929 combined to keep Mexicans informed about goings-on and conditions in Mexico and in Chicago. Even social gatherings appeared to aid in making ties across areas of settlement. Dances given by Hull-House, for instance, drew Mexicans from all over Chicago.[88]

Like their countrymen on the West Side, South Chicago Poles also worked to hinder or even prevent Mexican settlement in the area either by outright refusing to rent to them or by raising the rents beyond the means of Mexican workers.[89] Max Guzmán, a prominent South Chicago resident, recalled trying to rent a house in 1937. "Polish woman [said] to me, 'You Mexican?' 'Ya, I'm Mexican.' She said, 'No, Mexicans ain't allowed here. No Mexicans allowed here.'"[90]

Raymond Nelson, who interviewed South Chicago residents for the Congregational Ministry, experienced the density of Mexican living conditions firsthand. He wrote, "The average South Chicago Mexican[s] live like cattle in their flats . . . three to four families occupy the space ordinarily used by one American family."[91] Henry Matushek, an agent of a building and loan company the area, elaborated: "[W]e have to charge [the Mexicans] higher rents than others because more families occupy a flat or house at the same time."[92] He cited a typical example of a flat on Green Bay. The "white folks," he said, on the lower floor paid ten dollars per month in rent, but the three Mexican families that were living together in the flat above paid twenty dollars.

Mexicans logically responded by joining together in denser groups to pay those rents. Property owners then countered by further raising rents. Contemporaries often failed to perceive the economic motivations for the density of Mexican concentration in flats and apartments. They chose instead to explain this settlement pattern in terms of "being Mexican"—that is, somehow Mexicans preferred to live in such close quarters.[93] Extended family groups often lived together, including unmarried and married siblings and their families or cousins. Adolfo Moseda and his wife, for instance, took care of his two younger sisters, Josefina and María.[94] In another representative example, two brothers and their families lived in two small rented rooms in the rear basement of a ramshackle building at 748 DeKoven Street on the Near West Side. These four adults and five children shared a small cooking stove and a bed in one room and a trunk and old bedsprings supported on boxes in the other room.[95]

While it is unclear who the "white folks" were that Matushek mentioned, it is clear that in the minds of many Mexican men, all their neighbors were *güeros* (whites), lumping all nationalities into one—"Polack." When asked about his *güero* neighbors, Manuel Bravo recalled, "I don't know their nationalities . . . to us they were all Polacks. . . . we just call[ed] them all Polacks and that's it."[96] Despite the obviously derogatory use of "Polack," it is notable that Mexicans were making no distinction between white and Polish. Even Mexican women described all the Polish people as "white." After describing how she enjoyed visiting with her Mexican neighbors, for example, Plácida Gonzales remarked, "I likes to talk with white folks too." When asked to whom she was referring, Plácida explained, "white like Polish."[97]

Although this brand of discrimination against Mexican settlement became increasingly pervasive, it was also significant, as the contemporary researcher George Edson noted, that Mexicans were even allowed to live in these areas at all.[98] During this period, Blacks coming to Chicago found that they were not allowed to rent or own property outside a few limited areas.[99] The net result of these pernicious practices was to segregate Chicago's Black population, concentrating it primarily along what was called the "Black Belt" on Chicago's Near South Side and in certain blocks near the Calumet Steel mills in South Chicago. For the most part, Mexicans only experienced this degree of residential segregation in South Chicago.

In South Chicago, the Polish, like those in the Stockyards area, tried to influence where Mexicans settled, and since they tended to control real estate, they could do so effectively.[100] Polish attempts to keep Mexicans out of certain areas helps explain two patterns of Mexican settlement in the area: their initial tendency to live among Blacks, and the extreme density of the Mexican population. In South Chicago, Poles owned enough real estate to keep Mexicans from renting in certain areas, which meant that Mexicans and blacks had to live in close quarters. A contemporary observed, "[T]he Negroes and Mexicans live together—Negroes upstairs, Mexicans below, or Mexicans occupy shacks in the backyard[s] of Negro dwellings."[101] As Clementina Rodríguez recalled, when they first moved into South Chicago in the early 1920s, there "was one *prietito* [black man] living upstairs and we Mexicans downstairs."[102] There was even some suggestion of a literal hierarchy in which Blacks ranked above Mexicans. It is noteworthy that the relationship between these neighbors may have been friendly, since the assignation "prietito," with the diminutive ending of "ito," connotes a certain warmth ("a nice black man").

Yet living in such density often erupted in conflicts between Mexican men and Black men. The police in South Chicago reported that the few arrests of Mexicans they had made were mostly for carrying weapons. Mexicans carried these weapons, reported Miss Yates of United Charities, because "they [were] afraid of trouble from the Negroes."[103] A desk sergeant at the South Chicago police station confirmed her claim. Mexicans, he explained, "carr[ied] knives and guns . . . their excuse generally is that they are afraid of trouble from the Negroes."[104] Mr. Parkin, an assistant to the Reverend O'Neil of the Methodist church in South Chicago, also noticed the conflicts between Mexicans and Blacks, commenting that "a few Mexicans have been shot and a few Negroes have been cut up."[105] Parkin attributed the troubles between Mexicans and Blacks to "moonshine." While this may have been the case on the surface, deep tensions likely reflected ongoing Mexican desires to distinguish themselves from Blacks. As many Mexicans recognized, "[T]he white resident . . . has a very low opinion of the [N]egro,"[106] and as many discovered, the consequences of being taken for Black could be severe.

Mexican settlement also was concentrated in Black areas by other kinds of policing at the hands of Polish men engaged in practices that helped to reinforce Mexican exclusion. Some resorted to violence to regulate Mexican mobility in the area. *México* spread the news in January 1924 for Mexicans to be wary of the area around Forty-seventh and Ashland, as it was patrolled by a group of Poles.[107] The area lay in the turf of the notorious Ragen's Colts, a gang sponsored by Cook County Commissioner Frank Ragen that had been active in the race riots of 1919.[108] The gang masqueraded as an athletic club but in fact controlled and protected their turf, particularly from Blacks who worked in the area or traveled through on their way to and from work.[109] It is likely this group about which the newspaper was warning its Spanish-language readers. Like the white mobs of the 1919 race riots, Ragen's Colts targeted Mexicans as well as Blacks in marking the racialized boundaries of "their" space. Other white gangs that patrolled the area included several suggestively named ones like the White Club, the Mayflower Club, the Hamburgs, the Emeralds, and the Our Flags Club.[110] The Hamburgs were sponsored by the Bridgeport alderman Joseph McDonough.[111] In 1924, this particularly tough gang was led by an Irish youth named Richard J. Daley, who later became the longest-serving mayor in the history of Chicago.[112] Reportedly, young Irish men, particularly on the east side of the Yards, applied violent tactics similar to those of Ragen's Colts, "waylay[ing] Mexicans and beat[ing] them up."[113]

Other assaults on Mexicans vividly communicated the motives of some European immigrant men. In 1934, Luis Vargas was assaulted upon crossing 108th Street by "an enraged mob of Polish people."[114] The mob reportedly tore up Mr. Vargas's passport papers and stole two dollars from him. Though it is unclear from the description what kinds of papers Vargas carried, the significance of the act of destroying them was clearly to contest his claims of legitimacy. Without papers or passport, Vargas could not prove his rightful "belonging" in Chicago. He was even stripped of whatever legitimate claims he could make to belonging to a nation. Removal of these papers was particularly damaging during the Depression, as the danger of deportation or repatriation to Mexico was very real.[115]

Poles, and less frequently Italians, in Packingtown resorted to enforcing curfews for Mexicans in the area, times after which they were not "supposed" to be out and places where they could not go. As Carlos Roberts reported, "[T]he Polish residents . . . have designated a certain street as a line which no Mexican shall pass after sunset under penalty of being beaten up."[116] On January 22, 1927, a Mexican man walking home at night was attacked by a group of ten Italians.[117]

Occasionally, Mexican women too found themselves enmeshed in interethnic conflicts. Señora Arredara, for instance, was walking along the street with her husband and two children when a Polish youth, Joseph Jopek, knocked down her young son, Salvador. "She then hit Jopek to defend her little Salvador. Just then [another man, named] Grabinsky jumped out of his automobile, approached her and said, 'Miserable Mexican, you are a. . . .' Seeing herself so affronted she drew a .32 calibre revolver which she carried and fired several times." Grabinsky died on the way to Deaconess Hospital. "Many witnesses saw all the details of the incident and admitted that Sra. Arredara acted in legitimate defense of her outraged honor," and she was not found guilty.[118] She transgressed norms of decorum (not to mention femininity) to defend a much stronger belief, her own honor. This assertive move must have been a surprise to bystanders, particularly as her husband was beside her and did not act in her defense.

Work and Labor Relations

As seen with José Blanco and Elizondo González in 1919, Mexican fears of being mistaken for Blacks—and their fears of the consequences of such confusion—were not unfounded. The historian Alexandra M. Stern has described deftly how eugenicists worked to protect their notions regarding the purity of the body politic from the perceived threat of "hidden and hereditary 'unit characters' which determined human capacities ranging from degree of skin pigmentation to musical talent, from criminal proclivities to intellectual acumen."[119] As whiteness increasingly became the measure of intellect, desirability, talent, and purity, many loudly proclaimed that Mexicans were "'[e]ugenically, as low-powered as the negro.'" Eugenicists took these arguments to the U.S. Congress, first to secure passage of the 1924 National Origins Act and later to plug a supposed hole in the act by limiting immigration from "the new world."[120] The employment manager of a Chicago steel plant interviewed in the late 1920s echoed some of the most vitriolic of these eugenic views. He proudly relayed that he could see some "Negro" blood in Mexicans. "'You can tell . . . they seem to be thicker through the temples.'"[121] Far from benign, these views in an employment manager could impact the lives of Mexicans in tangible ways as they searched for jobs.

As if to confirm Mexican fears of their nonwhiteness, occasionally Blacks tried to pass for Mexicans.[122] In the early 1930s at one of the numerous employment agencies on Canal Street, an *enganchista* approached two dark-skinned men reading the sign in his window.[123] "Ship tonight Minnesota? Nice cool there. No mucho calor [heat]. Vamos upstairs," he said to them in broken Spanish. One of his fellow agents asked him to confirm that these men were in fact Mexicans. The first agent asked the two men again and was assured that they were in fact Mexicans. The second agent, however, dismissed them. "They are not [Mexicans] . . . they're Negroes trying to pass for Mexicans." Beyond noting one of the men's straight black hair, it is unclear from the account how the second man established that they were Blacks.[124] However, the agents' initial confusion and their willingness to believe that these men were Mexican highlight the instability of Mexican racialized positioning while also confirming the nonwhite status of these "Mexicans." The second agent went on to explain that if he had shipped those men to the beet fields, they would have been fired immediately and would have been quickly sent back to Chicago. "Nobody will work with them, not even the Mexicans."[125] Mexican resistance to working among Blacks in the fields could also be understood as active attempts to distance themselves from Blacks so as not to be taken for Black, or even so as not to be in direct economic competition with Blacks by working alongside them.

Motivated by the discriminatory, and at times violent, consequences of being taken for Black, Mexicans worked to secure their desirability as workers and residents. These efforts, however, were undercut by a sinister threat: the ever-present possibility of forcible deportation. In the recession of the early 1920s and again during the Depression in the early 1930s, federal, state, and local bodies throughout the United States instituted deportation programs to rid the country of Mexican "foreigners" and to ensure what few jobs remained for "Americans," usually European ethnics.[126] In many parts of the United States, such deportation programs devastated Mexican populations, cutting them by over half. In Chicago the population declined by one-quarter.[127] As jobs grew scarce during the Depression, employment managers in Chicago also preserved jobs for "Americans." Despite the fact that some of the Mexicans who came to work in the steel mills were U.S. citizens from the Southwest, especially Texas, employers often refused to hire them, and Mexican unemployment soared. As Benny Rodríguez recalled, "Why if the Polacks [were getting hired,] why couldn't we get a day at least? . . . [T]hey used to get two or three days sometimes four days. We didn't used to get nothing."[128]

In fact, fears of forcible deportation prevented most Mexicans from taking part in any labor activities that might jeopardize their jobs, even into the late 1930s. Relatively few Mexicans joined unions because of citizenship requirements, unsupportive leadership, and fears of deportation.[129] There were the occasional exceptions. Max Guzmán of South Chicago, for instance, was not a U.S. citizen and still became an early member of the Steel Workers Organizing Committee (SWOC; organized in 1936, in 1943 it became the United Steelworkers of America). Yet he did face harassment because of his citizenship status, particularly at the hands of policemen who threatened to deport him. "They told me as long as I was not a citizen of the United States they could send me back to Mexico any time they felt like it."[130] José "Joe" Alcala was more typical of the few Mexicans who did participate in labor. Joe ran an orchestra group in South Chicago called Los Charros, which played regularly at SWOC events.[131] As a Texas-born Mexican, Joe was not as vulnerable to threats of deportation as Mexican nationals.

Even if Mexican workers were U.S. citizens, and even if they were able to prove U.S. citizenship, many found themselves unable to support union strike efforts for fear of being deported. These fears were born out by real experiences; nearly 60 percent of those repatriated and deported to Mexico were U.S. citizens, many of them children born in the United States.[132] Union organizers were aware of this impediment to Mexican unionization. In 1936, Joseph Roth of the International Worker's League spoke to a regular meeting of Mexicans in Back-of-the-Yards, explaining how deportation was used as a strikebreaking weapon.[133]

Many employers, however, saw Mexican disenfranchisement and lack of labor power as a bonus. According to the "majority of employment managers, [this gave Mexicans] superiority over the eastern or southern European."[134] Mexicans, however, employed their own forms of resistance to intolerable labor conditions. Instead of changing citizenship or unionizing, the tool of choice for most Mexicans was voting with their feet—literally walking out of jobs or other situations that they could not tolerate. As one employment agent explained, "'A Mexican will never kick . . . if he doesn't like it, he just leaves.'"[135] This practice particularly infuriated employers and often left Mexican workers with a reputation for unreliability and laziness. It likely also exacerbated tensions with other ethnic groups who, ignoring high rates of Mexican unemployment, resented Mexican workers taking scarce jobs.

Unwilling to support strikes and in need of jobs, some Mexicans became scabs, providing yet another reason for European ethnics to harbor ill will against them. Benny Rodríguez described how the steel-mill employers in South Chicago brought in Mexican workers to keep the mills going during the steel strikes of September 1919. "They used to bring a lot of people from Mexico and put them in a boat [on Lake Michigan], put them around the back [of the plant], and put them in [to work]."[136] Lucio Franco recalled being involved in similar strikebreaking activities when he came to Chicago to work at the Carnegie Steel plant in South Chicago during the strikes of 1923.[137] "Mexicans came to shut down the strike," he said, "yes, the Mexicans came to break the strike." For years this was a common practice in industry, until passage of the National Labor Relations Act (the Wagner Act) in 1935 and the subsequent formation of the Congress of Industrial Organizations (CIO) stopped the common practice of using Mexican labor to break strikes.[138] In the meantime, however, Mexicans came to be perceived as strikebreakers by their immigrant neighbors, thus intensifying tensions between them.[139]

Violence erupted over European immigrant fears that Mexican men would take their jobs. One contemporary observer noted, "The Lithuanians and Poles thought the Mexicans came in to lower wages. . . . [So] they beat up Mexicans coming home at night."[140] The perception that Mexicans undercut European immigrant laborers did have some real basis, as evidenced in the marked changes in the pool of available workers. Between 1912 and 1928, the ethno-racial composition of the workforce in various industries in Chicago changed dramatically. Mexicans had gone from comprising 0 percent of the steel industry's workforce in 1912 to being 9.4 percent of the workers in 1928.[141] A similar shift took place in the packinghouses. In 1909, the Polish and "native white" were the most represented groups, followed in decreasing order by the Lithuanians, Germans, and Czechs. By 1928, the largest group was the "Colored," followed by, again in descending order, "native whites," Polish, Lithuanians, and Mexicans. While no Mexicans worked in the packinghouses in 1909, by 1928, 5.7 percent of the labor force was Mexican.[142] Interestingly, the story of Black workers in the packinghouses roughly parallels that of Mexicans, albeit in a much more concentrated period of time. While there were very few in 1915, by 1918 Blacks numbered nearly 20 percent of the workforce in the Yards. The huge boom in employment ended in 1921, as Blacks, like Mexicans, were laid off during the recession of that year. Unlike Blacks, however, Mexicans were subject to deportations during this, the first—and little-known—deportation program.[143] Like the repatriations of the early 1930s, public opposition to hiring Mexicans and pressure on Mexicans to leave from municipal governments forced many to accept help for repatriation offered by the Mexican government.[144] Employment opportunities revived during the national meatpacking strikes of 1921–22, where Blacks, like Mexicans, were hired as strikebreakers.

Demographic changes in the composition of the industrial workforce certainly intensified tensions between Mexican men and their immigrant co-workers. Moreover, that Mexicans were predominantly unskilled workers placed them at the lowest rungs of the employment ladder, in direct competition with those least-skilled of European workers.[145] Mexican predominance in the unskilled labor pool continued over the course of the interwar period to such an extent that the category "Mexican" came to mean "unskilled," as the contemporary sociologist Paul S. Taylor emphasized.[146] A Mexican man explained, "'If you are a mechanic, they won't believe you if you say you are Mexican.'"[147] Another Mexican clarified the point: "'[W]hen people see that I am a machinist, they say to me, "you are not a Mexican,"'"[148] as though no Mexican could hold a skilled job.

Even skilled workers found that prejudice from foremen limited their work opportunities. A Mexican who had been a machinist and locomotive engineer on the Mexican National Railway illustrated this point. "'The foreman said to me, "If you have not worked as a machinist in this country, then you are not a machinist."'"[149] Because the foremen in the steel and packing industries in Chicago tended to be at least second-generation ethnic Europeans, such a sentiment could easily be understood to be further evidence of the jostling for position between Chicago's immigrant groups.[150] By denying the legitimacy of the Mexican machinist's skills, the foreman was at once reinforcing the Mexican's foreignness and solidifying his own position of belonging and of Americanness.[151] In addition, by ignoring his skills, the machinist was conveniently positioned beneath the foreman, thus reinforcing the foreman's higher status and economic potential.[152]

Mexicans also grew increasingly aware of discrimination against them in the types of work they were assigned. A man working at a cement plant noted, "'[T]he dirtiest and hardest work is given to the Mexicans.'"[153] Often they found that not only were Mexicans given the hardest work, but their European neighbors got easier and better work. "The Poles get all the good jobs," complained Mr. Díaz of Packingtown. "The Mexicans have to do all the dirty jobs."[154] Revealing much about the racial bias of supposed allies, the noted Chicago anthropologist Robert Redfield commented that Díaz was "a bright, intelligent looking fellow, perfectly white. He might pass for a native American."[155] Interestingly, while his physiognomy could pass, he still experienced job discrimination at the hands of European foremen and supervisors, suggesting that more than physical differences were at work in constructing Mexican racial identity in Chicago.

A Mexican steel worker concurred with Díaz: "'They give the Mexicans the heavy work and the Poles the *suave* [easy] work with better pay.'"[156] Occasionally the prejudicial treatment was more subtle, as in the case of one foreman who asked his Mexican workers to work in his home garden and clean up around his house. "'He never asked the Italians or the Irish,'" recalled one man. The foreman didn't actively force the men to take the work, but "'if you didn't do it . . . you certainly paid for it on the job the next day.'"[157]

Contrary to the fears of their immigrant co-workers, Mexicans progressively found that most employers instituted policies against hiring them, and Mexican women had even fewer options than men. In 1928, only fifty-eight industries and businesses in Chicago employed Mexicans. Of those, only twenty-five employed Mexican women.[158] According to Mr. Oberhart, superintendent of the Illinois Free Employment Bureau, employers couldn't "mix Mexicans with other workers. The white workers won't stand for a Mexican in their camp."[159] Though it is unclear who the "white workers" were, it is plain that Mexicans were not included. A plant manager confirmed this, making an implicit equation between "white workers" and Swedes: "'We haven't any Mexicans; our workmen are practically all Swedes and object to the Mexicans.'"[160]

The separation of Mexicans from other workers continued throughout the period. Even the City of Chicago would not hire Mexicans to shovel snow in the winters. "'They demoralize a crew,'" explained one foreman.[161] Mexicans increasingly found themselves isolated from whites and from Europeans, a segregation that only helped to solidify the whiteness of the Europeans in the minds of the Mexicans and the "separateness" of the Mexicans themselves. In a move that underscored how pervasive anti-Mexican sentiments had become, the Chicago municipal court judge Thomas Green imprisoned the Mexican consul in Chicago because of the burden his people supposedly were placing on Americans. "'Mexicans,'" the judge said, "'come here to take work away from the Americans and later become vagrants and create a problem.'" When the judge was informed that the consul could not be imprisoned because of diplomatic immunity, he reversed the sentence and had the whole case stricken from the record.[162] Nevertheless, his sentiments and those of the institutions he represented were clear: Mexicans were not Americans; Mexicans took American jobs; Mexicans became vagrants and problems. In some views, Mexicans became even more disliked than the Blacks. Henry Matushek of Yates Building and Loan expressed the idea that Mexicans "are the most undesirable citizen that there is in the area and they are worse than the Negro."[163]

Yet a few employers did hire Mexicans and found them particularly desirable because they were not Blacks. When Clyde Brading of Wisconsin Steel hired light-skinned Mexicans, not only was he favoring a degree of whiteness, he also was actively *not* hiring Blacks. "I don't hire Negroes," he explained, "and [I] bro[ugh]t in the light-colored Mexicans to keep as far away from the color line as possible."[164] Clearly, the repercussions of the race riots in 1919 continued and helped to shape opportunities for Mexican workers in Chicago.[165] By hiring Mexicans, Brading could avoid the potential "race troubles" of hiring Blacks. He could also pay Mexicans much less than whites, which made the light-skinned Mexicans ideal for his purposes.

In some cases, Mexican racial positioning in Chicago worked for them in curious ways: Dr. Ellis of the Sherwin-Williams Paint Company preferred to hire Mexicans because their "pigmentation" made them "not so liable to skin disease induced by working with paint."[166] Informed by contemporary eugenics, Ellis believed that the skin color of Mexicans "hid" the toxicity of paint.[167] While Clyde Brading seemed to suggest a gradation of skin color among Mexicans, Ellis appeared to conflate Mexican and dark skin—though in actual hiring practice, he must have favored dark-skinned Mexicans over lighter-skinned ones. Again, Mexicans were ideal—dark enough but not Black and not as expensive as whites. Ellis was not alone. The Marshall Field Mattress Company, for example, "employ[ed] no colored," though the firm increasingly hired more Mexican workers.[168] Mexicans were not deemed "colored," but neither were they white.[169]

Police Relations

Mexican experiences with their immigrant neighbors increasingly solidified their positioning outside the ethno-racial hierarchies of Chicago. The Irish, and increasingly the Poles, controlled legal institutional structures that regulated Mexican life in Chicago with consequences always undergirded by the reality of deportation. These structures, particularly the police and the courts,[170] influenced the everyday life of Mexicans, and they reflected the mounting discrimination against Mexicans at the hands of their immigrant neighbors.[171]

Like Judge Green, the police also reinforced Mexicans' understanding of the prejudicial workings of the law in Chicago.[172] During the 1919 race riots, one of the areas of highest Mexican concentration, Packingtown/Back-of-the-Yards, had the highest incidence of reported injuries and lowest level of police protection.[173] As one Mexican in the Stockyards area explained, even when the police were present, "'[T]he average policeman's attitude is still against the Mexicans; the police are largely Irish and Polish.'"[174] While noting the distinction between Irish and Polish, Mexicans gave little weight to that difference, casting the police, whether Irish or Polish, as against them. This is notable in light of work by the historian Dominic A. Pacyga that highlights tensions and hierarchies between the Irish and Polish in Packingtown and South Chicago.[175] In the eyes of Mexicans, however, both groups seemed interchangeable in their shared preferential treatment against Mexicans.[176] Another man commented that when a Mexican man was caught drinking alcohol, he was arrested; however, if "a Pole gets drunk . . . the policeman takes him home."[177] A contemporary noted, "'[T]he Mexicans get little protection in the courts. . . . [and] are now learning that you must buy justice.'"[178] A Mexican in South Chicago confirmed this, relaying that sometimes the police "'take money from [Mexicans] instead of arresting them.'" He described the common practice of police taking bribes: "'[T]he police hold out their hands, spreading five fingers and say "sabe?" [you know?].'"[179] Even Spanish-language newspapers reported incidents of this kind of police corruption. In one such instance, the reporter himself was riding in a friend's car when a mounted Chicago policeman pulled them over for speeding. The Mexicans argued that their car could not go faster than the twenty-five-mile-per-hour speed limit, to which the policeman responded, "'[T]ell it to the judge.'" He did add, however, that they "could 'settle up' by means of money." When the pair offered him two dollars, the policeman refused, so they gave him four dollars, which he accepted. The two Mexicans were thereby able "to avoid the bother of appearing in court" by having "greased his palm."[180] Sidney Levin, interviewed years later, recalled seeing a policeman demand a bribe from one of the local poolroom owners. "Mr. [Manuel] Bravo permitted gambling in the back of the poolroom."[181] As Levin mused, "[T]he guy [the policeman] didn't even have the decency to turn his head."

This kind of police corruption certainly was not unique to Chicago. In Los Angeles, for example, police protection of organized crime, including liquor, gambling, and prostitution, was legendary. As the historian Edward Escobar notes, during this period in Los Angeles, "every mayor and almost every chief of police left office under a cloud of scandal."[182] When William Dever came into office as Chicago's mayor in 1923, he refused to turn a blind eye to the collusion of politicians and police with organized crime. During his term, he promised often that he would clean up Chicago vice and rid the city of crime.[183] He chose Morgan A. Collins, a veteran member of the police force who was known for his honesty, to be his new chief of police. And unlike most contemporary city mayors, Dever directed Collins to actively enforce the laws of Prohibition. "Eventually," wrote the historian Douglas Bukowski, "Morgan A. Collins declined bribes of as much as $100,000 a month because he refused to be bought, at least by organized crime." He reportedly had no problem, however, accepting two hundred thousand dollars' worth of Sears-Roebuck stock from Julius Rosenwald, then president of the company, to "enforce the law as Rosenwald believed right."[184] The stridency of the leadership's anti-bootlegging stance appeared to give license to Chicago's rank-and-file police to conduct unannounced vice raids at their discretion. The opportunities to abuse this power were legion. The apparent predominance of Irish and Poles in the force only exacerbated tensions, as their targets often were Mexican working-class homes, businesses, and people, as confirmed by Mexicans themselves.

Police frequently arrested Mexicans without charging them with any crimes. Rafael Guardado Valadez recalled a memorable incident in the 1930s in South Chicago when police swept through the area and arrested as many Mexican men as they could find. Apparently a woman had died of a large lump that the police suspected must have been the result of some form of Mexican male brutality. The men were finally released when Dr. Alejandro Treviño, who worked for the Mexican consulate in Chicago, intervened and explained that the woman died of illness, not from anything the men had done.[185]

In another instance, the police arrested over twenty Mexicans who were standing outside the hall doors at a dance one Saturday at Hull-House. "There was no crime for which to prosecute," but they were imprisoned until the following Monday.[186] In yet another incident, a shopkeeper, Enstolio Aviña, had his store windows broken by a group of Poles in the middle of the night. Although it was between 2:00 and 3:00 AM and the group of young Poles still stood around the store, the police rounded up several area Mexicans, including a family who was sleeping in their home nearby. The police arrested the randomly selected Mexicans and kept them overnight. They were released the next day after each paid a fine of eleven dollars without even being accused of any crime and without benefit of a lawyer or a phone call.[187] Three months later, a Polish policeman killed a Mexican in South Chicago.[188] In Back-of-the-Yards, Mexican men grew to associate police brutality with the brutality of Poles. Mexicans interviewed years later recalled that in those days, they referred to all policemen as "Polish."[189]

Periodically the police would raid Mexican commercial establishments. In January 1931, several Chicago policemen reportedly entered El Gato Negro, a Mexican billiard parlor, with their guns drawn and their "profane language" running, "abusing . . . our compatriots who were peacefully playing billiards." Then, "without any explanation," reported Chicago's leading Spanish-language newspaper, the police "took with them innocent Mexicans." Editorial commentary urged the Mexican consul to protest this treatment of Mexicans by the Chicago police, and reportedly he did.[190] Not until 1935, however, is there any record that these efforts to obtain better treatment of Mexicans had any impact. In September 1935, after significant lobbying by the Mexican consul and the Mexicans of South Chicago, there were unspecified changes made in the police department in the South Chicago district. The consul reported diplomatically to his government in Mexico City that he had begun to see better protection of "nuestros paisanos" (our countrymen) in Chicago after these changes.[191]

The Memorial Day Massacre in May 1937, however, proved the fragility of such negotiations. After at least three years of organizing steel workers around the country, union leaders finally got U.S. Steel (known colloquially as "Big Steel") to sign a contract with them. Republic Steel in South Chicago, however, like other smaller steel companies (known colloquially as "Little Steel") refused to do so. The SWOC, affiliated with the CIO, called a strike against Little Steel. On Memorial Day, supporters and sympathizers from all over Chicago assembled at Sam's Place, a local restaurant and the SWOC's headquarters during the strike, to hear speeches and rally to the cause. The group, then several hundred strong, decided to parade to Republic Steel in a public show of support for the strikers. Just shy of the gates, paraders and strikers clashed with police. Many were injured, clubbed by police, and ten were killed by police bullets.

Two locally prominent Mexicans, Guadalupe Marshall and Max Guzmán, were injured and carted off in a paddy wagon to jail. Both later testified before the U.S. Senate subcommittee investigating the incident, headed by the prominent Senator Robert LaFollette.[192] "The policeman on the front clubbed me down as soon as the first shots started," recounted Guzmán. "When I was just about to pick myself up, another policeman grabbed me by my jacket . . . when they picked me up they struck me twice on the shoulders—once on each shoulder."[193]

Lupe Marshall's testimony was even more graphic. As she wandered dazed through the crowd, bleeding from her head after being clubbed by a policeman, she watched as another policeman clubbed a man who kept trying to get up. "When the man finally fell so he could not move, the policeman took him by the foot and . . . started dragging him . . . the man's shirt was all blood stained . . . so I screamed at the policeman . . . 'Can't you see he is terribly injured?' And at that moment . . . somebody struck me from the back again and knocked me down. As I went down . . . a policeman kicked me on the side here."[194] Once thrown into the paddy wagon, she described bodies being thrown on top of other bodies next to her. All were injured, a few gravely. She tried to help them as best she could, even holding one man's head as he died in her lap. This seemed to be police brutality at its extreme and leaves one wondering about the hopeful tone of the Mexican consul who believed that police brutality was under control.

Police brutality extended to those in jail as well. Of the ninety-eight inmates interviewed by the researcher Paul Warnshuis in 1928 and 1929, nineteen reported being tortured in jail. "J. D." was starved for three days before he broke down and made a confession, while "R. R." reported being punched "about a hundred times" in the face and claimed that "they stuck a revolver in his mouth and threatened to blow his head off."[195] "J. G." reported being punched repeatedly the first day, then being put in ice water the second day for about half an hour before being beaten with a rubber hose for about an hour.[196]

Mexicans became embroiled in various aspects of the legal system at much higher rates than their proportion in the population would suggest. As the sociologist Paul S. Taylor noted, in 1928, 1929, and 1930, Mexicans constituted 1.4 percent of those arrested, even though they were only about .57 percent of the total population of Chicago.[197] Historians have also noted that arrest rates and conviction rates of Mexicans "did not necessarily measure comparative *offence rates* (the real rate of crime)," which only added to already biased views of Mexicans as prone

Fig. 2.6: Lupe Marshall being arrested, Memorial Day Massacre, May 1937. Digital still photo taken by the author, from newsreel footage provided by Les O'Rear, Illinois Labor History Society, Chicago.

to criminality.[198] Mexicans understood this, and also understood that they were targets for "'rascals, petty lawyers, and pettifoggers of the district who wanted to "fix up everything.""'[199]

In some instances, Mexicans found themselves saddled with lawyers they did not even want. In 1925, an AB&O Railroad detective arrested two Mexicans for stealing old lumber from a viaduct that was being torn down. They reportedly spoke no English, so "an Italian runner for an Irish lawyer, speaking Spanish, went to the Mexicans" and persuaded them to take this Irish lawyer. When Methodist missionaries investigated this incident, they discovered not only that the Italian runner who spoke Spanish was mistranslating the proceedings but also "that the Mexicans had not [even] wanted this [Irish] lawyer" in the first place.[200]

Gradations of an emerging group hierarchy appear in this exchange. The Irish lawyer was positioned as the representative of the legal system within which the Mexicans had inadvertently become embroiled. The Italian runner had been acting as a kind of intermediary. By building on linguistic similarities between Italian and Spanish, and being fluent in English, the Italian ingratiated himself with the Irish lawyer by bringing in clients, while at the same time establishing himself above the defendants themselves. That the Mexicans could not decline the services of the lawyer reinforced their subordination. The absence of women again signals the extent to which these dynamics played out in gendered-male interactions. In sum, as one local American noted, "The Mexicans get little protection in the courts . . . the Mexican is in the same position as the Negro in the South. He is always wrong unless there is a white man to speak for him."[201]

Many other Mexicans found themselves similarly enmeshed in a complex system of ethnic hierarchies that came into focus in their everyday experiences. Something as seemingly innocent as taking trash wood to fortify one's shack of an apartment exploded into multi-ethnic dealings involving several aspects of formalized legal structures and less tangible aspects of ethnic group powers.

In another incident, at the Proviso railroad camp, police arrested thirty-seven Mexicans and allegedly beat several of them. Not only did Mexican communities protest this treatment by police, but the Mexican consul came under fire for "display[ing] insufficient activity in behalf of his countrymen."[202] The consulate was also criticized for not intervening on behalf of Mexican nationals who reportedly received "unequal severity in sentencing" from judges.[203] Mexican mutual-aid societies, for instance, turned to the consulate alleging that "in almost all cases involving Mexicans accused of homicide, the judges give out the death sentence, and it is applied with all severity, and they use great partiality against the Mexicans during all stages of the trial."[204] The *mutualistas* insisted that the consul, as the representative of the Mexican government, demand the enforcement of treaties made between Mexico and the United States that promised nondifferential treatment of Mexicans (although they did not explain to which treaties they referred).

The instability of Mexican racial position continued to be shaped by daily experiences with Blacks and with their other immigrant neighbors. Over the course of the interwar period, the contours of Mexican positioning began to emerge. Mexicans were gradually becoming not-white and not-Black. Tensions continued, however, with each of the groups with whom they came into daily contact. Such tensions were indicative of the stresses of each group's attempts to adjust to and find a place in the ethno-racial orders of Chicago.

Heterosocial Relations

As has been evident in settlement, work, and legal/police relations, a significant amount of intergroup jostling was concentrated in gendered-male conflicts. Similar tensions erupted around heterosocial relations. That is, the frequency of these hostilities, particularly between Mexican men and Polish or Italian men, suggests that ethno-racial identities and attempts to "belong" were framed inherently by expressions of a kind of heterosexualized manhood. These were particularly evident in intergroup heterosocial struggles over women. Relations with women came to be a central source of intergroup male friction and a principal means for explaining such conflicts.

According to Mexican accounts in Packingtown, their mobility on the streets was dictated by relations between Polish men and Mexican men regarding women. "Now we cannot stop [at] 47th and Ashland Streets. And all because our countrymen have happened to cross the Polish gentlemen, in such simple matters as skirts."[205] Even workplace tensions between Mexicans and Poles were credited not to threatened notions of proletarianizing manhood but rather to competition over women.[206] When asked about the sources of the rivalry between Poles and Mexicans at work, Carlos López, for instance, reflected that it was really because Polish women preferred Mexican men to Polish men.[207]

Throughout the 1920s, the high concentration of single Mexican men often meant that these men looked to their neighboring groups for heterosocial contacts. A dance in South Chicago reportedly had three Mexican men to every one woman—and there were more Polish women than

Mexican women.[208] Contemporary observers also noted the scarcity of Mexican women, which raised concern for the few Mexican women who resided in Chicago. Noted one social worker, "[T]he scarcity of women in the community leads to many temptations for the young girls. Although only children in years, they find young lovers eager to marry them."[209] Another noted, "Mexican women are very scarce. There were many fights for the ones that were here."[210] The scarcity of Mexican women meant not only that they often married very young but also that it was not uncommon for older Mexican women to marry significantly younger men. Mr. Martinez, for example, was twenty-two and married a Mexican woman who was "about fifty."[211]

Despite the implicit assumptions of social workers and reformers that Mexican men should only couple with women of their own group, the unequal sex ratios of Mexican men to Mexican women encouraged cross-group heterosocial and sexual contacts. Such relations were thought by social reformers and aid workers to be "a strain on the moral health" of Chicago and were read as social pathologies. As one explained, "[T]he thwarted sex life of the [Mexican] man is all too apt to break across the normal social restraints." This thwarting was due, he continued, "to the great proportion of single men and the small number of women."[212] Occasionally the fears of social workers were confirmed, as in the case of Pedro López, who landed in Cook County Jail for raping a young Polish woman (he was released after the Mexican consulate intervened).[213] For the most part, however, cross-group social relations did not give rise to such extremes. In fact, Paul S. Taylor determined from Chicago Police Department records from 1928 through 1930 that the majority of convictions of Mexicans were for larceny and for disorderly conduct. Of the 141 Mexicans convicted of felonies in the Chicago Municipal Court, 132 (92.2 percent) were for various forms of larceny; of the 1,826 misdemeanor convictions, 1,231 (67.3 percent) were for disorderly conduct.[214] There were even rare instances of Mexican-Polish marriages. In 1924, for example, Mexico-born Justino Cordero married Poland-born Caroline Kon, and together they came to be longtime leaders in the South Chicago Mexican community.[215] In another example, Guadalupe Rios, born in Mexico City, married Poland-born Louise in 1933.[216] Interestingly, she was fourteen years older than him! She was fifty years old when they married, and the couple had no children.

Other kinds of interactions were much less clear-cut, as with instances where husbands knew their wives were "turning tricks" to make financial ends meet. Mrs. LaBetts, for instance, a Mexican woman married to an Anglo, "up till three y[ea]rs ago . . . turned tricks in the building with the knowledge of her husband, her boy never knowing it."[217] Reportedly, "[S]he never was a professional prostitute, but just turned tricks for pin money." Interestingly, the account claimed that she no longer got any business because she grew too fat "and her complexion has darkened so," but it is unclear who offered this explanation.

There were other cases where husbands knew their wives were "accommodating" the boarders in their houses.[218] Contemporary outside observers immediately viewed this behavior as prostituting, whether or not money was exchanged. There were questions about the legitimacy of the married relationship and allusions to the "business" of a boarding house. Though it is unclear how many of the Mexican boarding houses were used as brothels, the practice of taking in boarders was widespread throughout all the areas of Mexican settlement. Once in a while there were accounts of real dangers to the women of a household that rented to boarders. In one example a Mexican couple took in boarders, and one of them raped the woman, forcing her "to yield to him on the threat of killing her husband. When the other boarders found out that she had yielded they also forced her. When the husband found out what had happened, he shot one of the boarders and took his wife back to Mexico with him."[219] In another extreme instance, a Mexican man shot another Mexican because "it was claimed that the Negro wife of the first 'gave liberties' to the second."[220]

In South Chicago, Mexicans reportedly patronized Black female prostitutes. Two doctors serving Mexicans in South Chicago reported venereal disease to be common among Mexican men and "complained of the sordid relations that existed between the Mexican men and the Negro women of the Strand-Green Bay District." Like the social workers and reformers, their explanation for such "sordid relations" rested on the lack of Mexican women. "Because of the absence of numerous unmarried Mexican women, the men seek out the Negro woman."[221] It appeared that even in the "commercial" relations of prostitution, Mexican men's sexual relations with Black women threatened to "blacken" them in the minds of their white contemporaries. Nevertheless, the occasional marriage did occur between a Mexican man and a Black woman. In 1924, for instance, a Mexican named Aristeo Rios married a "Negro" woman in Chicago.[222]

No statistics exist on the rates of Mexican intermarriage with other groups, but interviews with contemporaries provide "the very real impression that . . . the proportion of intermarriages far exceeds those which take place in rural areas of the Southwest."[223] Mexican applications for U.S. citizenship contain some data on rates of intermarriage. While only an estimated 1 percent of the Mexican population in Chicago actually applied for U.S. citizenship, those who did were overwhelmingly male and married to non-Mexican, typically European ethnic, women. The low, though notable, rates of Mexican intermarriage with other groups during this period, however, do not reveal the tremendous amount of intergroup contact and socializing that existed.

Contacts occurred in formal and informal venues, including pool halls, club dances, parties, and parades. In the Packingtown neighborhood, Juan Martínez and his male friends often spent their evenings at a local billiard room. This hall was owned by a Polish man, but most of the clientele were young, single Mexican men.[224] As in the pool halls in South Chicago, these men were often joined by groups of young Polish women with whom they danced and socialized.[225] A young Mexican man admitted, "'I like the Polish women very much. They are physically attractive and their golden hair fascinates me.'" He went on to note another of their apparent attributes: "'[T]hey must be very affectionate wives, because they have a lot of children.'"[226]

As in the multi-ethnic dancehalls in Southern California described by the historian Matt García, these venues "provided youths the unique opportunity to challenge racial prejudices," that is, to partake of opportunities for interracial mixing that otherwise were rarely available.[227] Through dating, socializing with, and romancing Polish women, Mexican men learned about a group that was often hostile to them. Mexican men also repeatedly described Polish women as "white," suggesting that, in part at least, these men placed value on whiteness in coupling with Polish women. Yet the "whitening" effects of such behaviors were elusive. As Jesse Escalante recalled, "[Y]ou dated *güero* girls . . . but when it came down to it . . . we [were] still Mexicans."[228] Implicit herein is the understanding that Mexicans were not *güeros* and that "being Mexican" meant not being white. These men dated *güeras,* but when it came down to it, they didn't marry these girls. Even socializing at dances, however, could splinter along ethnic lines. At some dances held at the University of Chicago Settlement House in 1928, there were few women for the Mexican men to dance with. The local Polish women refused to dance with Mexicans, so social workers recruited university students to dance with them.[229]

That Mexican men sought the company of Polish women proved to be an added source of tension between Mexican and Polish men. As one reporter wrote in *México,* "The Polish males have a very bad impression of us Mexican men, but the Polish women have a different understanding."[230] The clear implication here is that Polish women preferred

Mexican men over Polish men. Occasionally these stresses erupted into extreme responses, as in one case of a Polish man who killed a Mexican man because he had "given attentions" to his wife.[231]

Mexican men knew that the Poles maligned them as "drunk and low." Mexicans responded by claiming that Polish men were worse: "'We do not want to associate with them.'" The Poles were worse in these men's eyes because they "'allow[ed] their women to appear drunk in public and act like wild women.'"[232] In other words, Polish men were diminished by not controlling their women. Ironically, given their preference for "white" women and the shortage of Mexican women, Mexican men sought out these "wild women" at the dance halls. Nevertheless, such strains between heterosexual men suggest that Polish manhood became threatened by the involvement of Mexican men with Polish women.[233] Mexican manliness also appeared bolstered by their ability to win over "their women." Perhaps, too, these tensions built on emerging hierarchies of male power and signaled anxieties of both groups as they sought to secure and legitimize their own claims to the privileges of whiteness.[234] As whiteness and manhood became conflated during this era in the United States, these kinds of gendered-male interactions revealed the negotiation involved in making such claims. The historian Gail Bederman's work, like many scholars of what is now known as "whiteness studies," demonstrates how race privilege became a critical tool for easing the anxieties white men experienced when immigrants permeated their workplaces and neighborhoods.[235] By extension, as subsequent immigrants entered these areas, they too struggled to claim their whiteness and thus to establish themselves "above" other nonwhite groups and partake of the opportunities available as whites. Bederman further argues that early twentieth-century redefinitions of manhood in the United States conflated white supremacy and male dominance. Read through this lens, Polish manhood was diminished by their lack of dominance over "their" women, thus also threatening their claims to whiteness. The conflation of white supremacy and male dominance can result in the blurring divisions of class. This is perhaps a useful trope for understanding how Irish and Polish policemen could become interchangeable in the minds of Mexicans, for example, or how Polish women could become *güeras* regardless of their social positioning within their own communities.

Mexican men also bemoaned Polish and Italian male behavior toward the women themselves. Mr. Guerrero, a shoemaker on the Near West Side, explained, "I do not like the manners of the Italian and Polish people; they are too disrespectful toward women . . . they want to touch them all over, even their breasts; they are too free, and this is repulsive to me."[236] Guerrero perceived Polish and Italian men to be taking liberties with women, but he failed to consider the roles of women themselves in such behaviors. Perhaps, like the women in the dancehalls and billiards rooms, they actively experimented with sexual freedoms opened to them by the shifting sexual order. Freedom itself seemed to hold meanings structured in gender.

Echoing Guerrero, Carlos López explained, "The Polish men are more coarse and less generous than the Mexican . . . [who is] generally more timid with the white woman."[237] Polish women were clearly "white" in López's mind. His words, however, implied derision for Polish men that did not extend to Polish women. This instance further demonstrates that Mexican and Polish "whiteness" and their notions of manhood were relational and in some ways mutually constitutive; it underscores Mexican attempts to "other" the Polish men.

In spite of obvious conflicts, Italians frequently occupied a position that mediated between the Mexicans and their neighbors. When Mrs. Quintero's sons had trouble with the Polish boys, "[T]he Italian boys always defend[ed] them and escort[ed] them home."[238] Another Mexican reported that an Italian family lived upstairs from her, and "whenever one of the [Italian] girls [saw] one of the Polish boys bullying a Mexican boy, [the Italian family] chase[d] him out."[239] Some Mexicans seemed to consider Italians to be both part of their community and outside of it.[240] Mexicans did not have their own bank, but they did place their hard-earned savings in the Italian State Bank.[241] Mr. Mugnaini, the head of the bank's "Spanish Department," reported that he not only helped Mexicans send their money orders to their families in Texas or Mexico, but he also held any letters that came for his clients until they came to retrieve them. He did this because many of his Mexican customers lived in railroad boxcars and had no address. In rare instances, individual Italians were embraced throughout the Mexican areas of Chicago, as in the case of Victor Lupiano. Lupiano, a labor activist, founded a Mexican workers' mutual-aid society in South Chicago, the Sociedad Mutualista Obreros Libres Mexicanos de Sud Chicago. In 1930, Mexicans all over Chicago mourned his death. The newspaper *México* eulogized him as a "well-liked and highly esteemed member of our colonia [community]."[242]

Commercial Relations

Intergroup competition also extended into commercial realms. In Brighton Park, for instance, a Mexican tailor, Mr. Mena, moved into the neighborhood and opened a tailor shop. His business was located on the same block and directly competed with a much older, established shop, that of a Jewish tailor named Rubin. Rubin kept his prices low to get business, charging sixty-five cents to clean and press a woman's coat, while the going rate was reportedly seventy-five cents. Mena, however, charged even less than Rubin—only fifty cents for the same service. In this way, "Rubin . . . undercuts the market price, but the Mexican undercuts Rubin."[243] An interesting permutation of this was a tailor shop on Green Bay in South Chicago, the Sastreria Mexicana, that was "run by a Negro, but all the signs in his window are in Spnaish [sic]."[244] Perhaps the Black merchant was undercutting the Mexicans, or perhaps he was encouraging Mexican patronage. Several merchants reportedly courted Mexican customers, because, as one Jewish clothing dealer commented, "'when they have money they spend it.'"[245] A Polish grocer in Back-of-the-Yards, however, countered this sentiment. "'No, the Mexicans don't spend much money; they live on a sack of flour.'"[246] Perhaps the conflicts between the Poles and Mexicans generally kept Mexicans from patronizing his store. Or perhaps Mexicans preferred stores owned by Mexicans. The largest and best-known of the Mexican *bodegas* before World War II was La Tienda Colorada, with locations in South Chicago and on the Near West Side.

Many Mexicans willingly bought on credit, a practice that garnered mixed reviews from their immigrant neighbors. One Jewish clothing dealer encouraged this practice, believing Mexicans to be "'better pay than the colored.'"[247] A dry-goods merchant, however, refused to extend credit to Mexicans.[248] Another shopkeeper explained that Mexican mobility and lack of permanence was a constant problem, an observation that prompted yet another comparison of Mexicans with Blacks: "'The Mexicans change names and move, and for these reasons, and because of language, it is harder to trace them than the colored.'"[249] Neighbors even complained about the kinds of customers Mexican businesses drew. A Mexican pool hall that opened on Union Street in 1929 reportedly closed only two months later, "owing to the opposition of neighbors to Mexican and Negro clientele."[250]

By most accounts, Mexican men and Black men rarely played pool in the same hall. Mexicans struggled to distance themselves from "blackness," and socializing with Black men would surely have marked them in ways Mexicans did not desire. The comparisons of Mexicans with blacks are notable in their frequency and as a chronicle of the increasingly racialized nonwhite status Mexicans began to occupy. Mexicans themselves were certainly aware of this trend and worked instead to mark their whiteness. Recognizing the discriminatory consequences of blackness, for instance, the editors of the Spanish-language newspaper

La Defensa warned their readers not to patronize the black undertaker near Hull-House. Instead, they encouraged, "[L]et us place our dead in the hands of our own people, the white race."[251] Even Mexican children absorbed these distinctions, for they reportedly refused to play with the "colored" kids in their neighborhoods and had to be separated from them.[252]

Such claims to whiteness, however, had proven to be of little use to Mexicans like Elizondo González and José Blanco during the 1919 race riots. Even then, segregation dictated the burial of victims, as white undertakers refused to accept black bodies, and black undertakers prohibited white bodies from entering their establishments.[253] The erasure of Elizondo González's murder and the circumstances surrounding his death—his outrage at being taken for black—provide a useful metaphor, as he remained in a kind of limbo, neither black nor white.

Conclusion

Over the course of the interwar period in Chicago, contemporaries began to observe that Mexicans were not incorporating on the expected trajectory set by previous waves of European groups. Mexicans did not experience residential and economic stability, much less upward mobility. Ironically, in working to separate themselves from blacks while continually experiencing racializing incidents painting them nonwhite, Mexican women and men continued to live segregated lives in Chicago. Ongoing intergroup conflicts gradually led social workers and reformers to advocate separation of Mexicans from the other groups. In Packingtown, social workers and settlement-house workers formed separate activity groups for Mexicans. As one wrote, "[I]t was deemed advisable to form clubs and classes for Mexicans only," since "the antagonism of the other racial groups which took root as the Mexicans came" meant that "the Mexican boys were not even allowed to mix with the whites."[254] As an Italian woman in the Hull-House area explained, "'[I]t is better for each nationality to live by itself.'"[255] An Irish woman, Mrs. McAvoy, agreed: "[T]hey're a harmless people if you leave them alone."[256] This strategy of leaving them alone increasingly meant segregating Mexicans from "whites." So, in Davis Square in 1938, Mexicans played in the small athletic field, while Poles and Italians occupied the large field to play softball.[257]

Through racializing experiences in a variety of sites in their everyday lives—and their own responses to them—Mexicans came to understand the significance of their "looks," that is, how their "markings" came to have racialized meaning to those around them. And their evolving status as neither white nor black underscored the relevance of meaning ascribed to such looks in mediating their circumstances and opportunities. Clearly, the ethno-racial dynamics of Chicago during the interwar period were much more complex than a simple dichotomy of white/black might imply. Mexican contacts with other groups, however, did highlight the currency of white and black as categories. While meaning was loaded into physiognomy and physical "markings," other elements certainly factored into the construction of these racial categories for Mexicans, including language, dress, birthplace, and even job seniority. These categories were also very much in negotiation among a variety of groups.[258] The frequency of conflicts among these groups, and particularly the concentration of tensions in male-male interactions, reflected deeper connections between masculinity, nation, and racial identification. Moreover, the erosion of largely gendered-male interactions into gender-neutral conflicts raises significant questions for understanding the circumstances of a growing female Mexican population.

Clearly, to understand the dynamics of Mexican adjustments to Chicago, one must consider Mexicans' experiences with their neighbors. This ethnic context was crucial, for their experiences of whiteness rested in these exchanges that charted the trajectories of *each* of these peoples's adjustments to Chicago. Mexicans jostled with their neighbors to mark their whiteness and to lay claims to their American identity, all the while sharpening their sensitivity to the emerging hierarchies that increasingly racialized Mexicans as nonwhite and non-Black, marking them as "Mexican," not American, ultimately placing them outside the ethno-racial orders of Chicago.

Mexicans were not blind to the consequences of their growing isolation. Rafael Aveleyra, the Mexican consul in Chicago in 1929, investigated a report from a German hospital worker that Mexicans received poor care at Cook County Hospital. He decided to try to get a hall designated specifically for Mexicans, but he received a speedy note from the central office in Mexico City instructing him not to attempt to separate Mexicans in the hospital "in order to not expose Mexicans to a negative [consequence]."[259] Clearly, separation of Mexicans would not have guaranteed them equal treatment and would probably have only added to the growing moves to separate Mexicans already under way in Chicago.

Mexicans were similarly aware of the negative consequences of the occasional "bad seed" for all Mexicans in the area. A Mexican store owner, for instance, refused to pay his rent to the Irish landlord, who then shot him dead. Mexican sympathy in the neighborhood was with the landlord, since the store owner was not well liked. What Mexicans lamented most, however, was the wide publicity that this "bad" Mexican received, because "few can deny that a few bad Mexicans are used as basis to judge us all."[260]

As Mexicans jockeyed for position with their immigrant neighbors, they were presented with a moment that held at least the possibility of a process of adjustment with the potential for Mexicans to "become white" and thereby become "American" alongside their newly arrived Polish and Italian neighbors. Over the course of the interwar period, however, that moment faded, and Mexicans found themselves increasingly becoming racialized as nonwhite. In a place where American identity was based on whiteness, Mexicans in Chicago found themselves increasingly removed from the possibility of incorporation. They became aliens—outside the borderlands between white and black.[261]

3   The Mexican Problem

In the June 5, 1926, issue of *México*, Armando Amador wrote, "Yo no soy ni hispano-americanista ni pan-americanista: soy, simplemente, americanista" (I am neither a Hispanic-American nor a pan-Americanist; I am simply an Americanist). America, he continued, stretched from Alaska to the straits of Magellan, making the peoples who inhabit the entire region Americans.[1] Presenting himself as simply an Americanist, a Mexican who believed himself already an American, Amador appeared to be arguing against the ever-present pressures on Mexicans to Americanize and become American citizens. Why, the logic went, should Mexicans Americanize when they were already Americans?

Armando Amador, however, was the Mexican vice consul in Chicago, a detail that he failed to mention in his article. Serving under the Mexican president Plutarco Calles, Amador surely meant through this editorial to combat the Americanization of Mexican citizens in Chicago. With a neat linguistic turn, he tried to make readers feel confident in their nationality, bolstering their defenses against Americanization by assuring them of their Americanism even as he tried to ensure that these *Mexicanos de afuera* (Mexicans outside Mexico) remained loyal to Mexico.

The general appeal of various definitions of "American" among Mexicans in Chicago is difficult to gauge. Yet it is clear that several notions of "American" coexisted among the city's diverse Mexican population. This is evident even in Amador's formulation of Americanism—he was not a hyphenated American (as, by implication, others believed themselves to be), nor was he a pan-Americanist (as, again by implication, others thought they were). Others of Chicago's Mexicans expressed their *con-*

tinental Americanism, stressing their native North American roots. In 1926, for instance, Atanasio Casares declared that "a Mexican is as much an American as any Polak [*sic*] or Italian that carries a mere certificate of naturalization in his pocket, for he was born on the North-American continent."[2] Casares laid claim to being American by birth—that is, by virtue of nativity on this continent. This continental vision of "American" also stressed the unnatural Americanness of Poles and Italians. Afterall, they had to *naturalize* their American citizenship. Mexicans like Casares, in contrast, considered themselves native-born Americans. Casares mocked the notion that one could "become American" simply by filing citizenship papers with the U.S. government.

These distinctions—continental Americans versus Americans of the Americas versus Latin/Hispano Americans versus U.S. Americans—formed the backdrop to Mexican encounters with U.S. exceptionalist visions of Americanism in Chicago during the 1920s. They evidence Mexican attempts to establish themselves as authentic Americans in order to partake of the benefits that this brought, while marking their ethnic neighbors, especially the Poles and Italians, as somehow not authentically American.[3] Their focus on authenticity reveals the pain Mexicans must have experienced as they felt strong pressures to belong, to Americanize. Amador's formulation of Americanism spoke to this discomfort and sought to console in order to persuade Mexicans to remain Mexican citizens.

Mexicans drew their understandings from Mexican nationalist ideologies, filtered through Caribbean and Latin American political activists and intellectuals whose writings on continental Americanism permeated the revolutionary contexts of Latin America during the early twentieth century.[4] This rhetoric of Americanism permeated postcolonial Mexican history. As early as 1811, Padre Mier (Fray Servando Teresa de Mier), a historian of the insurgency and a clerical patriot, wrote his *Cartas de un americano* (Letters of an American) to assert the rights of those born in what is now Mexico. "Americans!" he proclaimed, "We have the same right over America as the Indians, who came from Asia, had . . . that of being born here."[5]

The varied notions of Americanism that coexisted among Chicago's Mexicans, particularly in the 1920s, were similar in two respects: first, an American was someone whose "belonging" was not circumscribed by formalized legal status; and second, America was not contained by nation-state boundaries.[6] These flew directly in the face of the U.S. brand of Americanization. In the United States generally, and Chicago specifically, the national boundaries of this country were imbricated in the meaning of "American." Moreover, one's legitimacy, indeed one's right of "belonging," was circumscribed by the attainment of U.S. citizenship.

In Chicago, the experiences of previous European immigrant arrivals defined the model that framed the expected trajectory of Mexican assimilation to the area. Moreover, many of those who worked in and controlled the institutions and structures with which Mexicans came into contact had either traveled that path themselves or were the children and grandchildren of those who had. Social workers, reformers, employers, academics, and politicians all expected Mexicans to Americanize, as had previous waves of immigrants. The experiences of those groups, including the Germans, Norwegians, Swedes, Bohemians, Czechs, and Irish, indicated to contemporaries three central points: first, immigrant adjustment could be charted through specific indicators, including upward economic mobility, enfranchisement and political organization, proficiency in reading and speaking the English language, and geographic mobility from cramped, rundown tenements near the center of town to more solid homes with working amenities; second, as immigrants adjusted, as evidenced by these markers, they would become American;[7] and third, obtaining U.S. citizenship was fundamental to this process of Americanization.

Mexicans, however, increasingly presented a problem. As the lawyer, social critic, writer, and editor Carey McWilliams explained so insightfully nearly twenty years later, "'The Mexican Problem' has been defined in terms of the social consequences of Mexican immigration. . . . The whole apparatus of immigrant-aid social work . . . was thereupon transferred to Mexican immigration with little realization that this immigration might not be, in all respects, identical with European immigration."[8] The Mexican situation turned out to be critically different from that of the Europeans who preceded them, and this became apparent throughout the late 1920s and into the 1930s. Mexicans did not follow the expected trajectory of assimilation as outlined by previous European immigrants, and the primary sticking issue centered on citizenship.

Unlike other immigrant groups to Chicago, Mexicans overwhelmingly did not become U.S. citizens, did not vote, and therefore held little, if any, political power.[9] Over the course of the interwar period, their experiences with rising discrimination and prejudice did nothing to convince them to change their citizenship. Moreover, they perceived that the expected means of incorporation, the predominant model of becoming American, was fundamentally about attaining "whiteness," a condition most found unchangeable by citizenship. Their daily experiences increasingly convinced them that attaining that whiteness and becoming

American on the Eurocentric model would be impossible. This chapter surveys that model of Americanization and how it worked in the daily lives of Mexicans in Chicago. In addition, it explores many of the reasons for Mexican reluctance to change flags and demonstrates their ultimate understanding that "Mexican" came to hold derogatory connotations and negative consequences.

Americanization

A fundamental premise of the Eurocentric brand of Americanizers was their belief in the need to train immigrants, in this case Mexicans, to become proper Americans. Their faith in this method shaped many of the social and cultural efforts to Americanize newcomers. Father James Tort at Our Lady of Guadalupe Church in South Chicago, for example, received approval from Thomas Wall of the Royal Building and Loan Company because he "'intends to do much to promote American ideals and provide the training for the Mexicans that will enable them to become the highest type of citizen.'"[10]

Implicit in the expectations of clergy, reformers, and social workers involved in what they termed "Mexican work" in Chicago was the assumption of eventual Mexican "Americanization."[11] Thus, many of their efforts were geared toward encouraging Mexican men and women to naturalize their citizenship, to learn English, and to enroll and keep their children in school. As elsewhere in the United States, they targeted women specifically and taught them "proper" means of keeping their homes and families clean and healthy.[12] Ideological debates flared over the nature of poverty, child delinquency, and crime and over the relationship of these factors to ethnic and immigrant peoples.[13] Social workers, academics, church people, and reformers tested their theories and developed their practical applications in the laboratory of Chicago itself.[14]

Like many of his contemporaries, the University of Chicago sociologist Robert Park believed in the inevitability of immigrant inclusion. Founded on the premise that this process was natural, predictable, and desirable, Park developed his notions of the interaction cycle of Americanization in the United States.[15] As the scholar Henry Yu has convincingly portrayed, Park's understanding of immigration, informed by earlier work by William I. Thomas, was based on a model of European immigration.[16] The process entailed four steps: initial competition, leading to conflict, then to accommodation, and finally assimilation. Those groups who did not adhere to this trajectory became problems. Park was interested particularly in the "Negro Problem" and the "Oriental Problem." Because of the isolation and segregation these groups faced from race prejudice, they became exceptions to his interaction cycle. He might just as well have concerned himself with Mexicans. As academics, social workers, reformers, and Mexicans themselves discovered, Mexicans, too, became exceptions, or "problems," as they experienced growing levels of racial discrimination and isolation.

There is little indication, however, that Mexicans were caught up in the specifics of such debates.[17] They, like Mexicans in El Paso's Houchen House, availed themselves of what medical and social programs they could—though reportedly with lower incidence than other immigrant groups to Chicago.[18] Many did, however, work to obtain an education, inspired by potential mobility that they did not yet have in Mexico, for education was only just coming to rural areas in Mexico during these years. As if proving the worth of education and touting its values, the editors of Chicago's major Spanish-language newspaper optimistically wrote in February 1925, "In the United States, they do not consider 'nationality'; [rather] they consider the education of the individual."[19] The optimism lay in the expectation that education would triumph over divisions of nationality. Of course, this begs the question of U.S. nationality—the implication is certainly that "other" nationalities would be subsumed through education into a greater whole, the premise of contemporary "melting pot" ideologies.

Many of the reformers and aid workers with whom Mexicans came into contact in Chicago believed that to properly become Americans, Mexicans needed to be actively stripped of their "otherness" and taught how to be Americans.[20] The comments of one researcher for the U.S. Department of Labor revealed this bias. The Mexicans, he wrote, "have not yet learned to eat proper food, heat and ventilate their homes and to wear sufficient clothing."[21] In this view, the condition of Mexicans in the tenements of Chicago was due not to their extreme poverty or to their destitute surroundings but instead to their lack of knowledge, training, and education about how proper Americans conducted their lives.

These assimilationist views gained great popularity in the postwar years, and by the 1920s, as the historian Gary Gerstle has argued, cultural pluralist visions largely lost out to assimilationist perspectives.[22] In part this was spurred on by provisions in the 1917 Immigration Act that authorized federal funding to promote the acquisition of U.S. citizenship. According to the scholar Desmond King, Americanization organizations sprang up after 1917 and received funding from the Office of Education to provide English language classes, to promote literacy and knowledge of civic affairs, and to marshal state and federal agencies to particular immigrant needs.[23] The Bureau of Naturalization (Department of Labor) also launched citizenship-education initiatives, primarily through public school systems.[24]

Those involved with Americanization efforts in the churches, settlement houses, and aid societies were inclined to understand the "Mexican problem" as based in culture. This view drove many of the formal and informal Americanization programs. Some institutions developed and guided particular aspects of immigrant culture even as they pressured them to take English and citizenship classes. Hull-House's famous Mexican pottery, for example, was made in the settlement house's own kilns and grew out of efforts to foster immigrant self-help through an appreciation of homeland traditions.[25] Other efforts targeted more directly elements of immigrant culture that "needed changing." Robert Jones, a Protestant pastor and professor in divinity at the University of Chicago, studied the Mexicans in Chicago in the hopes of converting them to Protestantism. Like many religious workers, he believed that organizing Mexican spiritual life around a solid Protestant center would aid in the process of Americanization. By actively recruiting Mexicans into the Protestant churches, Jones and his colleagues believed they were helping Mexicans to not "go wrong." In addition, they could "win over" Mexicans who were either lapsed Catholics or who felt unwelcome in the largely Irish-controlled Catholic parishes.[26] Like many of their contemporaries, these Americanizers were concerned with creating and ensuring civic order by curtailing what were believed to be sources of potential unrest and turmoil. In his report on Mexican religious life, Jones wrote, "[S]ocial workers and others acquainted with the Mexicans agree that the disorganization of their religious life makes delinquency, crime, and other vice more easy."[27] Jones's views reveal the limitations of contemporary understandings of the religious context out of which many of Chicago's Mexican immigrants came. The reforms mandated by the 1917 Constitution in Mexico mandated a separation of church (the Catholic church) and state, and the subsequent tumultuous decade and a half reflected various attempts to actualize these changes. Leaving the unrest of the Cristero Rebellions did not mean, as Jones implied, that their own religious life was "disorganized." Indeed, it was more likely that they had found a measure of religious peace upon reaching Chicago.

In their work with Mexicans at the Central Free Dispensary, the leading Chicago social workers Gertrude Howe Britton and Kate Constable noted that "the average Mexican has unusual native intelligence, a very pleasing courtesy and a marked ability to get along happily in very poor surroundings." These qualities made Mexicans "a very desirable addition to our American mixture."[28] Clearly, Britton and Constable expected the Mexican population in Chicago not only to stay but also to become part of the general mix of Americans. As Anita Jones, a social worker with the Immigrants' Protective League, wrote in 1928, "[O]n the whole, the Mexicans have been much like the other immigrant groups in many respects."[29] She went on to enumerate the similarities. Like other groups, Mexicans live "under hard conditions when necessary and gradually find their condition improving with their period of American life." She cited increased Mexican participation in recreational activities and the growing numbers of Mexican children in schools. Like classic assimilationists of her time, Jones expected Mexicans to assimilate as had other groups before them.

Those few employers who hired Mexicans also anticipated that Mexican laborers would rise in the ranks of slaughterhouse or steel-mill jobs.[30] When interviewed in the late 1920s, for instance, the personnel supervisors of Illinois Steel and Wisconsin Steel facilities in South Chicago expected "the Mexicans to advance to the better paid jobs as they merit[ed] and qualif[ied] for them just as the Germans and Poles have in the past."[31] The superintendent of Marshall Field mattress factory also sketched out a gradual progression of immigrant workers in which Mexican laborers were expected to be just another wave. "The first workers were Germans and Scandinavians . . . then came Italians and Poles. With the war the Mexicans began to come, and the factory has had an increasing proportion of them."[32]

Industries at which Mexicans found employment often already had in place Americanization classes for the foreign-born immigrants who made up their workforce. Mattress factories, meatpackers, and steel mills, among others, offered classes at day and evening schools set up with the help of social workers, reformers, and the Board of Education of the city of Chicago.[33] Usually classes were held either on site at the factories or nearby at settlement houses or school buildings. Instruction was usually free at the lower levels, while high-school subjects required up to a five-dollar deposit. Refunds were issued to those who attended 75 percent of the class meetings if students retained the receipt of their original deposit.

Courses in Americanization were structured into seven categories. The groupings included English-language instruction, classes in citizenship, and high-school subjects like French, Spanish, chemistry, and physics. Other categories included "commercial subjects" for men and women and covered such topics as bookkeeping, stenography, typewriting, commercial English, business arithmetic, accounting, secretarial work, and comptometry (comptometry involved working with a comptometer, an electromechanical calculating machine and precursor to the electronic calculator).[34]

Immigrant men were steered towards another category of Americanization class, the technical course. This covered subjects related to trades and industries in Chicago in which men were expected to work. Topics included automobile repair, baking technology, freehand and machine drawing, sheet metal, electricity, foundry, machine shop, oxyacetylene welding, pattern making, printing, tailoring, and woodworking.[35]

Immigrant women were directed toward instruction in home economics, trade millinery, and dress making. In home economics, women were encouraged to take "interest in the home and in the spirit of real homemaking . . . to give them an insight into the hygiene of the home and of the person."[36] Furthermore, immigrant women were taught "the benefits of sunshine, fresh air, and cleanliness; and to insist on neatness of person and a neat method of work; to show the worth of economy."[37] Clearly, immigrant women were subjected to more than learning particular—gender-prescribed—job skills like dress making or sewing. They were subjected to less tangible forms of acculturation that sought to reshape normative beliefs: "The elements of good taste in dressing, in selecting suitable material, and in the proper laundering of the garments."[38] Implicit in such strictures, of course, was a subtext of cleanliness—that is, cleanliness was understood as part of "American-ness." Immigrants, by extension, were coded as dirty. Many were treated as though they preferred to be unkempt and unwashed, as though poverty, filthy work, and substandard housing situations played no role in their circumstances.

Efforts also concentrated on proper nutrition and diet. A sample menu for "good standard quality" meals from 1920 speaks volumes about the level to which social workers and reformers tried to standardize treatment and shape immigrants into "100 percent Americans."

SAMPLE MENU FOR ADULTS[39]

Breakfast—
   Cornmeal mush with top milk, toast, bacon brisket, coffee
Dinner—
   Pot-roast with potatoes and onions, Home-made bread,
   Deep pie of raisins, coffee
Luncheon or Supper—
   Thick soup of dried peas, Bread with Oleomargarine,
   Stewed rhubarb

By the mid-1930s, Mexicans apparently were still eating "Mexican" foods, gathering supplies at local bodegas like the popular Tienda Colorada (located on the Near West Side and in South Chicago). In a 1937 handbook, a menu similar to that of 1920 existed for the "American family," but new menus were also included.[40] These menus provided a kind of blueprint showing which immigrant groups had most recently arrived in Chicago. In addition to the standard "American family" menu, there were menus for the "Italian family," the "Mexican family," the "Negro family," and the "Polish family."[41] The only exception to this trend was a menu for the "Jewish family," which was built around long-standing religious observances: "[T]he Jew will eat no pork products."[42] Though the foods vaguely reflected the tastes of each of these groups, welfare workers were told that the most striking "variations in diet [were] due to differences in preparation." Thus from the same allotment of grain, Italians made macaroni, Poles made dumplings, "Negroes" made biscuits, and Mexicans made tortillas.

As with other aspects of life in Chicago, Mexican responses to Americanization programs often divided along gendered lines. When interviewed about the various social agencies of which he was aware, one Mexican man replied, "'The Mexicans don't like the Visiting Nurses Association, Infant Welfare, etc.'"[43] His wife quickly jumped in, however, and contradicted, "'Mexican women do like these agencies.'" The interviewer then mentioned that he knew one Mexican woman who "no longer wanted to return to Mexico" because of the work of such agencies. The man was outraged: "'She is a traitor to her country! She denies her mother because they get more wages and aid here! She tramples on her flag!'"[44] This revealing exchange suggests a disjuncture between men's and women's views on life in the United States. Another Mexican woman interviewed remarked, "'I like the United States. The United States is good protection for me. If my babies are sick, the Welfare takes care of them. I can go to the dispensary. The nurse and the doctor come, and when there is no money we don't pay. It is better here than in Mexico.'"[45] Women tended to see the pragmatic benefits of remaining in the United States and did not view such a decision as denial of home. They did not change their citizenship, but neither did they express the patriotic fervor of the men. Most spoke of conditions in the United States as clearly better for them and their children than those in Mexico, and they appeared to make choices in light of this reality. The outraged husband, however, apparently believed it was acceptable for Mexicans to receive higher wages in the United States—so long as they eventually returned to Mexico; that is, so long as they did not "deny their mother." Of course, the ultimate denial was changing one's citizenship, and it was apparently this prospect that fueled his outrage and accusations of treachery. Ironically,

Table 3.1 Typical Menus for Different Nationalities Which May Be Secured on the Budgets Allowed

AMERICAN FAMILY

Breakfast
Tomato Juice, Whole Grain Cereal with Top Milk, Toast with Butter or Butter Substitute, Milk for Children, Coffee or Milk for Adults

Lunch
Navy Bean or Split Pea Soup, Vegetable Salad, Bread and Butter Substitute, Apple Sauce or Dried Fruit, Milk

Dinner
Liver Loaf, Pot Roast of Beef or Egg Dish, Potatoes and Carrots, Bread and Butter Substitute, Milk for Children, Coffee or Milk for Adults, Rice Pudding

ITALIAN FAMILY

Breakfast
Orange, Italian Bread, Egg, Milk for Children, Coffee or Milk for Adults

Lunch
Vegetable Soup (Minestrone), Italian Bread, Apples

Dinner
Spaghetti with Tomato or Meat Sauce and Cheese, Salad of Greens with Oil, Italian Bread, Milk for Children, Coffee or Milk for Adults

JEWISH FAMILY

Breakfast
Orange, Oatmeal with Top Milk, Rye Bread and Butter, Cocoa for Children, Coffee or Cocoa for Adults

Lunch
Beet Borscht, Boiled Potato, Cottage Cheese, Rye Bread, Milk for Children, Coffee or Milk for Adults

Dinner
Pot Roast with Potato and Carrots, Coleslaw, Stewed Prunes, Rye Bread, Tea

MEXICAN FAMILY

Breakfast
Tomato Juice, Oatmeal and Milk, Tortillas, Milk for Children, Coffee or Milk for Adults

Lunch
Eggs, Potatoes, Cabbage, Tortillas, Milk

Dinner
Sopa with Fideo, Pinto Beans, Tortillas, Milk for Children, Coffee or Milk for Adults, Dried Fruit

NEGRO FAMILY

Breakfast
Tomato Juice, Grits, Hot Biscuit, Milk for Children, Coffee or Milk for Adults

Lunch
Scrambled Eggs, Biscuit, Apple Sauce, Milk

Dinner
Black-eyed Peas, Collards with Salt Pork, Baked Sweet Potato, Dried Peach Pie, Milk for Children, Coffee or Milk for Adults

POLISH FAMILY

Breakfast
Orange, Oatmeal and Milk, Rye Bread, Milk for Children, Coffee or Milk for Adults

Lunch
Cottage Cheese, Sauerkraut, Rye Bread, Milk for Children, Coffee or Milk for Adults

Dinner
Smoked Fish, Sauerkraut and Potatoes, Rye Bread, Apples, Milk

Source: Nesbitt, *Chicago Standard,* 7.

he accused Mexican women of denying their mother even as he denied them their maternal prerogative of choosing what they thought best for their children.

Citizenship

The accusation of being traitors was powerful and certainly influenced many not to change their citizenship. As social workers at the Rush Medical College dispensary, a facility serving the Mexicans of the Hull-House and Stockyards areas, noted in 1925, "[P]ractically none of the Mexicans are citizens or contemplate becoming citizens."[46] Robert Jones concurred in 1931 when he wrote, "The Mexican is not inclined to seek citizenship."[47] During this period in Chicago, contemporaries began to observe that Mexicans did not assimilate on the expected trajectory of settlement and mobility, English-language and citizenship acquisition set by previous waves of European groups.

Mexicans naturalized their citizenship at a lower rate than any other immigrant group in Chicago during this period. In the winter of 1924–25, when there were an estimated twelve to fifteen thousand Mexicans in Chicago, not one Mexican was reported to have applied for naturalization to the Office of the Clerk of the Superior Court.[48] Even organizations with large branches in charge of Americanization noted the lack of Mexicans willing to change their citizenship.

Abraham Bowers, the head of the YMCA Americanization Department in the mid-1920s, found himself working effectively *against* Mexican incorporation into a paradigm of upward mobility because of his inability to find employers willing to hire Mexicans. His job was to help newly arrived immigrants find jobs. However, since most employers only hired a few Mexicans "to help keep down wages and avoid strikes," Bowers could rarely place Mexicans in jobs.[49]

Bowers, like other Americanizers, believed that with U.S. citizenship came rights, better jobs, social and economic mobility, and ultimately political access.[50] Consequently, Mexican indifference to their urgings to change their citizenship indicated to Americanizers a fundamental disinterest in the means of becoming Americans and a basic lack of desire to assimilate. Consequently, attempts were made to channel Mexican activities into so-called Americanizing venues like adult schools.

Even before more formalized discriminations of Depression-era relief programs, local institutions acted to restrict Mexican activities and to channel those into acceptable Americanizing venues. The Union State Bank in South Chicago, for example, cooperated with other banks in

Chicago to actively discourage its Mexican clients from sending their savings out of town.[51] By sending their earnings out of Chicago, and predominantly to Mexico, Mexicans indicated their continuing orientation toward Mexico and a lack of commitment to Chicago. Several other banks in Chicago also reported that their Mexican clients sent most of their savings out of town. Arthur Hansen, vice president of South Chicago Savings Bank, and F. A. Tinkham, vice president of Calumet National Bank, noted that Mexicans were saving money but not investing in the area. Rather, they sent money back to Mexico or Texas. The U.S. Post Office in South Chicago estimated that in 1927 upwards of fifteen Mexicans per day sent around forty dollars each to Mexico or Texas.[52] In spite of the actions of the banks, however, Mexicans did send much of their earnings "to the plateau states of central Mexico and very few to Texas."[53]

This continuing orientation toward Mexico further underscored the ambivalence with which most Mexicans regarded their stays in Chicago. For instance, the Chicago branch of the Naturalization Bureau (Department of Labor) reported a grand total of forty-eight Mexicans naturalized between 1924 and 1928.[54] Similar numbers were confirmed in the "Mexican Work" reports of 1930–31 from the Mary McDowell Settlement.[55] Even the Naturalization Petitions and Record books of the U.S. District Court reveal only a few Mexicans who naturalized during this period.[56] Of over a thousand cases that the YMCA reported assisting with citizenship papers between 1925 and 1928, only twenty-five were Mexicans.[57] To be fair, however, the YMCA had a history of actively discouraging Mexican participation in the organization's activities.

Nevertheless, as one social worker in Packingtown noted, the Mexicans "[were] difficult to help because they [were] unwilling to become American citizens."[58] Their refusal to succumb to Americanization occasionally translated into emotional resistance. As one Mexican man explained, "'The more wrong they say about Mexico, the more I love it and the less I want to take out my United States papers.'"[59] Financial pressures did not shake the determination of others, including women. Thus, "[O]ne woman, almost penniless, with three small children, when told she would have to take out first papers in order to secure a mother's pension, said she was unwilling to do this, and apparently preferred to relinquish the pension."[60] Mr. Grabozo expressed similar sentiments. Before the economic crash of 1929, Grabozo, his wife, and their six children had received relief aid from United Charities several times during 1928 and 1929. Neither Grabozo nor his wife had naturalized their citizenship. In 1930, when asked about doing so, one of their children, who acted as an interpreter, explained, "My father would not think of changing flags."[61]

During the early 1930s, in the most desperate years of the Depression, access to many sources of relief aid was formally tied to proof of U.S. citizenship. Consequently, well-meaning social workers stepped up their efforts to encourage Mexicans to become Americans. In an attempt to convince the Gonzáles family to change their citizenship to that of the United States (and thus to free up limited privately donated funds), a case worker at United Charities explained to them that their neighbor, Mrs. Díaz, would not be receiving her Mother's Pension monies had she not planned to become a citizen. The Gonzáles family was aghast: "Did Mary Díaz change flags?!"[62] Clearly, the critical issue for the Gonzáles family was Díaz's disloyalty and not their own need to become American citizens to be eligible for aid.[63]

Mexicans reported that employment opportunities also began to be bound to U.S. citizenship. Juan Martínez reported that as early as 1924, the railroad company that employed him had started requiring workers to "make [an] application for their first papers . . . [and that] no one could continue working who did not intend to become an American citizen." To try to convince him, the foreman told Juan that "it was to his advantage to be an American citizen because he would get a better job, and get it quicker." Juan later explained that he quit the job, for he "would not change his sentiments for his country for any job."[64]

Barriers of Prejudice

Why were Mexicans in Chicago so resistant to "changing flags"? For some, taking out citizenship papers was a mere formality. As Mr. Reed at the YMCA explained, "[T]he average Mexican considers himself an American now and so can see no reason why he should have to take out papers. This formality, the Mexican thinks, does not make him any more American than he is now."[65] This sentiment was echoed by some Mexicans themselves, including, as noted earlier, Armando Amador. Pressures based in the revolutionary ideologies of patriotism, unity, and tradition served as another deterrent against Mexicans, forsaking their Mexican citizenship and becoming U.S. citizens. The effect of these pressures on the ground was to set those who chose to change flags against those who did not, with those who changed flags perceived as traitors. Any status Ingeniero ("Engineer") Gordínez held in the community, for instance, was undermined by his constant urgings "to stay here and become citizens." As the organizer and president of the Benito Juárez Mutual Aid

Society, his attempts "to introduce American practices" were met with resistance. "The other Mexicans," explained Manuel Bueno, "resent this and his status is much impaired on account of this view he takes."[66] Similar sentiments surfaced at a meeting of the Sunday Afternoon Discussion Group at the University of Chicago Settlement House in February 1936.[67] A motion to exclude all Mexicans who had taken out their U.S. citizenship papers was reportedly met with great enthusiasm until Mr. Paz, one of the directors at Hull-House, made an eloquent speech against the motion. The motion failed, but the sentiment remained a deterrent to those considering taking out papers.

Another reason for the unwillingness of Mexicans to change their citizenship centered on their awareness of the growing stridency of prejudices against them. Many knew that merely changing citizenship would not relieve them from discrimination and hateful acts. After working their way through the U.S. Southwest, and Texas in particular, many had seen the extreme discrimination faced by Mexicans who had been U.S. citizens for generations.[68] The sociologist Paul S. Taylor discovered instances of Texas-born Mexicans who took out Mexican citizenship papers because the anti-Mexican prejudice was so strong.[69]

Mexicans recognized the history of Mexicans in the Southwest and the continued discrimination against them despite the fact that they had "lived 80 years under the civil, administrative, and educational laws of the U.S. and although . . . they are citizens of the United States."[70] As one Mexican resident of Chicago explained, "[E]ven if we do become citizens here, we always remain Mexicans."[71] Another explained, "[T]he few Mexicans who have taken American citizenship have not changed from their former condition." He went on to clarify, "[E]ven the Mexican[s] born here and hence American citizens suffer by the working of those same prejudices," and those prejudices had real consequences that put Mexicans "at a great disadvantage with the other citizens of this great country."[72] In 1932, for example, two agents of the Immigration Department burst into Ignacio Romero's home in Chicago without a warrant. Although Romero was a naturalized citizen of the United States, he was arrested without cause.[73] Romero was later released, but his experience and the fact that it was published in the large local Spanish-language newspaper served to reinforce for many the lack of protection citizenship accorded Mexicans. Expressing frustration, Mexicans asked, "[H]ow are [we] to become identified with th[is] country when a barrier of prejudices is opposed to it?"[74]

The longer they stayed in Chicago, the more Mexicans experienced discrimination and prejudice against them, which did nothing to convince them that they should change their citizenship. Many employers enacted "a general rule against hiring Mexicans" regardless of their citizenship, so Ruth Camblón, a case worker at Hull-House, "had learned not to waste time with them." Instead, when she was trying to find work for a Mexican, she called one of a small group of employers whom she knew to be "in the habit of hiring Mexicans."[75] Even if they did secure employment, Mexicans understood that employers used their mobility to discriminate against them. As Mr. Díaz explained, Mexicans got all the worst jobs because "the boss says, 'I cannot give a good job to a Mexican when pretty soon he goes away and I have to break in a new man!'"[76] In 1928, the employment superintendent at Wisconsin Steel claimed to benefit from this tendency. "We used to get a good many [Mexicans] from Illinois Steel, especially when they had the twelve hour day." Wisconsin Steel, he clarified, was "a straight 8–hour plant."[77] Clearly, Mexican workers were leaving the less-desirable job for one that paid equal wages for fewer hours of work. In one revealing comment, an employment manager even rationalized his hiring of Mexicans because they had a "habit of disappearing when out of work."[78] Thus, Mexican mobility rendered them invisible when work was scarce and saved the employer from having to rid himself of extra labor.

This version of voting with their feet, however convenient for the occasional job boss, added to the prejudicial treatment of Mexicans at the hands of employers. As one noted, the first Mexicans employed in Chicago "were not satisfactory" because they "showed no inclination to learn English. . . . and were disposed to quit at any time."[79] The superintendent of the Illinois Free Employment Bureau testified that "the Mexicans are an unreliable class of laborer."[80] Here, the mobility of Mexican workers came to be associated with unreliability. Just as employers learned to segregate Mexicans from other workers, they found that Mexicans themselves "insisted on being allowed to work in gangs by themselves," perhaps to thwart conflicts with other immigrant workers.[81] As "Mexican" came to hold such meanings (e.g., unreliable, unsatisfactory), Mexicans, aware of their vulnerability, again found little incentive to become citizens. After all, they knew that much of the unskilled work they performed was not constant, and "if work slack[ed] up. . . . [they] were] going to be the first one[s] released."[82]

Moreover, dead-end jobs meant that Mexicans suffered immediately if economic conditions were tight. By 1930, Mexicans had the highest unemployment rate of any immigrant group in Chicago (second only to that of Blacks, who were not considered immigrants by statisticians). This was due in part to employer hiring practices but also to many Mexicans' minimal education and lack of industrial work skills. During the 1930s, 66 percent of Chicago's Mexican working-age population was unskilled. This rate was the highest of all groups in Chicago: 53 percent of Blacks, 35 percent of foreign-born whites, and only 33 percent of native-born whites were unskilled. Mexicans also had, on average, the lowest number of years of formal education: 3.2 years, versus 4.7 for Blacks and 5.3 years for European whites.[83] Without skills or much education, Mexicans were often confined to the most menial and least secure jobs (first fired in any economic downturn).

Separation of Mexicans from other groups came to be an increasingly common practice. Statistics on attendance and graduation rates from classes at Hull-House and the University of Chicago Settlement House always listed Mexicans separately from "other foreign groups." In 1921, a survey of twenty-three night schools for the foreign-born in Chicago listed 129 Mexicans enrolled in English classes at twenty-one of these schools. By 1926, there were reportedly only 492 Mexicans, 80 percent of whom were men.[84] Out of an estimated population of twenty to thirty thousand Mexicans, only a small part of the population was availing itself of this assistance. Moreover, few of the "needy" Mexicans could even access other kinds of services, notably public relief and welfare aid, as both by the early 1930s were restricted to those with U.S. citizenship. This may have accounted in part for the observations of numerous social workers that Mexicans were less willing to take charity. "The Mexican peoples ask for less and receive less than other families from charitable agencies."[85] The low numbers of Mexicans accessing relief aid may also have been tied to elements of cultural pride. As one Mexican in Chicago observed, "'A Mexican will starve or steal before he begs.'"[86] He went on to compare Mexicans with their immigrant neighbors: "'In Chicago I have never seen a Mexican asking for money . . . or begging for food . . . like I have seen Poles, Italians, and others do.'"[87] More likely, however, reluctance stemmed from wariness and fears of deportation as a "public charge."[88] As Jane Addams of Hull-House reported, "[T]he Mexicans . . . are simple family men who are afraid of being deported and are even afraid of receiving relief for fear of being sent back to Mexico as public charges."[89] Data from the Illinois Emergency Relief Commission, as cited by the historians Francisco Balderrama and Raymond Rodríguez, confirm the low levels of Mexicans receiving unemployment relief. Between 1933 and 1934, for instance, 85.1 percent of those receiving unemployment assistance were "white"; 14.1 percent were "Negroes"; and only 0.8 percent were "Mexicans and Others."[90]

Rising unemployment and swollen relief rolls spurred local representatives of steel and meatpacking industries, along with protectionist nativist groups like the American Legion, to repatriate Mexicans. The American Legion, for instance, negotiated cut-rate train fares to Laredo, Texas, to facilitate removal of Mexicans.[91] "In the Chicago area, the steel companies that had stimulated Mexican migration . . . in the 1920s now actively encouraged repatriation."[92] As in Los Angeles, local officials "expected that several well-publicized deportations would provoke a mass exodus of Mexicans receiving relief," thus lowering the burden on sources of relief, especially municipal relief rolls.[93] The Immigrants' Protective League (IPL), other private relief groups, and even Cook County shared these views.[94] Unlike many other groups, however, the IPL took some pains to look out for the welfare of repatriates. They even contacted the Mexican government in Mexico City repeatedly on behalf of those they helped to repatriate. Specifically, they were concerned that the Mexican government was not providing for its citizens once they reached the U.S.–Mexico border. The workers at the IPL worried that repatriates would become indigent and negatively impact communities on the border. Copying their response to the Mexican consul, the Secretaria de Relaciónes Exteriores (SRE) responded that provisions already existed to transport Mexicans at Nogales (on the border with Nogales, Arizona) and at Ciudad Juárez (on the border with El Paso, Texas). The consul then telegrammed back to the SRE to explain that the majority of repatriates from the IPL could only get to Nuevo Laredo (on the border with Laredo, Texas). Ultimately, the Mexican government agreed to make arrangements for repatriates from the IPL arriving at Nuevo Laredo to be transported to their desired destinations in the interior of Mexico.[95]

The Mexican government reinforced these kinds of practices by offering free or cut-rate train passes and encouraging states to provide food and shelter to get repatriates to their hometowns from the border.[96] Chicago's principal Spanish-language newspaper, *El Nacional* (formerly *México*), reported that "the Mexican National Railroad Company, cooperating with the Mexican government in this movement, has agreed to fix its transport rates at one cent per mile for those who will travel from Laredo [Texas] to points in Mexico."[97] The Mexican Foreign Relations office also arranged "for all Mexican families who find themselves in economical straits to return to Mexico at the cost of $15 by way of the Missouri Pacific Railroad Lines."[98]

Approximately four thousand Mexicans repatriated or were deported from the Chicago area.[99] As reported by Antonio L. Schmidt, the Mexican consul in Chicago in 1937, not all Mexicans who repatriated to Mexico registered at the border or notified the consulate of their departure. In fact,

"[O]nly persons who are carrying with them certain instruments, such as radios, washing machines, typewriters," had to clear them with the consulate before leaving to prove ownership.[100] Thus the statistics from Mexico's Migration Service are not entirely accurate. Nevertheless, using those numbers, Paul S. Taylor estimated that an estimated 3.6 percent of Mexicans in the United States lived in Illinois, Michigan, and Indiana in 1930, yet "these states furnished 10.5 percent of all repatriates during 1930–1932!"[101] Clearly these areas furnished more than their share of re-patriated Mexicans, and "repatriations occurred somewhat unevenly from the Mexican colonies of the country."[102] From an estimated population of nearly twenty-nine thousand Mexicans in Illinois in 1930, 5.3 percent, or nearly 5,500 people, were repatriated. For comparison, nearly half, 48.1 percent, of all Mexicans in the United States lived in Texas, from which an estimated 49.7 percent, or nearly 13,800 people, were repatriated.

The Mexican consulate in Chicago played an active role in facilitating those repatriations. *El Nacional* reported in May 1932 that "the reduction in transportation rates has met with great approval by the Mexican colony of Chicago and that many of our countrymen will take advantage of the opportunity."[103] Beyond providing funds for transportation to the border, the consul updated the SRE on conditions for Mexicans in the greater Chicago area. Consul Rafael Aveleyra appeared to be especially

Table 3.2: Distribution of Mexicans in the United States, 1930, and Departures of Repatriates, 1930–32

State	Mexicans in USA		Departures of Repatriates Percent
	Number	Percent of All Mexicans	
Texas	683,681	48.1	49.7
California	368,013	25.9	19.6
Arizona	114,173	8.0	6.9
New Mexico	59,340	4.2	2.4
Colorado	57,676	4.1	3.1
Illinois	28,906	2.0	5.3
Kansas	19,150	1.3	1.2
Michigan	13,336	0.9	2.7
Indiana	9,642	0.7	2.5
Oklahoma	7,354	0.5	0.5
Wyoming	7,174	0.5	n/a
Others	54,088	3.8	6.1
Total:	1,422,533	100.0	100.0

Data compiled from U.S. census and Mexican Migration Service, Mexico. Source: Taylor, *Mexican Labor.*

diligent in his record keeping.[104] Aveleyra consistently monitored economic circumstances and conditions relating to possible deportations or repatriations. In May 1930 he wrote an open letter to the Mexicans of Chicago, published in *México*, explaining how the Mexican government was helping in the repatriations. "Our fellow countrymen," wrote the consul, "who desire to return . . . will not, therefore, have to pay custom duties on any type of household goods which they might carry with them, such as radios, pianos, phonographs."[105]

In 1935, the consul wrote to the Cárdenas government that Mexicans continued to experience discrimination in employment—that is, jobs were being "conserved in preference for North American citizens."[106] Rather than intervening on their behalf with the employers, the consulate often simply recommended repatriation. This strategy had been used before, most notably by the consul Francisco Pereda during an earlier period of repatriations in 1921–22, following the economic depression of 1920–21. Then, as in the 1930s, expediency seemed to be the operative theme for how consuls and the Mexican government dealt with Mexican nationals who sought their aid.[107] Consuls chose to intervene, advocate for, or facilitate repatriation based on the circumstances of individual cases. Most often, consuls, especially in the early 1930s, secured monies from their government for Mexicans who wanted to return to Mexico.[108] Among those the consulate supplied passage to the U.S.–Mexico border in 1935, for instance, were Heleodoro Cervantes, his wife, and four children; Santos Gonzáles, his wife, and son; and Señora Lazara Ruíz de Silva and her three children. Señora Francisca Alvarez and her two children were helped to return to Mexico with financial aid from the Atchison Topeka Railroad, for whom her deceased husband had worked.[109]

Those who chose to be repatriated did not make the decision lightly, for once they left, they knew they could not return until economic conditions improved. In addition, legal return to the United States was prohibitive, requiring a sponsor and the written guarantee of employment.[110] Sadly, many welfare recipients who chose to repatriate did not know—and aid workers conveniently neglected to mention—that having received aid qualified them as "public charges" and prevented them from ever entering the country legally again. Thus, "voluntary repatriation" became akin to deportation, for once deported, a Mexican could never re-enter legally.[111] When repatriates reached Mexico, they discovered that Mexico had little means with which to help them reestablish their lives, despite promises to the contrary.[112] The Mexican historian Fernando Alanis has discovered that many repatriates actually petitioned the Mexican government for their promised compensations. Though few ever received job offers, land, or promised funds, their petitions are evidence that they believed themselves to be entitled to protections and aid from the Mexican government.[113] Others became victims of scam artists like Juan Rojas, who duped people in 1931. Reportedly he contacted Mexicans in Chicago posing as a representative of the government of Pascual Rubio-Ortíz "with the purpose of helping all those Mexicans who wish to come back to Mexico and do agricultural work." Interested Mexicans paid him to make their travel arrangements, but he absconded with their funds. Consul Aveleyra warned all Mexicans in the area to not give this man money, even offering a general physical description to help people identify him.[114]

Reflective of the growing scale and intricacies of repatriation structures, the Mexican consul in Chicago began keeping statistics in October 1935 that were separated into new categories. Those categories now included "repatriated by Mexican government" (old), "repatriated by U.S. federal government" (new), "repatriated by local governments (state, county, or city)", "repatriated by U.S. benevolent societies," and "repatriated by Mexican benevolent societies."[115] That same month, Aurelio Alonzo, his wife, and four children were repatriated by "local governments," as were Josefina Ordorica de Farias and her three children. José Garza was deported to Lampazos, Nuevo León, from Cook County jail for drunk and disorderly conduct and carrying a weapon without a license.[116]

Because repatriation and deportation came to be used as ways to discriminate against Mexicans, the Mexican consul in Chicago also began keeping track of growing racial prejudice against Mexicans. The incidents he charted centered on segregation of Mexicans. His office lobbied against restaurants and other commercial establishments that were segregating Mexicans based on what the consul termed *prejudicios raciales* (racial prejudice).[117] He and his staff also noted that Mexican children were being segregated in schools for similar reasons but made no mention of specific instances. At the University of Chicago Settlement House in 1929, workers decided to segregate Mexican boys from other boys "because it has not proved highly successful where Mexican boys have been mixed with other boys."[118] They took this action after consulting with workers at Hull-House, who reported similar experiences. All agreed that it was the best way to protect Mexican boys from malicious name-calling and fights. Despite such good intentions, however, the net effect was to isolate these boys.

Given the paucity of evidence, it is difficult to gauge to what extent repatriations from Chicago were deportations, whether formal or informal.[119] The random sweeps and arrests so common in border states were reported in East Chicago, Indiana, and Gary, Indiana, but rarely in Chicago itself. It is clear, however, that news of forcible deportations and indiscriminate confiscation permeated the Mexican communities throughout the city, thus fueling already-growing fears of deportation. On January 14, 1930, for example, *El Nacional* ran a front-page story on the deportations occurring in other parts of the United States. The headline cried, "Mas deportaciones de Mexicanos." Reporting from Guaymas, Sonora, the article explained, "North American authorities continue their relentless persecution of numerous Mexicans who entered the United States without filling out the required papers."[120] Minimizing the degree of their offenses, the reporter then chronicled the dire economic circumstances of the deportees arriving in Guaymas, a city in Sonora, about 250 miles south of Arizona on the Sea of Cortéz (Gulf of California). Many of the deportees and their families "find themselves in complete misery, half-naked, and without a cent with which to eat."[121]

Stories such as these encouraged Mexicans to appeal to the consul to help them repatriate, in the hopes that they could get enough aid to mitigate their economic circumstances. Those Mexicans still fortunate enough to have employment after the economic crash of 1929 increasingly lost their jobs to "native whites" and Europeans. Representing "we the Mexicans in Rockdale," Nemécio Peña, Román Gomez, Jesus Rodríguez, Apolinar Castillo, and over twenty other men sent a moving letter to the Mexican consul in Chicago in December 1930. The letter itself, though typed, was full of misspelled words and grammatical errors, and, adding to its poignancy, many of the men who signed their names wrote in awkward and uneven scrawls. These Mexicans had lost their jobs at a local brick factory, positions some of them had held for nearly ten years, "simply for being Mexicans." Those jobs, they wrote, were given to North Americans and Europeans.[122] Their rhetoric harkened back to the Flores Magón brothers' socialist newspaper *Regeneración*. Working as an arm of the Partido Liberal Mexicano (PLM), the paper, published in Los Angeles during the Mexican Revolution, informed *Mexicanos de afuera* of events in Mexico while working toward political solidarity among working-class Mexicans.[123] Distributed widely in Mexican communities throughout the United States, the paper frequently contained accounts of "gringos" getting jobs over Mexicans and of Mexicans being paid less than "gringos" for equal work. The Mexicans of Rockdale used similar rhetoric in their appeal to the Mexican consul in Chicago. They beseeched him to help them repatriate to Mexico before they were driven to crime to provide their families with food and before they and their families died of cold or hunger. Nowhere did they mention becoming citizens to better access relief aid. Like many of the Mexicans in Chicago, they knew that "the few Mexicans who ha[d] taken American citizenship ha[d] not changed from their former condition."[124] "Moreover," another explained, "even the Mexican born here and hence [an] American citizen suffer[s] by the working of those same prejudices which put[s] them at a great disadvantage with the other citizens of this great country."[125]

Clearly, these Mexicans did not view U.S. citizenship as a means for creating opportunity; rather, they believed that prejudices against Mexicans canceled out whatever benefits one could attain. An editor of Chicago's principal Spanish-language newspaper asked, "How are [we] to become identified with th[is] country when a barrier of prejudices is opposed to it?"[126] A man in Packingtown concurred, "What advantages do you get by becoming naturalized? We are going to be subjected to the same difficulties that we are now suffering, in spite of our citizenship, because our looks cannot be changed by our nationality."[127]

Herein lay the crux of the citizenship issue for Mexicans: becoming American on the nationalist model of the Americanizers meant more than changing their citizenship. Becoming American required a "look" that would free them of the "barrier of prejudices" they experienced in their everyday lives.[128] For Mexicans, the required look was "whiteness," and they experienced the truth of this in many aspects of their daily lives. When they went to church on the Near West Side, the Protestant pastor required Mexicans to go to the segregated services, "although," he admitted, "there are a few who are as white as the ordinary American."[129]

Not only was the equation of whiteness with American identity increasingly obvious, but so too was U.S. citizenship equated with American identity. Not having it jeopardized a variety of economic and social aspects of Mexican life in Chicago, including obtaining city licenses to conduct business. Felipe Martínez, for example, applied on February 13, 1924, for a billiard-hall license from the City of Chicago.[130] The intended poolroom would have replaced a defunct soft-drink parlor run by John Skoden.[131] Martínez's application was initially denied because he was not a U.S. citizen, so he declared his intention to become a citizen by taking out what were commonly called "first papers," the first step in the process of filing for citizenship. The process changed somewhat during this period, but it generally began with filing a declaration of intention. Within seven years, an applicant filed "second papers," the petition for naturalization. Once two upstanding U.S. citizens (usually co-workers or neighbors) were deposed in support of the applicant's petition, the oath of allegiance was administered, and citizenship was granted.

In spite of having made a declaration of intention to become a U.S.

citizen, however, Martínez still could not obtain a license. A Chicago police officer, Christian Radden, after investigating the application, recommended against the license because the applicant "is a Mexican . . . and as a general rule people of this kind are undesirable characters."[132] The policeman feared that allowing a pool hall in the area would attract more Mexicans. If he could prevent the opening of an establishment catering to Mexicans, then he could prevent bringing any more of those undesirables into the area.

The Chicago municipal court judge Thomas Green shared Radden's anti-Mexican sentiments. When a Mexican appeared before him and happened to complain that he needed a larger size pants than what the local relief agency provided, Green shouted, "'You have a lot of nerve. After being in this country nineteen years without becoming a citizen and after living on relief for five years, you kick about it. If you don't like this country—or the pants—get out!'"[133] Recall that Judge Green achieved some degree of notoriety when he imprisoned the Mexican consul because of the burden his people were allegedly putting on the state.[134] Mexicans themselves were well aware of Green's views of them. As Max Guzmán recalled years later, "Judge Green . . . he didn't want nothing to do with the Mexicans. He, he hated the Mexican people."[135]

Alderman Joseph McDonough, in his capacity as chairman of the billiard commission, wrote to Mayor Dever about Felipe Martínez's attempts to obtain a license for his billiard hall. Writing nearly a month after Radden's comments, McDonough reversed the opinion of the policeman by recommending the license be issued immediately. In the month after the rejection of Martínez's initial bid for a license, the Mexican consul had telephoned McDonough's office, apparently intervening on behalf of Martínez. The consul "complained to the [billiard] Commission with reference to discrimination between citizens, and non-citizens, applying for licenses." The commission and the chief of police agreed "that there should not be any discrimination whatsoever," and the license was issued. Rather than keeping Mexicans away, as the policeman suggested and as Judge Green advocated, Joe McDonough settled on allowing Mexicans a place of their own to play pool. His major concern was that "Mexicans are now playing pool mixed with the white people just a few blocks away." With their own billiard room, he reasoned, the white people would be freed of the undesirables Radden hoped to keep out. As the alderman stated, "[T]he Commission ha[s] tried to prevent Mexicans [mixing] with the white people."

As early as 1924, Mexicans experienced prejudicial treatment at the hands of earlier immigrants who had risen into positions of power within local institutions. Through those institutions, like the billiard commission, earlier immigrants also worked together to segregate Mexicans from those considered white. Separation, the strategy used in the case of Felipe Martínez's pool hall, served to concentrate Mexicans in their own recreational venues. The police too reportedly took advantage of Mexicans' lack of U.S. citizenship, for without it, they had little recourse when abused by the police. As Max Guzmán recounted, "[T]hey didn't want . . . [to] hear nothing about becoming citizens or anything . . . and then the police, well, took advantage of it."[136]

Mexicans themselves occasionally advocated segregation and separation, particularly as a means of fighting anti-Mexican prejudices. For instance, in 1928, *México* discouraged its readership from joining in any of the upcoming Fourth of July events because of the racial prejudices they would be sure to face.[137] "While there is a barrier of racial hates, and while we do not know how to present ourselves and mingle with them [given this barrier], for our own good and for the name of our country we should stay away from their festivity." This was an interesting argument for the editors to make, as they employed the real threats of racial prejudice to encourage their readers to stay away from Fourth of July festivities and to isolate themselves. A convenient by-product of not participating in the country's quintessential expression of patriotic fervor was to shield Mexicans from any forces of Americanization that might be present at these events. Indeed, the paper reported that many of Chicago's Mexicans found themselves "incapable of being assimilated spiritually, mentally, and physically into the American people."[138] As proof of this, the editors of *México* in 1927 offered evidence of those Mexicans who had been living "under the civil, administrative, and educational laws of the United States" for over eighty years and yet still had "different ideals, customs, and temperament."[139] Clearly, their experiences and accounts of other Mexicans in the Southwest informed the views of many of those who came to Chicago.

Once again, their lived experience provided the context through which Mexicans explained their claims to and definitions of American identity. "The Asiatic immigrants come to the United States with the idea of establishing a home and staying . . . in what they call 'the promised land,'" proclaimed the editors of *La Prensa*, the leading Spanish-language newspaper in San Antonio. Reprinted in Chicago's *México* in 1926, the editorial completed the comparison: "[N]ot the Mexicans. Except for very rare exceptions, those who come to this country set their hopes on returning to their country, . . . the only . . . promised land."[140] A year later, the editors of *México* clearly shared this perspective as they explained that the Europeans came because of a perpetual evil, the overcrowding of their countries. Therefore, they came predisposed to becoming permanent "U.S. citizens, to adopt the English language, to dwell with their progeny under their new roof, identified with and faithful to their new flag."[141] Mexicans, in contrast, were "not prepared to make such a transcendental change." Indeed, the editors noted, most Mexicans came to the United States only temporarily, ready to return "easily by the rails which unite the two countries without any geographical break."[142] Like the editors of La Prensa, the editors of México appeared to hold sympathies for Mexican nationalism and worked to keep their gente de afuera oriented toward Mexico.

Despite the relative proximity of Mexico, the barriers and constraints erected during this period greatly lengthened the distances to travel. During the interwar years, state and federal legislation increasingly formalized the Mexican position in the United States. The creation of the Border Patrol in 1924, for example, institutionalized a previously casual migratory process.[143] Initially, the "Registration of Aliens" report of the Immigration Committee of the U.S. Chamber of Commerce recommended requiring certificates of arrival and payment of fees of aliens crossing into the United States on its southern border. Certificates and fees were settled on in lieu of more formal registration programs. Such programs, the Immigration Committee argued, would not be "in accordance with American principles" because they would require monitoring and surveillance of individual aliens.[144] The Border Patrol was established as part of this certificate-of-arrival program. In its first year, it was appropriated one million dollars and 450 men.[145]

After 1924, Mexicans crossing the southern border of the United States were required to register, pay fees, pass literacy tests, and submit to health exams.[146] These border crossings themselves were increasingly prejudicial experiences. Ignacio Valle, the owner of El Arte Mexicano, a music shop on the Near West Side in Chicago, recounted that when he came to the U.S.–Mexico border from Guadalajara, officials let him across because he "look[ed] all right."[147] Interestingly, Valle chose to register himself with the Mexican consulate in December 1930, after at least five years of being a successful merchant in Chicago.[148] Perhaps in the changed economic circumstances of the Great Depression, that he "look[ed] all right" was not enough protection against rising anti-Mexican sentiments. During times of economic stress, officials were more willing to enact the provisions of the 1917 Immigration Act that denied visas on the basis of illiteracy or the "Liable-to-Become-a-Public-Charge" proviso. During the 1920s and 1930s, this provision was reportedly used throughout the United States to reduce the burden Mexicans were perceived to be placing on public schools, jails, and welfare agencies.[149]

More subtle forms of everyday discrimination were also evident. In 1930, the Illinois Governor's Commission on Unemployment and Relief issued new guidelines requiring local relief agencies to register all unemployed people. Several agents reportedly used this to encourage Mexican repatriation from Chicago to Mexico.[150] When a Mexican applied for relief, often a case worker was dispatched to the family to discuss how much happier they would be in Mexico, yet without mentioning that time on relief would blacklist them from ever reentering the country legally. As economic circumstances worsened, "an increasing number of families f[ound] their homes without electricity or gas"—a dire situation in December in Chicago![151] When Mexican tenants had trouble paying rent, landlords reportedly resorted to extreme measures to evict them. "One landlord," reported the workers at the University of Chicago Settlement House, "removed both doors and windows to force the family to move without the expense of a court notice."[152]

By 1939, the Works Progress Administration issued a ruling that closed off yet another avenue of employment for Mexicans in those difficult years. Aid workers lamented that "the ruling that all WPA workers must be citizens has affected many. . . . Many lost their WPA assignments because of their citizenship requirements."[153] At the same time, "Mexican" clearly came to mean a nonwhite racial group like Blacks, for even researchers of the Chicago Area Project segregated Mexicans and "Negroes" from the rest of the populations studied in the neighborhoods of the Near North, West, and South Sides of the city.[154] In spite of heavy pressures and the discriminatory consequences of not succumbing to them, Mexicans still did not increase their rates of naturalization throughout the 1930s.

Conclusion

The growing prejudices against Mexicans and the resulting moves toward segregation illustrate fundamental flaws in the process of Mexican Americanization in Chicago. By trying to inject Mexicans into a model of Americanization predicated on the attainment (and desirability) of U.S. citizenship, educational and social mobility, and on the supremacy of whiteness, it became clear during this period that Mexicans did not fit the model.

Mexicans' own growing understanding of this insular Americanism came at the cost of other visions of Americanism that had operated among Chicago's varied Mexican communities. As early as the mid-1920s, discussions of citizenship and Americanism among Mexicans in Chicago became supplanted by debates on how to defend themselves against the prejudices they faced. By the mid-1930s, their lived experiences of ever more racially charged discrimination ultimately determined the heart of the Americanism issue for these Mexicans. As "being Mexican" came to hold specific meanings in Chicago, being American became less and less tenable. The process of Mexican Americanization meant adjusting to expectations framed by European immigrant experiences even as it became clear that the Mexican experience did not conform to the expected trajectory of assimilationist Americanization. Mexicans thus became "problems" even as they struggled alongside European ethnic groups like the Poles and Italians who strove to mark their own belonging and hence lay claims to their Americanness.[155]

The Mexican situation was fundamentally different, however, from that of the European. Differences lay in issues of citizenship, looks, racial prejudice, and whiteness—or rather, Mexicans' nonwhiteness. As the Mexican consul in Chicago wrote to officials in Mexico City in the early 1920s, "[T]he situation of Mexicans in the United States is unique by virtue of the prejudice against our race, intensified a great deal over the last ten years."[156] As Chicagoans became more familiar with Mexicans, they came to reflect views like those outlined by the consul. Despite their varied claims to whiteness and American identity, Mexicans were segregated from whites with growing frequency. As one movie-theater operator made clear, "'[W]hite people don't like to sit next to the colored or Mexican . . . many of them are not clean and we can't separate them on the basis of dress, so we separate them [the Mexicans] on the basis of nationality.'"[157] Mexicans repeatedly found themselves marked pejoratively as "Mexican," a term that by the end of the 1930s reflected the conflation of race and nationality into a derogatory, nonwhite racial category.

The growth of this racialized prejudice against Mexicans helped to crystallize Mexican immigrants as nonwhite. As a worker at the Chicago Chamber of Commerce explained, "The Mexicans are lower than the European peasants. They are not white and not Negro; they're Mexican."[158] And so workers like the men in Rockdale lost their jobs to European immigrants "just for being Mexicans." By the mid-1930s, Mexicans clearly recognized the discriminatory consequences of "being Mexican." As one Spanish-language newspaper observed, the Depression "has made of us who compose the foreign element, the principal victims."[159] And yet they still did not change their citizenship.

For Mexicans in Chicago during the interwar years, a "barrier of prejudice" gradually emerged that could not be broken down with U.S. citizenship, nor could it be sidestepped through claims of continental, hemispheric, or Pan-American citizenship—despite prevalent rhetoric espousing Pan-American unity as high up as the presidency of the United States. Shortly after his presidential inauguration in 1933, Franklin Delano Roosevelt addressed the governing board of the Pan American Union, in which he celebrated the common ties—historical, economic, and social—shared by the forty-one republics of America. "Common ideals and a community of interest," he claimed, "together with a spirit of cooperation, have led to the realization that the well-being of one Nation depends in large measure upon the well-being of its neighbors. It is upon these foundations that Pan Americanism has been built." Like the proponents of the North American Free-Trade Agreement nearly sixty years later, however, his concern was not with the free exchange of peoples but was rather focused on trade, the free exchange of goods. This became clear as further restrictions were placed on relief aid while repatriations and deportations of Mexicans continued into the mid-1930s, and the threat of deportation hung over every Mexican, citizen and noncitizen alike, throughout the interwar period.[160]

Contemporaries like the sociologist and researcher Robert Jones occasionally glimpsed the double-edged quandary Mexicans faced. In his writings, he displayed clear sympathies with the Mexican condition. He wrote, "As the Mexican becomes Americanized he is separated from the non-assimilated group by customs yet often because of his race he is not free to join American groups."[161] The process of racialization that Mexicans underwent in Chicago rendered them not white and not Black but foreign, alien, not American. By the end of the 1930s, Mexicans in Chicago did not simply drift in the ethno-racial borderlands *between* whiteness and blackness.[162] They also hovered outside these borderlands, marked by their un-Americanness—indeed, their Mexicanness.

4 Striations Within

María Moreno Corona was born in the small, remote town of Arteaga, Mexico, on April 19, 1903.[1] The mountainous terrain around the village ensures that it remains isolated. Lying between Monterrey and Saltillo in the northern state of Coahuila, Arteaga is ten miles from the state capital of Saltillo. At some point during her early adulthood, María found her way to Saltillo. Just shy of her twenty-second birthday she traveled from Saltillo to the U.S.–Mexico border and crossed legally into the United States on the footbridge at Laredo, Texas. Although unclear from the records, she was likely not traveling alone, for she was eight months pregnant with her first child. Since she had been married two years earlier in San Antonio, Texas, this was clearly not her first time coming into and staying in the United States. She made it from Laredo to San Antonio in time to give birth to Fernando in March 1925. Just over a year later, while still in San Antonio, she gave birth to Amalia in July. By September, María had traveled with her newborn daughter and infant son through Texas, Oklahoma, Kansas, Missouri, and Illinois, all the way to Chicago.

Once in Chicago, María settled on the Near West Side and worked as a full-time housewife. In May 1928, her second daughter, Aurora, was born, and in May 1930 María gave birth to her second son, Roberto. Both were born in Chicago. Sometime during 1930, either just before or right after Roberto was born, María's husband of seven years abandoned her and their four children, all under the age of five. Somehow María persevered in Chicago through the harshest years of the Great Depression, and by 1937 she had filed her first papers, declaring her intention to become

certify that the photograph affixed to the duplicate

at
ani
sion
dec
by
nes

cover a portion of the photograph)

Fig. 4.1: María Moreno Corona, Chicago 1937. Petition for Naturalization No. 196261, National Archives and Records Administration.

a U.S. citizen. By 1940, shortly following her thirty-seventh birthday, María was sworn in as a U.S. citizen.

As the contours of María's life reflect, the geographies of Mexican women's lives were fundamentally different from those of men: from crossing international borders while eight months pregnant to giving birth multiple times in short succession, from traveling long distances with children in tow to being abandoned—or in some cases, widowed—by their husbands. Part of understanding the histories of Mexican women like María involves mapping these lived experiences, deciphering and paying careful attention to the whispers that remain of their migration processes, their settlement and adjustment experiences, and the decisions they made along the way. Doing so provides a very different lens through which to view and understand Mexican Chicago and brings into stark relief the extent to which that terrain was lived differently according to one's gender.

Previous chapters have drawn out the gendered nature of the migration process itself, the significance of gender, particularly masculinities, in Mexican relations with other ethnic groups in Chicago through heterosocial interactions, and even the different ways Mexican men and women reacted to Americanization programs. This chapter explores the gendered terrains of life in Chicago, specifically highlighting several aspects of social relations between Mexican women and men. It draws out the diversity of the Mexican population in Chicago and clarifies the elements along which the population divided. Shifting gender norms and rising mass culture further stratified the Mexican population along lines of generation, language, and looks. Generational tensions erupted as young Mexican women and men growing up in Chicago embraced activities and opportunities often against their parents' wishes. Issues of language and the quality of one's language further complicated relations between generations, classes, and those recently arrived versus those with some years in the United States. Looks continued to be an issue in the ongoing struggles with the processes of racialization and Americanization.[2] As movies, dime dances, baseball, and jazz music infused life in Chicago, Mexicans, like other residents, participated in these diversions. Yet experiences like having to sit in the "Colored" section of the movie theaters mediated the enjoyment of those Mexicans who couldn't "pass" while splintering them from others who could, episodes that again highlight the heterogeneity of Mexican racial positioning. Language too played a significantly divisive role in dictating the forms of recreation in which Mexicans could partake. As Manuel Bravo recalled in an interview years later, "[T]he guys were, you know, their English wasn't that good so they didn't go [to the movies]."[3]

One's appearance (from phenotype to manners to dress) also seems significant in Mexican attempts to positions themselves as Spanish. Such a move was certainly familiar in the histories of Mexicans in the U.S. Southwest; yet, claims to Spanishness in the context of Chicago were more problematic, particularly in the face of many recently emigrated Spaniards. Many of these had fled the rise of fascism and Generalismo Franco. Because of Chicago's history with anarchists and communists, claims to Spanish identity became potentially suspect, as such claims could associate a Mexican with transgressive political ideologies in which he or she may not believe.

The heightened awareness within the Mexican population of the diversity among Mexicans in Chicago hindered the creation of any sense of cohesiveness, particularly as individuals experienced differing levels of prejudice based in differences of language, skin color, and to some degree, class. Ironically, awareness of these striations rarely extended outside of the Mexican communities. As discussed in the previous chapter, "Mexican" in Chicago came to hold pejorative meanings and a homogenized identity, undifferentiated to those "outsiders" with whom Mexicans came into contact.

This chapter explores the tensions and conflicts among Mexicans themselves as they came to and lived in Chicago. In doing so, it reveals the diversity of the city's Mexican population. Mapping the gendered geographies of Mexican life in Chicago illuminates these internal striations, many of which were undergirded by changes in mass culture and economic development. The chapter highlights the extent to which some women experienced fragmented or unconventional relationships with men as single, widowed, abandoned, or divorced women. From the migration process to the settlement, work, and entertainment options, the experiences of Mexican women in Chicago were distinct from those of Mexican men. Most significantly, Mexican women discovered that life in the United States—in spite of its difficulties—provided them with freedoms unavailable in Mexico. Ironically, it was these same freedoms that men found most detracted from life in *el norte*. This chapter examines those internal striations, the divisions that erupted from the conflicted relationships Mexicans had with Americanism, with each other, and with their varied attempts to adapt while navigating the shifting terrains of race and gender.

Fragmented and Unconventional Relations

The lives of Mexican women who came to Chicago reveal much about their relationships with men. Many experienced fragmented connections with male partners, whether through death, desertion/abandonment, or divorce. Many of these women embraced options in their lives that challenged sociocultural conventions, and in doing so, Mexican women often gloried in the freedoms they could attain outside of Mexico.

Some women chose neither to marry nor have children. Delfina Navarro, for instance, left her hometown of Guadalajara, Mexico, and entered the United States at Laredo, Texas, when she was twenty years old. Delfina went directly to Chicago, where she remained a single woman with no children until at least the age of thirty-four, when she applied for and received U.S. citizenship.[4] Like Delfina, Concepción Pérez remained single and childless until she was at least thirty-one years old.[5] She, however, traveled much farther and seemed to be even more mobile than other women. She left her hometown of Mérida in the southernmost Mexican state of Yucatán when she was merely nineteen. Unlike most Mexicans, Concepción came to the United States by ship, traveling through the Gulf of Mexico and up the eastern seaboard to New York City. Nine days after docking, she arrived in Chicago to begin work as a machine operator, evidently in a garment shop.[6] When she applied for U.S. citizenship, she changed her name to Caroline, a more common English name (she kept Pérez as her last name).

Celia Hernández also became a U.S. citizen; however, her journey was different from Concepcion's in many ways.[7] Celia was born in No-

certify that the photograph affixed to the duplicat

at
an
si(
d(
b)
ne

(T   ...pressed so as to
cover a portion of the photograph)

Fig. 4.2: Delfina Navarro, Chicago 1937. Petition for Naturalization No. 195115, National Archives and Records Administration.

certify that the photograph affixed to the duplicat

a
a
si
d
b
n

(T
cover a portion of the photograph)

Fig. 4.3: Celia Hernández, Chicago 1936. Petition for Naturalization No. 176592, National Archives and Records Administration.

vember 1908 in the tropical mountains of the state of Guerrero in the capital city of Chilpancingo. After living for a time in Mexico City (over 170 miles away!), Celia entered the United States legally at Eagle Pass, Texas, on September 10, 1923. Only fifteen years old, she spent the next seven years living predominantly in the United States. By 1930 she had moved to the small suburbs of Cook County, Illinois, outside Chicago.

Celia spent her young adulthood in the 1930s in Chicago as a single woman working in what she termed the "beauty culture" and in "dancing." She continued in these occupations throughout the years of the Great Depression. Perhaps she was part of the Latin dance craze that hit Chicago and the nation during the 1930s. Headed by Alfredo Cano and Bertha "Rosita" Musquiz, performers donned brilliantly colored costumes and danced traditional Mexican and Spanish numbers to sold-out audiences. Like many young men of his time, Cano left the family *rancho* in Mexico to work in Chicago in 1922. He joined cousins already there and studied Spanish dance. Rosita was a U.S. citizen, a Mexican born in San Antonio. She and Alfredo met and began their lifelong dance in 1930. Rosita and Alfredo performed in the Spanish and Mexican villages at the 1933 Century of Progress Exposition in Chicago. Many years later, Rosita donated the costumes she and Alfredo used in their performances throughout the 1930s, 1940s, and 1950s to the Chicago Historical Society, who exhibited their costumes in "Flamenco! Latin Dance in 1930s Chicago" in the winter of 2003–4.

Mexican dancing had become widely popular in Chicago at least ten years earlier with the arrival of Paco Perafán, a professional dancer from Mexico City. After settling in Chicago he continued to tour throughout North and South America, performing traditional Mexican dances.[8] Perafán also taught Spanish dancing in his studio at 733 North Dearborn. He was especially known for his rendition of the "Jota Aragonesa." As Perafán himself explained, the dance was "expressive of the soul of the bullfighter."[9] At fiestas throughout the 1920s, Perafán taught many groups to dance the "Jaraba Tapatio, the famous 'Hat Dance' of Mexico, which is a gay and flirtatious dance."[10] His impact was clear when the newly elected Mexican President Pascual Ortíz Rubio came to visit Chicago in January 1930. Ortíz Rubio received a festive welcome that included four-year-old Emma Valle, the daughter of the notable music merchant Ignacio Valle, dancing "el tipico Jarabe Tapatio" for Rubio's family. She appeared on the front page of *México* in her beautiful dress.[11] Paco Perafán himself, appearing with his dancing partner, Herlinda Rodríguez, took part in the festivities for Ortíz Rubio's visit.[12] Clearly, the dancing community was vibrant, for other professional dancers moved to Chicago in the late 1920s. The Enciso family, for instance, came to Chicago in 1928 after dancing for two years in Los Angeles. A tailor by training, Señor Enciso made all the costumes for the family's performances. He taught his five children to dance the Jarabe Tapatio, and when the family arrived in Chicago, he sent the children to study at Paco Perafán's studio.[13]

Younger dancing teachers opened studios in the 1930s. The duo Tina y Nacho taught dance on the Near West Side. Reportedly, their style of dancing, especially boleros, was "more dynamic, and faster than the original dances."[14] Even Hull-House had several dance troupes, including the Club Recreativo, which offered public performances at bimonthly fiestas.

The fascination with Latin dance was part of the larger national fascination with Latin culture and stereotyping of Latin identity that contributed to the popularity of movie stars like Dolores del Rio and Lupe Vélez, all of which fueled the market for what Celia termed "beauty culture."[15] Perhaps too Celia participated in the modern dime dances so popular during this period. As was common, young girls were paid to dance with men, keeping a portion of the amount they charged for themselves. Given the unequal sex ratios between Mexican women and men, this form of controlled socializing helped to ensure heterosocial contacts among Mexicans themselves (with an eye toward reducing interethnic contacts).[16] Regardless to which "dancing" venue she referred, Celia continued enjoying the freedoms of modern womanhood by working for wages and remaining unmarried at least until she became a U.S. citizen in 1939 at the age of thirty-one.

There were not, however, many women like Delfina, Concepción, and Celia, as most Mexican women of their age married and bore children. In fact, booming birth rates serve as one indicator of a growing Mexican

Fig. 4.4: Mexican Fiesta: Jarabe Tapatio, Hull-House, 1939. Yearbook, 1939, Hull-House Reports, folder 443, Jane Addams Memorial Collection, University of Illinois at Chicago.

female population. Childbirth brought its own risks, and occasionally women died during childbirth, as did twenty-five-year-old Catalina Morales. Her son, Joseph Morales Jr., survived, and her husband Jose (who also went by Joseph), a shoe cutter by trade, brought him up on the North Side of Chicago.[17] More frequently, Mexican women were widowed with several children to raise.[18] Sofía Casso López, for instance, had five children, two of them Chicago-born. Her youngest was only seven years old in September 1930 when his father died. Sofía worked as a machine operator on the Near West Side during the 1930s, and by 1940 she had sought and gained U.S. citizenship.[19] María de los Angeles Navarro de Nuñez was widowed at the age of twenty-nine. With four children to raise (all born in Mexico), she eventually worked as a seamstress, also on the Near West Side.[20] Like María, Paz Fernández (Abundes) was a widow who worked as a seamstress in the 1930s, laboring as a sewing-machine operator to support her two Chicago-born daughters, Hortencia and Angelina.[21]

Even more frequent than widowhood among Mexican women in Chicago during this era, however, was desertion. Mexican women were not alone in being deserted by their husbands; other poor women in Chicago also faced desertion. However, many of them sought recourse through state institutions from which Mexican women were disenfranchised. The historian Michael Willrich has shown that, between 1923 and 1927, many deserted women appealed to the Court of Domestic Relations (a branch of Chicago's municipal court) or to Mayor Dever directly through letters.[22] In their letters, these women beseeched the state and its representatives to enforce laws against alcohol, which many blamed for their dire circumstances. Many of these women were from European ethnic groups long thought by contemporaries and historians to be against Prohibition, like the Poles, Irish, and Italians, a revelation that challenges scholars to rethink the politics of Prohibition in Chicago.[23] And some of the petitioners were Black women. These letters and petitions certainly indicate a level of enfranchisement, even if only a "'minimum form of citizenship.'"[24] This form of epistolary citizenship had been used traditionally by women (especially middle-class white women) in the United States before passage of the Nineteenth Amendment to the Constitution granted women the right to vote in all elections.[25]

Mexican women, however, turned not to the state to battle their desertion but rather relied on the network of other Mexican women and sympathetic families to augment their conditions. María Paniagua's husband deserted her and their children in Detroit in the early 1920s. María faced rearing children alone, a circumstance rarely shared by men. Relying on a network of Mexican women and men, María worked for other Mexican families in the boxcar camps providing child care and laundry service. The families paid her in food for her and the children. During the summer of 1923, María worked in the beetfields with a couple she knew from the boxcar camps in Detroit, José and Margarita Medina. She saved enough money to pay for carfare to Savannah, Illinois, on the edge of the Mississippi River. María and her children moved with another family, Guillermo and Nellie Villalobos, to Savannah. Shortly thereafter, her brother, already living in Chicago, sent money for María and the children to join him there.[26]

Though no statistics exist on rates of desertion during this period, it is clear that Paniagua's desertion by her husband was not uncommon among Mexican women living in Chicago. Desertion may in part have been tied to male adventurism.[27] One angle on the standard narrative of Mexican migration focuses on the adventurism of young men who headed *al norte* to try their luck in the various jobs available in the United States during the 1920s. Again, this adventurism often was a gendered-male experience, as evidence suggests that few women took off on such trips, likely because of the cultural and institutional constraints on the mobility of Mexican women. What is absent from that narrative is the human toll in the lives of the Mexicanas who entered into the adventure with those young men.[28] María had married her husband in her hometown of San Antonio, Texas, against her family's wishes and joined him on the adventure north. He had obtained work on the Rock Island Railroad, and the couple lived in boxcars in Des Moines, Iowa, Kansas City, Missouri, and finally in Detroit, Michigan. When her husband deserted her, María and the children lived in a boxcar in Detroit.[29]

Like María Paniagua and María Corona, Eva Guerrero found herself an abandoned woman after only three years of marriage.[30] Married at thirty-four, she was considered an older bride during that era, yet she had traveled far before marrying. She left her home in Oaxaca at the age of twenty-four. After some time in Chiapas, Eva crossed legally into the United States at Calexico, California, as Genoveva L. de Benavidez. For thirteen years she lived on the West Coast, not coming to Chicago until May 1937. While in Los Angeles, Eva married Frank Guerrero in 1934, a U.S. citizen born in the mining town of Morenci, Arizona. It appears that he did not come to Chicago with her. Once in Chicago, Eva lived in South Chicago and worked as a cook.

A few women challenged expected trajectories in other ways. Raquel Chávez, for example, was not single, nor abandoned by her husband. She was a divorced woman.[31] Like other women in these narratives, her life transgressed many conservative cultural norms. Divorced in her mid-twenties and left with a young son to raise, Raquel Chávez Velasquez toiled as a factory worker to make financial ends meet. Raquel was born in Torin (a.k.a. Torim), a small village on the Yaqui River in the Sonoran desert on the northwest coast of Mexico. During the Mexican revolutionary years, several military regiments were stationed in the area. Raquel left town in 1919 at the age of nine (presumably with family), just as an epidemic of yellow fever broke out.[32]

After entering the United States at Laredo, Texas, Raquel (and her family?) came to Chicago two years later. In September 1930 she married her soon-to-be-ex-husband, Manuel Velasquez, in Chicago, and the following year her son, Renato, was born. Only four months into her marriage and a couple of months into her pregnancy, twenty-one-year-old Raquel found her way to one of the Eleanor Association clubs and befriended the secretary of the association, Bernice Durkee. Under the auspices of the Eleanor Foundation, the Eleanor Association ran residential clubs for working women and girls, providing them "with safe spaces for growth and development . . . expand[ing] opportunities for women and girls to learn, collaborate, and serve each other and the greater community."[33] Because the women of Eleanor were primarily single working women (with or without children) in Chicago, Raquel's ties to the association so early into her marriage suggest how short-lived that union must have been. She maintained her link to Eleanor clubs

Fig. 4.5: Raquel Chávez, Chicago 1938. Petition for Naturalization No. 214000, National Archives and Records Administration.

for at least the following ten years, as her friend Bernice became a witness for Raquel's (now known as Rachel) bid to become a U.S. citizen in late 1940.

Juana León evidently presented an unusual case, but she nonetheless represented a life whose passion for learning helped to transcend many sociocultural constraints. Aspects of her life were captured in a 1928 University of Chicago thesis by Anita Edgar Jones.[34] Juana's father was a schoolteacher in Mexico and provided ample opportunity for Juana, his oldest child, to gain an education far better than what was typically accorded Mexican women in the 1910s. She became such a notable and successful teacher herself that in 1916 she was among one hundred teachers the Mexican government sent to study in the United States. When the strains of the revolution forced the Mexican government to recall the teachers, Juana returned to Saltillo with the dream of one day studying again in the United States to become a pediatrician. Four years later, Juana managed to convince her father to move the family to Chicago so she could pursue her medical education. They arrived in Chicago in 1920, where Juana promptly began taking classes to learn English and prepare for medical school. Her father took night classes after working at Marshall Field's during the day, her sister worked as a milliner, and her brother entered school. By 1928, Juana had finished medical school despite having to support herself the last two years after the death of both parents. Her siblings were married, and Juana took a full-time job with a social-service agency in Chicago providing medical care to newly arrived immigrants. It is unknown whether Juana ever finished her medical internship to become a certified pediatrician.

It is striking how resilient these women were in their life choices. While many of them found their lives contoured by expectations of men, they managed to persevere and nagivate those worlds without the expected male mediator. Whether they were abandoned, widowed, divorced, or single, these *mujeres*, like those brought to life in Vicki L. Ruiz's *From Out of the Shadows*, raised children, worked as single women in modern factories, and availed themselves of limited resources around them to survive.[35] Their resilience is lost in the standard gendered-male narrative of settlement of Mexicans in the area.

The unequal sex ratios between Mexican women and men, along with rising female participation in the wage-labor economy, clearly shaped gender relations. The backdrop of newly emerging mass culture and women's enjoyment of newfound freedoms only further exacerbated gender tensions.

Shifting Gender Norms

Mexican women and men struggled with the shifting gender norms and freedoms of this era. Moreover, the explosion of mass culture and its attendant consumption provided new venues for women and men to identify with "American" identity.[36] These new sites of exchange were further complicated by Mexican women's embrace of these new freedoms and Mexican men's overall resistance and even rejection of them. Coupled with shifting gender behaviors and expectations, generational cleavages also erupted throughout the Mexican communities in Chicago. These kinds of ruptures tore through American society generally during this period, yet because (in part, at least) Mexican women and men encountered these stresses concurrent with their adjustments to Chicago, they perceived the shifting gender and sexual norms to be part of American identity itself.

By the mid-1920s, nearly a quarter of Chicago's Mexican population was female.[37] Evidence of this growing female population became evident in the items targeting women that began to appear in Chicago's Spanish-language newspapers. Weekly columns geared toward women began in 1926: one was entitled "The Doctor of the Home," the other "The Woman of the Home."[38] The first mostly carried nutritional information, the second primarily recipes and cooking advice. While acknowledging women's growing presence in the community, such features reinforced their subordinate position.[39] Women as cooks and caregivers were presented as acceptable female roles—both of which were explicitly defined within the home.[40] The byline of the column on medical advice was male, the one with recipes female. Interestingly, the man's full name, Gustavo Carr, and his degree credentials were printed in the byline, but only the woman's first name, María Luisa, was mentioned—a subtle detail that speaks volumes about the respect accorded the writer and ultimately to her (presumably) female readers. The column of medical advice also attested to the growing professionalization of medical practice.[41]

While reinforcing traditional gender roles for women and opening new possibilities for men, these kinds of columns and advertisements also worked to marginalize traditional *curandera* (healer) remedies as quack concoctions and were also indicative of modernizing trends already under way in Mexico.[42] A trenchant example of this was an advertisement for Sal de Uvas Picot. It pictured a young boy paying a male pharmacist for a bottle of this product. The text read: "This boy knows what's good. When his mother tries to give him some antiquated, horrible tasting concoction . . . the little boy prefers to . . . buy himself some delicious Sal de Uvas Picot that effectively and gently purges him."[43] Clearly, the audience was to eschew traditional folk remedies in favor of modern pharmaceuticals. The young boy served as the symbolic agent in the implied transformation.

Alongside efforts to control women's roles was the increasing incorporation of Mexican women into the wage economy of Chicago. Some women entered the wage economy through informal channels. Recall María Paniagua, for instance, who lived in a railroad camp near the Santa Fe tracks in Corwith and worked for other women in the camp.[44] She helped with child care, cleaning, and laundry while the women provided María with food and bit of spending money. Other women also began working for wages outside the home.[45] The wage-labor opportunities available to Mexican women, however, were severely limited. At Inland Steel, for instance, only 10 percent of the workforce was female in 1928. The bulk of jobs available to Mexican women in industry involved what employers termed "typically female" tasks, which often served to reinscribe traditional gender roles.[46] Clotilde Montes, for instance, sewed mattresses at a factory in Chicago.[47] Mr. Belcher of the Marshall Field mattress factory explained, "[T]he [Mexican] women stitch . . . [they] seem to have a natural aptitude with the needle."[48]

Overall, industrial work paid more than agricultural or railroad work (few railroads hired women). Generally, steel was the highest paid during the 1920s, and the average wage in factories of the Midwest for unskilled Mexicans ranged from forty-three to fifty cents per hour.[49] Packinghouses paid forty-three to forty-seven cents per hour, while average wages in railroads for unskilled Mexican laborers ranged from thirty-five to forty-one cents per hour.[50] As was common elsewhere, the jobs Mexican women performed paid lower wages than those of Mexican men. Minimum-wage men in these industries earned on average forty-four cents per hour, while women earned only twenty-five cents per hour. Their wages were more on par with those of agricultural laborers, the lowest-paid of all. Consider, for example, that the berry pickers in El Monte, California, even after they settled their strike in 1933, only made twenty cents per hour "'where the employment was not steady,'" or $1.50 for a nine-hour day.[51] Some Mexican women, however, labored in factories at skilled jobs. Herlinda de la Vega, for instance, was a milliner, originally from Guadalajara, Jalisco, Mexico.[52] Nevertheless, while reifying particular gender roles, these kinds of labor practices, like those throughout the U.S. Southwest, worked to racially code certain kinds of employment as being particularly "for Mexican women."[53]

[likely prepared by Dept. of Public Welfare
to hand out to Mexicans seeking work, original in Spanish]

"We can no longer give a card of recommendation for work to any person and all that we can do is to give you this list of companies who are in the habit of hiring Mexicans. We do not know if they are hiring right now, but you can go and see."

COMPANIES HIRING MEXICAN MEN

American Bridge Company	208 S. LaSalle Street
Barrett-Cravens Company	1328 W. Monroe Street
Crane Company	4100 S. Kedzie Avenue
Chicago Milwaukee & St. Paul Railway Co.	44th Street & Central
Illinois Steel Company	3426 E. 89th Street, South Chicago
Illinois Central System	135 E. 11th Place
McCormick Twine Mills	2557 Blue Island Avenue
Sloan Valve Company	4300 W. Lake Street
Wisconsin Steel Works	270a E. 106th Street, South Chicago
Santa Fe Railway Company (Round House)	W. 40th & S. Central Park Avenue
Santa Fe Railway Company (Scrap Yard)	44th & S. Central Park Avenue

COMPANIES HIRING MEXICAN WOMEN

American Finishing Company	500 S. Peoria Street

COMPANIES HIRING MEXICAN MEN AND WOMEN

Armour & Company	W. 43rd Street & S. Racine Avenue
Blackstone Hotel	S. Michigan Blvrd. & E. 7th Street
Walter O. Birk Company	500 S. Des Plaines Street
Cracker Jack Company	512 S. Peoria Street
Congress Hotel	S. Michigan Blvrd. & E. Congress
Curtiss Candy Company	750 Briar Place (& N. Halsted)
The Drake Hotel	Lake Shore Dr. & N. Michigan
Griess Pfleger Tanning Company	884 N. Halsted Street
Marshall Field & Company	Harrison & S. Des Plaines
Montgomery Ward & Company	Chicago Ave. & Larrabee
Olson Rug Company	1520 W. Monroe Street
Omaha Packing Company	2320 S. Halsted Street
Peanut Specialty Company	400 W. Superior Street
Sears Roebuck & Company	Arthington & Homan Ave.
Stevens Hotel	S. Michigan & 7th Street
Stewart-Warner Speedometer Corp.	1828 Diversey Parkway
Swift & Company	4100 S. Halsted Street

Fig. 4.6: Chicago Employment Flyer. Box 1, folder "Mexican Labor, Gary, IN.,"
Paul S. Taylor Papers.

Fig. 4.7: Herlinda de la Vega, Chicago 1936. Petition for Naturalization No. 171129, National Archives and Records Administration.

As many scholars have demonstrated, the family economy was thoroughly integrated into urban industrial labor.[54] In Back-of-the-Yards, for instance, packinghouse work included the paid and unpaid labor of women and children.[55] Of the estimated two thousand women who worked in the stockyards in 1930, the majority were unmarried. The bulk were Polish, but among them also worked substantial numbers of Mexican, Bohemian, and Lithuanian women. Married women of the area, including Mexican women, contributed to the family economy in ways familiar to Mexican communities throughout the southwestern United States. These included keeping a family garden during warm seasons and foregoing modern conveniences like clothes washers to save money by doing their own (and often neighbors') laundry.[56] Even families who lived in boxcar camps, like the Gresham Camp at Ninety-first and Halsted, reportedly had garden plots.[57]

New Freedoms

As scholars have shown over the past two decades, women's wage labor, however small, did provide working women with new freedoms. Women participated in new heterosocial commercial activities and redefined notions of family and female sexuality. Mexican women shared in these new freedoms. Yet these new opportunities also heightened frictions between Mexican women and men. One Mexican man sought an explanation for these tensions in strictly practical terms. "'In this country,'" he explained, "'everything costs so much that women have to work.'"[58]

Interestingly, as in Mexico, once a woman got married, it was no longer acceptable for her to work outside the home, particularly if she had children. An elderly Mexican woman, reflecting older norms, agreed. "'How would you like you[r] wife to work?'" she asked, and then explained the impossibilities of such a situation: a woman "'can't serve two masters, and one of them has to be your husband.'"[59]

Other women reflected curious mixtures of bowing to older norms yet desiring to participate in new freedoms. Mrs. Grabozo, for example, attended the dances at the local settlement house, yet "my husband he is like stick—no dance."[60] She also reportedly wanted to participate in other social groups, but respecting norms in Mexico, she would not attend them without her husband. Interestingly, one aspect of American identity—the attainment of English proficiency—also factored into the accessibility of these new freedoms for women and men. Mr. Grabozo, for instance, had a difficult time participating in activities at the local settlement house because of his limited English. Since his wife would not participate without him, his lack of English skills handicapped them both.

Mrs. Grabozo's nod to older norms required her to be in the company of her husband when she went out socially. This notion was part of a larger belief system laced with Catholic dictums of purity and chastity that protected a woman's honor and decency. Other Mexican women, however, especially younger women, seized opportunities to go out socially and expressed pleasure at getting to work outside the home. As one woman explained, "'Women like to work here [in the United States]. At home the man is boss, but not while you are at work.'"[61] Clearly, getting out of the house helped to put Mexican women into spaces unregulated by their husbands, fathers, and sons. Sidney Levin, who grew up during this era in South Chicago among many Mexican families, noted years later, "[T]he Mexican culture is so strongly male oriented, male dominated that they are reluctant to give that up. . . . Mexican women don't want to put up with this. Just because they're Mexican descent, don't mean they're going to put up with all the machismo."[62]

Some women performed wage labor to contribute to the overall family income. In those cases, men often failed to consider the social and economic freedoms for the whole family that often accompanied a woman's working outside the home for wages.[63] More frequently, Mexican men seemed threatened by the freedoms working women experienced. Thus, some prohibited their wives from working for wages and controlled family monies themselves. Mr. Quintero, for instance, "[held] the purse very tightly," forcing his wife, who was not working for wages, to ask him for money.[64] Some Mexican men, like Raul DuBois, explicitly associated a woman's freedom to spend her money with being American. "The American woman is freer in the first place," he explained. She "never arranges to regulate how her money is spent," whether she receives that money "from her husband [or] from her work."[65] Another Mexican man agreed: "'Mexican men don't like freedom of women. It is all right for the Americans, but not for the Mexicans.'"[66] Perhaps by highlighting the sentiments of Mexican men regarding these new freedoms for women, they betrayed a recognition, if only implicitly, that Mexican women enjoyed those freedoms.

The freedoms associated with Americanism and the meanings Mexicans attached to those freedoms were fundamentally imbued with gendered interpretations. In the minds of Mexican men in Chicago, American women were assigned a panoply of seemingly outrageous behaviors. One Mexican man recounted, "'I have an American friend who in his own house can't even . . . order a couple of fried eggs.'" The man's wife reportedly sent him to a restaurant, telling him that "'she did not get married to be a cook for any[one] . . . including her husband.'"[67] The legal recognition of divorce in the United States was perceived by Mexican men to be another source of women's downfall. The reputed ease of divorce was deemed to be "nothing but the first step that a woman takes toward her own perdition," as it supposedly allowed women to change husbands so frequently that their lives would become "a succession of 'husbands' only comparable to the lives of those unfortunate ones called prostitutes."[68] Clearly, the legacy of Catholic doctrine remained in such views, but perhaps they were also symptoms of the significant demographic imbalances in Chicago during this period. With so many available men and potential suitors for his wife, a man might worry that she would partake of the new freedoms afforded her. Moreover, his own inability to exert control in his own life or to control effectively his wife (as he *believed* he'd been able to do in Mexico) added to his insecurities. This was particularly true if a man believed that women used divorce to "fix" conflicts between them. The American woman, explained another Mexican man, "always has present the recourse of divorce in that it is not seen with horror as with us[;] rather [it is seen] as a medium for fixing difficulties."[69] Perhaps the stigma of divorce added to the numbers of deserted wives. Many men were likely Catholics who would not have seen divorce as an option; thus desertion offered them a viable way to get out of a marriage. Many women would not have wanted to be known as divorced women, given the negative social connotations. For them, male desertion may have been the lesser of two evils. The ease of desertion would have tempered men's desire for divorce. It must surely have been transgressive, then, for women like Raquel Chávez to divorce only months after her marriage, even before the birth of her baby.

Interracial Marriages

While many heterosexual unions were between Mexican women and Mexican men, there is ample evidence that Mexican men, in particular, did marry women of other ethnic groups. Fueled by unequal sex ratios between Mexican women and men (some estimates were four men to every one woman), such interracial marriages ran counter to the expectations of contemporaries—Mexicans and non-Mexicans alike—that Mexicans would or should marry other Mexicans.

As discussed in chapter 2, infrequent marriages did occur between Mexicans and African Americans. No statistics exist on rates of Mexican intermarriage with other groups in Chicago during this era, but interviews with contemporaries provide "the very real impression that . . . the proportion of intermarriages far exceeds those which take place in rural areas of the Southwest."[70] The most common interracial unions were between Mexican men and first- or second-generation white ethnic women.[71] Manuel Bravo, for instance, met his wife, Alma, a woman of German descent, at a dance in South Chicago. As he recalled, "The community was so small of young people that I think everybody went . . . and they drew a lot of these outsiders, these outside girls."[72] They dated for three years and then got married. Manuel's father supported them, but his mother "wasn't too keen about it."[73] Neither were Alma's parents happy with the union. "My folks resented it," she recalled, "because at that time Germans married Germans and Mexicans married Mexicans." Manuel and his father-in-law eventually "turned out to be very good friends," but for a time, Alma's mother had to sneak around to visit the newlyweds because "it took my dad a while to get over it [the marriage]."[74]

Mexican applications for U.S. citizenship contain some data on the intermarriage of Mexican men with non-Mexican women. While only an estimated 1 percent of the Mexican population in Chicago actually applied for U.S. citizenship, those who did were overwhelmingly male (which might account for the lack of data on Mexican women marrying non-Mexican men), and the bulk married non-Mexican, European ethnic women. Like Manuel Bravo, Juan (John) Ramírez also married a German woman, Ida Flake, who was five years his senior.[75] Unlike Alma, Ida was not a U.S. citizen, having been born in Lage, Germany. Juan and Ida emigrated as young adults: Juan at the age of twenty-five in 1925, Ida at the age of thirty-one in November 1926. By January 1929, Ida had moved from New York to Chicago, and only six months later, she and Juan married. Guillermo León Gómez (William Leon Gomez) also chose to marry a non-Mexican woman who was five years older than he. His wife, Anna Mathias, was born in Hungary and came to the United States when she was sixteen years old. Guillermo emigrated at the age of fifteen from Zacatecas, at the height of the Mexican Revolution. The couple married in 1928 in Chicago, where Guillermo worked as an elevator operator.

Fig. 4.8: Ida (Flake) Ramírez, Chicago 1934. Petition for Naturalization, National Archives and Records Administration.

Fig. 4.9: Guillermo León Gómez, Chicago 1936. Petition for Naturalization, National Archives and Records Administration.

José (Joe) Flores married a woman named Ella, born in "Boheimia, Czecho-Slovakia," who came to the United States at the age of two in 1912.[76] Joe too came to the United States in 1912, though he was already twelve years old. Joe lived in the Chicago area continuously for eight years before he and Ella married in 1931, and Joe worked as a shipping clerk in a mail-order company. Enrique Aguirre married a woman from Rome, Georgia, named Zephyr, who was seventeen years younger than he! Enrique worked as an unskilled laborer, a machinist's helper, until later in the 1930s when he became unemployed.[77]

Fig. 4.10: José (Joe) Flores, Chicago 1936. Petition for Naturalization, National Archives and Records Administration.

Fig. 4.11: Enrique Aguirre, Chicago 1934. Petition for Naturalization, National Archives and Records Administration.

The young men who married non-Mexicans in some ways challenged norms that expected them to marry Mexican women. Undoubtedly, these unions contributed to generational tensions within extended Mexican families. Some of these men, however, transgressed other kinds of social constraints. Salvador Martín del Campo, for instance, married Susan, a native of Hungary, a year and a half *after* the couple had their first child, Antonia. By waiting so long after the birth of the child to marry, the couple apparently were not concerned with trying to fudge the dates of her birth to maintain the appearance of her having been born in wedlock, as was customary. Evidently their union remained strong, for in 1935, three years after their marriage, Salvador and Susan had their second child, Richard. By 1939 Salvador had become a U.S. citizen.

While comprising a little under 1 percent of the Mexican population in Chicago, it nevertheless is significant that there were these Mexican men who "married out" of their ethno-racial group. Legal restrictions on the women who married these men kept marriage from being a tool through which noncitizen men could gain legal access. This is underscored by the fact that a majority married first-generation, noncitizen women. Demographic realities like the dearth of Mexican women in Chicago surely shaped rates of interracial marriage. The fact that any Mexicans, however, could marry non-Mexicans only fueled fears of Mexicans as potential threats to the color line that many whites tried to delineate so carefully during this period. As the historian Neil Foley has written, "[M]any whites considered Mexicans inferior to Indians and Africans because Mexicans were racially mixed, a hybrid race that represented the worst nightmare of what might become of the white race if it let down

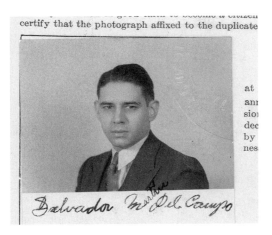

Fig. 4.12: *Salvador Martín del Campo, Chicago 1935. Petition for Naturalization, National Archives and Records Administration.*

its racial guard."[78] The ultimate impact of these marriages, of course, would be on any children born into them and would likely be especially notable as they came of age in the late 1940s and 1950s.

Generational Cleavages

Even before the Second World War, however, signs of generational struggles and conflicts were clearly evident. New opportunities to identify with Americanism through mass culture proved to be the locus of tremendous intergenerational conflict. In addition, the new social terrain that was being negotiated was fundamentally gendered. It was complicated further by Mexican women's general welcome of new freedoms available and Mexican men's overall resistance or even rejection of them for women.

In 1927, Ignacio Sandoval, a Mexican man living on the Near West Side, stated the problem succinctly: "[H]ere . . . women want to be boss and the poor man has to wash the dishes while the woman goes to the movies."[79] Mass-culture venues like movies and dances did provide Mexican women with new arenas for individual freedoms and identification with American identity. As one young Mexican girl explained, she went to dances and movies, "just like other American girls."[80] Reportedly, upon returning from these events, the young girl "was slapped and beaten by her mother." Perhaps the mother depended on her daughter for income, thus explaining her outrage with her daughter's "stepping out." Conceivably, interwoven with her outrage at broken moral codes, the mother might have been expressing her own frustration at the difficulties of monitoring her daughter's behavior in this densely populated urban world full of temptations.[81] As with Mexican families in other parts of the United States and Mexico, here the family oligarchy existed in part to maintain the girl's purity and the family's honor. As the historian Vicki L. Ruiz points out, "A family's reputation was linked to the purity of women. . . . Since family honor rested, to some degree, on the preservation of female chastity [which was tied to *vergüenza*, or shame], women were to be controlled for the common good, with older relatives assuming unquestioned responsibility in this regard."[82]

It was also likely that this mother shared the sentiments of many older Mexicans living in Chicago, who disliked many aspects of "modern" youth culture. Mass culture helped to challenge the control of family oligarchy by providing myriad ways for youths to engage in new opportunities that again proved how difficult it was to police youth behaviors in a complex urban space. The "modern" dime dances often emerged as targets for concern and generational tension. At one such dance at the

Hall of All Nations on Mackinaw Avenue in South Chicago, "[G]irls as young as twelve years . . . were hired to dance with Mexicans." The girls earned five of the ten cents they charged per dance. The organizers were jailed thirty days for running a dance to which minor girls had been encouraged to come, and the organizers were fined one hundred dollars each.[83] Newspaper editors admonished their readers, particularly fathers or mothers, to "maintain the high dignity of the Mexican woman and prevent her from attending these kinds of dances."[84]

Some of the earliest Mexicana arrivals to the area recalled having strict rules at home to maintain the dignity of young girls. Agapita Flores, for example, came to Chicago with her family in about 1923, and she remembered, "[M]y father was very strict . . . he wouldn't even let us [go] to the movies . . . nope, no dancing, no movies. . . . [T]hat's how it was." Agapita's family had come from Torreón, Mexico, and entered the United States in March 1919 when she was nine years old. She married her husband, Rubén, in Chicago in 1927 at the age of seventeen. Two years later she had a daughter, Ruth. She had her son, Rubén, in 1933. Ruth, who came of age in the early 1940s, not only was allowed to go to the dances but "would have gone anyways" if her parents had tried to prevent her—a brash transgression that her mother wouldn't have contemplated twenty years earlier. As Ruth admitted, "[W]e had a little bit more freedom."[85]

The young Mexican men who attended these dances were also influenced by movies and fashion. During the 1920s, many wore their sideburns in *patillas*, the "short pointed side whiskers" made popular by Rudolph Valentino, "the late moving-picture star."[86] Dressed in stylish clothing and sporting *pantillas*, these youths reportedly called each other "sheiks" after Valentino.[87] And they too used a variety of ploys to attend these dances. Jack García, for example, recalled that friends would chip in money "for one guy [to get in]. The guy would go in the back and open the door and a whole bunch of guys would come in!"[88]

Perceived dangers to a young woman's dignity also lurked in the form of men from other ethnic groups. Sidney Levin, a young Jewish man who grew up in South Chicago, recalled meeting Mexican girls at dances. He learned quickly that according to Mexican custom, a proper man did not ask the girl herself to dance, but rather her guardian. "I had to be very careful," he said. "One time I got jerked back. I thought I was gonna get hit because I asked a young lady to dance."[89] His Mexican male friends then took him aside and explained the protocol.

Generational struggles also emerged between fathers and daughters.[90] One father recounted that his daughter had wanted him to buy her a bathing suit so she could join her friends at the beach. He refused, telling her, "'You can bathe . . . here at home. I will . . . not buy [you] a bathing suit. You can wait till I am dead and buy it then.'"[91] One can hear in the father's voice older norms of restraint confronting newer sexual orders in which individual sexuality—embodied in the daughter and her bathing suit—held the power of self-definition.[92] Ironically, in Chicago during this period, beaches were often segregated. Until 1932, Mexicans and Blacks could not go the the Twelfth Street beach (the one closest to this girl's home) because a private company had been charging admission to the beach to keep it "for whites only."[93]

Such seemingly headstrong young girls occasionally faced the dire consequences of their choices. Paul Esparza, for instance, murdered his daughter's husband, Tomás Castillo, reportedly because his daughter had married against her father's wishes at the age of fifteen. Apparently the courts sympathized with Esparza's feelings, for he was acquitted of the charges two months later.[94]

Some girls were clearly acting out intergenerational frictions in the extremity of their choices. In frustration at her parents' disapproval "of her recreational activities, especially her attraction to movies and dances," one nineteen-year-old "attempt[ed] to overcompensate for the old culture by accepting the most dramatic form of activities which differentiated her from her family." When her parents disapproved of smoking "and other immoral practices," she actively took up those practices. "She frequently stayed out late at night, and on several occasions stayed away from home for several days."[95]

Fathers and sons, too, struggled to navigate the strains of Americanization. In one example, the two sons of the "P" family (noted as such in case-worker files), one aged twenty-three, the other twenty-five, resented that they were "expected to contribute so much of their wages to the support of the family." Henry, the twenty-three-year-old, was married, and he and his wife lived with his mother and his two high-school-aged sisters in the house his father bought and left for his mother upon his death. He contributed fifteen dollars per week to the family, but his brother gave "very little to the home." Needless to say, there was a great deal of friction in the household, particularly as Mrs. P and Henry's young wife did not get along at all.[96]

In another case, a Mexican man in Packingtown, whose sons worked in the packinghouses, explained that he spent his evenings teaching his sons to play the violin and guitar they had brought with them from Mexico. "'The violin belonged to my grandfather, and the music of it makes me homesick. But when the boys try to pick out some of your jazz music, it makes me very angry inside.'" The sons told their father that they had to learn the contemporary music styles if they were to make any money playing at dances and festivals, to which the father responded, "'Do all Americans think jazz music beautiful?'"[97] Clearly, the father believed that traditional music would instill in his sons respect for and ties to Mexico. Yet the sons' attempts to play American jazz on the grandfather's instruments only intensified his fears that they would lose their Mexican identity. The question also arises whether the man also feared the stigmas of "blackness" commonly associated at the time with jazz.[98] Perhaps, too, the man worried about the associations of "jazzing"—a common contemporary term for sexual intercourse with illicit overtones.[99]

The influence of jazz even extended into settlement houses like Hull-House. The famous jazz musician, band leader, and clarinetist Benny Goodman, for instance, had grown up in the neighborhood and had spent much of his youth at Hull-House. He felt so indebted to the organization that he returned whenever his schedule allowed to play free jazz concerts for the children of Hull-House.[100] Generational divisions opened throughout American society during these years with the emergence of mass culture; yet, because Mexican women and men experienced these stresses along with their adjustments to Chicago, they perceived the changing gender and sexual norms to be part of America itself.

Fig. 4.13: Benny Goodman at Hull-House, 1939. Yearbook, 1939, Hull-House Reports, folder 443:46, Jane Addams Memorial Collection, University of Illinois at Chicago.

The significance of gender in understanding the lived experiences of Mexicans during the interwar period in Chicago cannot be understated. Mexican men in particular revealed their deep frustrations with the unstable terrains of workplace, home, and neighborhood. Mexican women, in contrast, overwhelmingly spoke hopefully about the changes and opportunities they experienced in Chicago during this period. Freedom itself seemed to hold meanings structured in gender.[101] Focusing on the lives of individuals clarifies the human dimension of the adaptation process and underscores the variability between Mexican women's and men's lives. It also reveals the notable degree to which women's lives varied from the standard narratives of Mexican migration and settlement to the Midwest. Considering the shifting terrains of gender that Mexicans experienced in Chicago further highlights the tremendous sociocultural upheavals at work within Mexican communities and between individuals.

Racial Geography: "Looks"

In 1928, when asked about his matches in the United States, the pugilist Eduardo Huaracha admitted, "In fights many times they [his fans] confuse me for an American, well they see me as white with light, chestnut-colored hair." This boxer from Michoacán elaborated, "[B]ecause of this I always tell the [North American] promoters to say I'm Mexican, so that *la raza* notices that I am Mexican."[102] Evidently, Huaracha hoped to increase the chances that Mexicans in the United States would come to his fights. His comments, however, highlight racialized aspects of Mexican and American identities. To Mexicans, his light skin and chestnut hair indicated elements of being an American. The confusion that Mexicans themselves experienced with respect to racial meanings reflects the instability of such categories.

Like Eduardo Huaracha, Mexicans quickly understood that "becoming American" in many ways meant "becoming white." Yet the instability of racial categories in this period created tensions and exacerbated conflicts between Mexicans in Chicago. Tensions arose as individuals sought to position themselves in the "best," or whitest, light possible while larger forces worked to mark them as nonwhite. As one Chicago Spanish-language newspaper editor lamented, referring to Americans, "[B]ecause their color is white, they classify us as 'colored people.'"[103] The ascription of "coloredness" held real consequences during the interwar years, and Mexicans increasingly became conscious of their effects.

Unquestionably, Mexicans came to Chicago already sensitized to questions of race and skin color. As Ramón Gutiérrez has described, a system of social status tied to skin color can be found as far back as the seventeenth and eighteenth centuries in (what became) Mexico. In this system, whiter skin was directly related to higher social status, and darker skin was "associated with physical labor and the infamy of the conquered."[104] Mexicans quickly learned, however, that the American racial order was more rigidly dichotomized than that of Mexico and did not allow for gradations and combinations.

Many recognized that there was a growing "prejudice against the Mexican" and that "in many cases the [white] people [did] not discriminate between the Mexican and the Negro."[105] Throughout the interwar period, Mexicans sought to distinguish themselves from Blacks, thus suggesting a growing recognition of the limits and discriminatory consequences of blackness in the United States. Even Mexican children in Chicago reportedly refused to play with the "colored" kids and had to be separated from them.[106] For Mexicans in Chicago, blackness seemed to represent the oppositional other against which Mexicans strove to mark themselves. They chose to measure themselves instead in terms of whiteness and American identity.

Attempts to distinguish a cohesive group, however, were undercut by the diversity among Mexicans. Skin color, for instance, separated those with lighter skin tones from those with darker pigmentation. Those with lighter skin found they could "pass" and often called themselves "Spanish." In doing so, they gained whiteness and an identity based in Europe. Claiming Europeanness provided them a tool for legitimizing themselves. "The Spaniards," one editorial explained, "have a certain supremacy, certain distinctions in this country which the Mexicans unfortunately haven't."[107] As a Mexican woman living in Packingtown explained, she was "Spanish, coming from Mexico."[108] She clung to a Spanish identity in spite of being "so dark in complexion one would take her for a negro."[109] In some cases, the label "Spanish" itself served to further confuse potentially significant divisions within Chicago's Mexican population. In 1926, a Mexican living in South Chicago, Carlos Pérez López, explained in an interview that Mexicans in South Chicago had recently acquired a Mexican priest.[110] In fact, the priest was Spanish, educated in Spain, and came from the Spanish Claretian orders.[111]

Some Mexicans wielded the tool of Spanish identification situationally. As Sidney Levin recalled about some of the young Mexican women he knew, "[T]hey were Mexicans. They probably died being Mexican. I mean, they wouldn't deny it when they were home in South Chicago. But, downtown, they were Spanish."[112] Claims to Spain were potentially divisive, as evident in the case of Ambrosio Castillo and José Saldívar. Both men worked for Illinois Steel and were well known for passing themselves off as Spanish. In fact, the editors of *México* felt compelled to expose them publicly as Mexicans because of the great injury they reportedly were committing against other Mexicans. "We have received various complaints of these gentlemen during the past three weeks . . . these gentlemen have denied their nationality, passing themselves off as Spanish before the authorities and before all who have had the disgrace to know them."[113]

The efficacy of positioning themselves as Spanish, however, was tempered by potentially undesirable associations with radical ideas and influences, given contemporary developments in Spain, or accusations of "foreignness." At a meeting of the Mexican Club of Unemployed Men in 1932, members voted against joining over twenty-five thousand other workers at a United Front hunger march protesting cuts in relief payments out of concern that it would be branded a Communist parade.[114] This, in turn, would have heightened the dangers of deportation, "since immigration officials are so active in seeking candidates for deportation."[115]

Fig. 4.14: United Front Hunger March, October 31, 1932. Mexicans in Pack-ingtown voted not to join these protesters. Courtesy of Chicago Historical Society, ICHi 20955.

Conversely, in 1936, Mexicans of Packingtown actively participated in a mass rally against the dictatorship of Franco.[116] This change in sentiment corresponded to a rise in El Frente's popularity among Mexicans in Chicago. Based in the University of Chicago Settlement House in Packingtown, El Frente Popular Mexicano, like Popular Front groups elsewhere in the United States, Latin America, and Europe, sought "to achieve the social and economic betterment of the working classes."[117] In Mexico, Vicente Toledano's confederation of industrial and agricultural workers, the Confederación de Trabajadores de México (CTM), founded in 1936, shared similar goals. As the historian Louise Año Nuevo Kerr points out, "Using Popular Front organizations to unify and pacify communists, leftists, liberals, and patriots, [Mexican president] Cárdenas and Toledano temporarily maintained worker support for radical national and international actions, including the nationalization of land . . . and the expropriation of oil resources from foreign . . . ownership."[118]

Representatives of the Popular Front in Mexico came to Chicago in January 1935 to spread the message of radical worker solidarity.[119] Only a year later, members of the newly formed CTM visited Chicago, and shortly thereafter the Chicago chapter of El Frente was founded.[120] Beyond fighting for the rights of Mexican workers in the area, the group also was sensitive to situations arising out of repatriation and deportation. Thus, they also sought "to protect the Mexican who returns to his own country."[121] The group only survived as El Frente for about two years. Though Kerr questions how much influence it really had, by 1939 the Lázaro Cárdenas Club in Packingtown reportedly delivered hundreds of signed union cards to the CIO-affiliated packinghouse workers union, the Packinghouse Workers' Organizing Committee (PWOC).[122] While it remains unclear how influential it was in Chicago, in other areas of the United States, El Frente did have tangible results. In California, for example, members of El Frente joined many other groups and activists like Louisa Moreno and Josefina Fierro de Bright to found El Congreso del Pueblo de Habla Española in 1938.[123] According to Vicki L. Ruiz, El Congreso, or the Congress of Spanish-Speaking Peoples, sought to end "segregation in public facilities, housing, education, and employment and to discrimination in the disbursement of public assistance. El Congreso endorsed the rights of immigrants to live and work in the United States without fear of deportation. While encouraging immigrants to become citizens, delegates did not advocate assimilation, but instead emphasized the importance of preserving Latino cultures."[124] Unfortunately, red-baiting ultimately devastated the organization.

When the Chicago chapter of El Frente focused on "the situation in

Spain" and took a stand against "war and fascism," it shared perspectives of others in the broad Popular Front movement. As the historian Michael Denning argues, "[T]he Popular Front was a radical social-democratic movement forged around anti-fascism, anti-lynching, and the industrial unionism of the CIO."[125] Regular meetings at the University of Chicago Settlement House discussed "the true story of the heroic fight of the Spanish people against the fascist invaders."[126] Mexicans who sympathized with the anti-Franco forces, whether as part of El Frente or not, faced criticism from Mexicans who were staunchly Catholic and in support of Franco. The Catholic church in Spain supported Franco through the fascist National Front. In Chicago, as Kerr notes, *El Ideál Catolico Mexicano*, a newspaper for Mexican Catholic workers, served as the voice of Chicago's conservative Mexicans. It was "particularly antagonistic to Cárdenas . . . defending Franco in the Spanish Civil War, it claimed, 'The Spanish people wish to see themselves liberated from the Bolshevik degradation which is aided by the powerful Soviet dictator and the ridiculous help from the Chicharronero'—a belittling reference to Cárdenas as a bacon-rind maker."[127] Anti-Franco forces and those involved in El Frente also risked being labeled radicals, socialists, or even communists, any one of which could bring harsh consequences.

The presence of "real" Spaniards must have complicated Mexican claims to Spanish identity. Naturalization petitions and citizenship papers suggest that many Spaniards in fact did live throughout Chicago.[128] Avelino López, for example, was born in Noceda, Spain, and lived with his Scandinavian wife in the Near West Side, not far from Jesus Lista Fraga, an elevator operator living in the Loop, from Cerceda, Spain.[129] Benjamin Rodriguez, from Aviles, Spain, lived in Packingtown, as did Mary Manuela Fernandez, who was born in Lugo, Spain.[130]

Spaniards themselves had a strong fraternal society, La Sociedad Española, that functioned much like the Mexican mutual-aid societies.[131] Founded around 1915, the Spanish Society sponsored regular meetings, had club rooms, and accepted anyone who learned Spanish and paid their dues. Members paid dues corresponding to the services they received, which included sick benefits and admission to social events. The weekly "authentic Spanish dinner" was a highlight and included Spanish music. It is not clear whether or not Mexicans participated in the group's events, but simply the presence of such a long-lived group speaks to the strength of Spaniards in the area.

Mexican claims to whiteness through a Spanish identity were also framed by the contours of class. In Mexico, the poorest and least powerful classes were predominantly the *indios*, who had the darkest skin;

the powerful elites tended to be the lightest-skinned and most European-looking.[132] "Mexicans of lower classes never give up their nationality," explained Carlos López, suggesting that the darkness of their skins precluded the lower classes from the possibility of becoming American. "Those of higher classes and who can by their appearance pass for Spanish," he continued, "call themselves Spanish."[133] At the same time, he actively reinforced the hope that if one were white enough, one would have the opportunity to become American.

Señor Galindo, a druggist in South Chicago, graphically described the more lowly of his Mexican customers: "[A] few are ignorant and haven't even noticed newspapers and when they buy ten cents of paper they take one page of the newspaper for [toilet] paper."[134] Galindo's words held a note of derision for the Mexicans of the lower classes. Galindo himself was likely the son of a Mexican cooper (barrel maker) and a white woman from New York named Emily Jane.[135] Citizenship papers for John Benjamin Galindo of South Chicago document that he and Emily had two children, one a son of Señor Galindo's approximate age. Galindo's father was well traveled, moving from port cities in Mexico to other port cities including Liverpool, England, and New York City. As a barrel maker, it is reasonable to speculate that he was connected in some way with shipping. The family settled in South Chicago in 1898, when Benjamin was only seven years old.

A few years later, an editorial in *México* echoed Galindo's scorn for lower-class Mexicans and lamented the effects of such people calling themselves Spanish. "Even though a little dark or clearly a Mexican, [he] replies in the worst possible English . . . 'Me? Oh, mister me be Spanish.' . . . [B]ecause of this," the writer claims, "the genuine Mexicans are being ruined."[136] The irony in this, of course, was that "genuine Mexicans" did not exist. The nationalist project in Mexico was attempting to create those very Mexicans. Moreover, the *indios* of the lower classes in Mexico had only begun to learn Spanish themselves under the Calles programs of rural education. Following much the same lines as those of the Americanizers, Mexican teachers believed that fluency in Spanish could ease the acculturation into the Mexican nation.[137]

The kind of sentiments expressed by Galindo, however, reflected similar attempts by middle- and upper-class Mexicans throughout the American Southwest to distinguish themselves from those darker-skinned, poorly educated Mexicans whose presence fed the racializing currents of American society during this period. The League of United Latin American Citizens (LULAC), for instance, founded in Texas in 1929, worked to defend the rights of Mexicans with U.S. citizenship.[138] The historian Richard García argues against those who had long dismissed LULACers as "sell-outs" or assimilationists. Instead, he shows how these people strategically injected themselves into the political system to better the condition of all Mexicans. Subsequent work has continued to add nuance to the goals, strategies, and outlooks of this largely middle-class organization.[139]

Scholars have shown that in San Antonio and Los Angeles, many of the social elites exiled from Mexico during the turmoil of the revolutionary years worked to maintain their positions in the hopes of returning to those positions when the political situation in Mexico stabilized—Ignacio Lozano and his family, for instance, founders of *La Prensa* in San Antonio and *La Opinión* in Los Angeles. Both newspapers were highly political, reporting on events in Mexico and remained staunchly anti-Calles during this period. Notably, the Lozano family never returned to Mexico and today continues to own and direct publication of *La Opinión*, the largest Spanish-language daily in the United States.[140] Dr. J. B. Medina of Chicago's Near West Side, however, suggested that those kinds of elites in Chicago played no active role in the affairs of Mexicans in this city. "Generally those," he said, "don't make themselves known and don't become part of the group nor do they give help." His explanation was that these were "Mexicans who in Mexico held a certain social position and through the revolution or through some other cause" were forced in Chicago "to occupy a more humble position." In effect, they were ashamed of their loss of position.[141] Though this was undoubtedly the case, particularly if they did not speak English, there seems to be little evidence suggesting that any notable number of expatriate elites lived in Chicago during this period.

Leaders in the community tended to be small-business people and professionals like Dr. Medina or Dr. Samuel Meixueiro, who came as a *soltero* from Oaxaca in the early 1920s.[142] Medina and Meixueiro quickly became members of the Benito Juárez Mutual Aid and Recreation Society, the first Mexican mutual-aid society founded in Chicago in 1918. It "maintains national and recreational fiestas," and by 1924, it "initiated . . . a system of life insurance and insurance for illness and accident without additional cost to its members."[143] Its board of directors in 1924 included an engineer, Manuel Godines, as president; Dr. Samuel G. Meixueiro, vice president; Dr. J. B. Medina DDS, treasurer; Camilo Alcántara, secretary; Augustín S. Fink, auditor; and Jesús Domingues, pro-secretario.

Language

The diversity of class and regional backgrounds among Chicago's Mexicans provoked further divisions beyond those of "Spanish" identity, involving problems of language. Mexicans swiftly discovered that success in Chicago necessitated at least some knowledge of English. As Dr. Medina of the Near West Side noted, "Even a Negro has more security [than a Mexican] because he speaks the language."[144] Social workers and reformers lamented that "so few [Mexicans] speak any English."[145] Throughout the 1920s, English classes were offered through charitable organizations, aid groups, schools, social clubs, churches, and settlement houses. In 1928, for example, a class in Trumbull Park Field House enrolled eighty-five Mexicans, although attendance only averaged thirty-five to forty per meeting. Steel companies in cooperation with the YMCA encouraged workers to take English classes and even offered incentives at work. Wisconsin Steel, for instance, provided higher wages to English-speaking laborers. By the late 1920s, however, those incentives had molded into discriminatory practices that worked against Mexicans, for some steel companies refused to hire anyone who did not speak English.[146]

Proficiency in English was clearly tied to citizenship. As they struggled to learn English, students in English classes did so with the Federal Citizenship book as their text. By the mid-1930s, states and the federal government funded such language and citizenship classes. Business interests also invested in these courses to the extent that many firms required proof of an applicant having taken citizenship classes and of having begun the process of taking out their citizenship papers before they could be hired.[147] Not only were Mexicans using the Federal Citizenship book to learn English, they also were pressured to internalize its contents.

These classrooms for learning English, however, presupposed a student body that was literate in its native language, and many of Chicago's Mexican population were illiterate in Spanish as well. Even the basics of everyday life in Chicago were problematic for someone who could neither read nor write. One man in the Near West Side described how he was "frequently out of work because he doesn't know how to go to his work, neither can he read the numbers on the train nor the names of the streets."[148] Though requirements for legal entrance into the United States at the Mexican border required men over age twenty-one to be literate at least in Spanish, this man's predicament suggests either leniency in enforcement of those rules or, more likely, the preponderance of undocumented migration across the border.

The quality of a Mexican's spoken Spanish signaled class divisions. The mocking tone of one writer in the local Spanish-language newspaper betrayed seemingly unbridgeable differences. He lamented the affected dress and pretentious behavior of some members of the working class as they sought to acculturate in this country. "They do not behave like that in their own country," he explained. "In crossing the [border] they acquire talents and an importance that exist only in their feverish imaginations."[149] Apparently, these pretensions crumbled as soon as they begin to speak. He warned, "[T]hey will say *'truje'* instead of *'traje,' 'estemago'* for *'estomago.'*"[150]

Adding to the potential for conflicts among Mexicans, some employers hired what they termed "a better class" of Mexican.[151] To illustrate this point, Mr. Belcher of the Marshall Field mattress factory noted "a wrapped copy of *El Universal* and said the addressee, Francisco Cárdenas, received it daily at the factory every day."[152] *El Universal* was published in Mexico City, and brought news of goings-on throughout much of Mexico. Clearly, Belcher thought that Francisco Cárdenas's subscription indicated not only a literate man but one who was educated and thoughtful enough to want to keep up with current events in his home country.

A Mexican man described similar structuring of his opportunities by his appearance. "All the time I got better jobs—you know, I was smart, looked all right, they gave me better jobs."[153] Yet the advantages of class in Mexico and "looks" did not frequently translate into similar circumstances in Chicago. Francisco Mata, for example, obtained a business degree in Mexico and had been working in Mexico City as a bookkeeper. He came to the United States in 1920, and because he could not speak English, he "had a great difficulty finding employment."[154] At the Barrett Company, Francisco Mata made twenty-three dollars per week, but he "had such difficulty supporting his family that they became charges of the United Charities."[155]

Conflicts around class and looks even emerged around employment status, particularly among men during the years of the Depression. Social workers at the University of Chicago Settlement House noted in July 1933 that entertainment among Mexican adult groups was difficult to organize because of "the reluctance of the unemployed to show up at events with the employed." They noticed that the real problem was "not because of immediate lack of money, which might have explained the paid affairs, but because of lack of proper clothes, and because of a general feeling of inferiority beside the others."[156]

Class conflicts also worked in the opposite way; that is, those of lower classes looked down on those who seemed to be adopting middle-class sensibilities or "American" aspirations. Sidney Levin recalled the hostility that "Boots" Garcia and his friend, Minnie, faced when they went to the junior college after high school. When asked why neighborhood Mexicans were hostile to these boys, Levin reflected, "[T]hey [other Mexicans] thought they were trying to lift themselves or something or become Americans or middle class or something. I don't know exactly what it was. But there's no question. In fact, one of the biggest impressions of my life was this tremendous hostility." When pressed to speculate about the source of this hostility, Levin thought that perhaps "people saw that . . . you were just going to wind up in the steel mills anyway, so why did you need an education?"[157]

For other Mexicans, the particular dynamics of Chicago prevented them from learning English, as Juan, a factory worker near Hull-House, made clear: he found it hard to learn more than the few words of English used in his work because he was in a group of Poles and didn't hear English all day![158] Juan's situation reflects one of the strategies used by employers to ensure control of workers. By interspersing Mexicans with other workers, employers believed they were diluting the potential for labor activism, since no one group predominated. This also potentially kept workers of similar language groups from talking with each other, a kind of divide-and-conquer strategy.[159] In Juan's case, interestingly, Poles were allowed to work together, perhaps indicative of management's lack of concern about Polish activism. These practices also created isolation and separation. Perhaps it was this practice of dilution that contributed to Mexican workers insisting that their employers allow them to work together.[160] Ironically, if employers heeded their desires to work alongside each other, then Mexicans traded-in single isolation for the segregation of the group.

Some Mexican workers evolved creative strategies to cope in situations where they did not speak the language. When interviewed years later, Lucio Franco, a worker who eventually settled in South Chicago, recalled that he communicated well with the *güeros* he worked with even though he only spoke Spanish. How did he communicate? "Oh pues, bien, bien, a señas" (Oh well, fine, fine, using signs).[161]

Even without a common language with which to communicate, Franco could make himself understood enough to remain on the work crew. Nevertheless, language was central to Mexican experiences in Chicago, and their differing relations to English-language acquisition in particular signaled the diversity of the Mexican population during these years.

Conclusion

From skin color and the shadings of American identity to the tensions and conflicts that striated an already diverse population, Mexicans in Chicago tried actively to distinguish themselves from one another in an effort to "mark" themselves more favorably. Ironically, the pressures they experienced to Americanize helped to bring some of these people together, if only in their resistance to the process. Those who were more successful in their Americanizing might have lost solidarity with those who resisted or had a harder time with it—except for one critical factor: anti-Mexican discrimination and segregation. Unlike areas of the U.S. Southwest during this period, in Chicago efforts to claim Spanish or Latin American identities did not translate into political organization and groups like LULAC. Without the history of Mexicans in the Southwest, Mexicans in Chicago wielded other tools, including language and Spanishness, to forge pride in a group identity. As one explained, "North American[s] saw only the crude Mexicans, los rudos, los Indios, and did not appreciate the true Mexico."[162]

Ironically, in working so hard to juggle the pressures of Americanization and in spite of the ongoing efforts to separate and segregate them, Mexicans in Chicago began to define the contours of a visible though fragile Mexicanidad, a Mexicanism rooted in the revolutionary context from which many of Chicago's Mexicans emerged. It was an identity that made sense of the ambivalence many of these Mexicans felt toward the permanence of their stays in Chicago and that helped to reconcile the growing prejudice and segregation they experienced in their daily lives.

Emanating through the fractious diversities of the Mexican population that emerge in this chapter were ever-louder calls for Mexicans to unify against the growing discrimination practiced on them. These attempts to shift people's energy into solidifying "the Mexican community" only served to exacerbate already-evident differences of class, origin, gender, education, language, race, opportunity, and means. These calls for unity paralleled and ultimately intertwined with similar calls for unity in Mexico. These factors and the subsequent attempts to create a unified identity of Mexicanidad are the subject of the next chapter.

5 Mexicans Emergent

In the fall of 1924, a grand fiesta was orchestrated at the swanky Edgewater Beach Hotel in celebration of Mexican Independence Day. Sponsored by the Mexican consulate and the Benito Juárez Mutual Aid Society, the festivities were "attended by the consuls of the Latin American republics of Chicago," including Argentina and Colombia. Local dignitaries, including the chief of police of Chicago, also attended, along with over one thousand Mexicans.[1] Commemoration of Mexican independence from Spain in 1821 could easily and properly have been a strictly Mexican nationalist moment. This seemed particularly true so early into the postrevolutionary years, when Mexicans of all stripes were still working out what it meant to be Mexican and how to create a unified nation-state. It would have been particularly understandable given how recently most of Chicago's Mexicans had come to Chicago and the limited number of gatherings that could bring together such numbers. And, yet, the celebration included other Latin Americans, as if expressing pan-ethnic solidarity. Given the discrimination and brutality the police practiced against Mexicans, the presence of the chief of police seems an ironic turn. After the party, the editors of *El Heraldo* wrote that the fiesta "ought to be continued year after year because in this way will be blotted out some of the prejudice which exists against us."[2]

This faith in the positive power of celebration and historical memory resonated in Chicago and in Mexico during this period. In Chicago, Mexicans deployed a collectively imagined historical past to combat rising discrimination against them. Even as they were treated increasingly as "Mexicans" and faced discrimination and prejudice, Mexicans also worked to define for themselves what it meant to "be Mexican." Multiple voices and perspectives floated throughout the population, often reflecting the many strains of *lo mexicano* in postrevolutionary Mexico. Having fought the revolution to give Mexico to the Mexicans, by the early 1920s they faced the task of unifying the country's heterogeneous population into some form of collective whole. After years of internecine war, the task was to bring together those who had fought against each other and to deliver into the national fold those who had never before held (or been allowed to hold) a stake in the nation-state. Put simply, they had to create a new nation called Mexico, peopled by Mexicans, those elusive yet collectively imagined national citizens.

In Chicago, Mexicanidad emerged as a fragile but proud identity that wove together elements of postrevolutionary Mexican nationalism and nostalgic conservative histories of "México Lindo" (Beautiful Mexico) with the acknowledgment of growing anti-Mexican biases.[3] It took the negative racialized connotations that "being Mexican" increasingly carried in Chicago and turned them on their head by celebrating Mexicanness. Played out in Chicago against a Latin American backdrop, Mexicanidad provided Mexicans with expressions of national allegiance. In Mexicanidad lay the groundwork for explaining and sharing—and imagining—common experiences and commonly expressed goals.

Unlike their European neighbors, Mexican communities in Chicago were continually reinforced by new migrations from Mexico and the U.S. Southwest, at least throughout the 1920s. Moreover, the geographic proximity of Mexico and the particularities of preexisting histories between Mexico and the United States—indeed, the very connectedness of land and histories—meant that Mexicans in Chicago lived in dynamic, ongoing ways with Mexico. Multiple migration routes flowed into and out of Chicago: up and down the railroad lines, through states in northern and western Mexico and the central United States, and snaking along transportation routes throughout the Midwest. Taken together, these ongoing movements of people (and thus of news, ideas, cultural and social practices, etc.) and the distinctiveness of U.S.–Mexico relations enforced a raw awareness of Mexico in Chicago's Mexicans. Building on the ideals of the revolution and the nationalist projects in Mexico, Mexicans in Chicago found themselves creating a Mexicanidad that was fundamentally transnational and imbued with the mandate to redress anti-Mexican sentiments. Because of the particularities of Chicago, Mexicans also understood themselves within a broader Latin American context.[4] This chapter demonstrates how Mexicans in Chicago became Mexicans—how the nationalist project of Mexico took root and began to grow outside the actual nation-state, emerging as a distinctive yet familiar version of *lo mexicano.*

Lo Mexicano in Mexico

Early twentieth-century Mexican nationalism contained several threads that attempted to define, create, and defend *lo mexicano,* "the Mexican essence."[5] As Matthew Gutmann has argued, by the 1920s masculinity was embedded in the meaning of *lo mexicano,* and thus the essence of the Mexican state was gendered male.[6] Yet the discursive rhetoric of nationalism and patriotism appeared inclusive and gender-neutral. At its heart, Mexican nationalism of that era focused on creating Mexicans out of its varied population. As one prominent nationalist voice, Moisés Sáenz, wrote: "It is preferable that Mexico concern itself with 'making Mexicans' out of its inhabitants, inspired by justice, loyalty toward tradition, and the principle of human rights."[7]

At the popular level, nationalists culled Mexico's histories for useful events, myths, and memories that collectively could be used to create and appeal to popular visions of "Mexican tradition." As the historian David Brading noted, "[T]he Revolution represented a revival and a re-valuation of fading traditions."[8] Much of this was captured in various flavors of *indigenismo* and in the celebration of particular, notably male, heroes from nineteenth-century insurgencies like the Niños Heroes and Benito Juárez.[9]

As a strategy, mobilizing an imagined past to throw off the mantle of oppression had deep roots in Mexican history. In the early nineteenth-century struggles for liberation from Spain, prominent ideologues like Padre Mier and Licenciado Carlos María de Bustamante effectively "proclaimed what was essentially a fiction, the myth of a Mexican nation, which was the lineal heir of the Aztecs."[10] The existence of a Mexican nation that predated the Spanish conquest provided justification for its liberation.[11] This brand of neo-Aztec nationalism created by and spread largely through the Catholic priesthood permeated many of the popular revolts that led to the destruction of Spanish control over Mexico.[12]

Indigenismo of the early twentieth-century postrevolutionary period moved beyond valorization of a neo-Aztec past to include a celebration of the *indio* specifically.[13] "Incorporation of the Indian into the Mexican family," proclaimed Sáenz, "should mean as much as incorporation of the Mexican family into the Indian. Mexico is an Indian country."[14] While nineteenth-century *indigenismo* saw little cultural value in the *indio* and largely excluded the Indian, postrevolutionary *indigenismo* found much to value and worked to guarantee the Indian a place within the nation-state.[15] Working toward agrarian reform programs, many *indigenistas* of the revolutionary era looked to the *indio* as the model member of a reconstructed Mexican state.[16] That is, the *indio* represented a gendered-male communalism that supported moves toward land reform and that challenged those Porfirian holdovers. As an ideology, *indigenismo* appeared to be progressive, yet *indios* themselves faced only two real options: remain frozen in time as representatives of an imagined pre-Columbian Mexican past, or incorporate into the Mexican state only if they could be transformed into homogenous *mestizos*.[17] It is important to note, as does the historian Alexander Dawson, that any form of *indio* resistance to the revolutionary authority of the state (in the form of assassinating rural teachers, for instance) made the resisters objectionable to the state.[18] This meant that particular Indian peoples were held up as examples over others. Those who participated in and cooperated with representatives of the postrevolutionary nation-state were deemed "more Mexican" than those who resisted. As Dawson concludes, "This was an inclusive notion of citizenship, in that it could include Indians from a variety of cultures in a multi-ethnic nation, but it was restrictive in that it demanded a certain modernistic orientation from those subjects who would be awarded full citizenship."[19]

The notion of the new *mestizo* arose concurrently and appealed to those who were not drawn to this brand of *indigenismo* and its celebration of communalism and an Indian or precolonial past. Notably, those least moved by this version of *indigenismo* at the popular level came from some of the regions most represented by Chicago's Mexicans, especially Jalisco and Guanajuato. "Neither the glories of the Aztecs nor the principle of communal land tenure attracted the ranchero, the miner, or the artisan of Jalisco, Guanajuato, and Zacatecas. They desired a greater degree of equality, a wider distribution of property; they resented the superior social status of the Spaniard and the Creole [*Criollo:* a Spaniard born in Mexico]."[20]

Unspoken yet very much a part of these ideologies were racial divisions. Being a much more explicitly classed society than that of the United States, social status in Mexico closely correlated to racial categorization. Markers of race included physiological indicators of *indio*-ness, including body type, physical strength, skin color, hair texture, amount of body hair, and facial features, but they also included other cultural features like dress, practices, and language.[21] Such markers also broke across gender lines. The contemporary anthropologist Manuel Gamio revered the "healthiness" of Indian women, finding little prostitution and promiscuity even as they commonly took multiple partners. Gamio saw this as proof of the errors of Mexican Catholicism, which demanded virginity and chastity in women.[22] His seemingly progressive critique, however, did not extend to his own hand in nation building.

Race in Mexico, however, as in the United States, was a malleable and unfixed phenomenon, and *indigenistas* like Gamio and Sáenz came to realize that *mestisaje* better captured the realities of the Mexican nation-state. "Racially," Sáenz wrote, "the mestizo is the real American, and his number is on the increase. . . . It is inaccurate, therefore, to refer to Mexico as a nation of Indians; it is, rather, a nation of mestizos."[23]

If *mestizos* constituted *lo mexicano* and *mestizos* were the "real Americans," what broader implications did this vision have, and where did it leave women? In Chicago, if Mexicans were already American, why Americanize? As Robert Jones noted, "The Mexican . . . has a strong feeling . . . he, too, is an American and proud of that fact."[24] Mexican nationalist ideologies of unity, whether of *indigenismo* or *mestisaje*, harmonized with an understanding of American identity that echoed the continental Pan-Americanist rhetoric of Latin American and Caribbean intellectuals and activists.[25] As early as the turn of the nineteenth century, Simón Bolívar had written of unifying the former colonies of Spain into a continental republic.[26] By the turn of the twentieth century, this brand of continentalism took on a new flavor in the emergence of arielism, so called after the Uruguayan José Enrique Rodó's book *Ariel*, published in 1900.[27] In this, his most famous work, Rodó pursues his goal of political modernism by calling on Latin America to resist the rise of U.S. imperialism by embracing common beliefs and cultural values that he believed were shared across Latin America. This Hispanofilia, grounded in a critique of U.S. imperialism, also provided the political and ideological mortar for other Latin American and Caribbean revolutionaries and thinkers like Cuba's José Martí. One of Latin America's most famous political philosopher-activists and considered the father of Cuban independence, Martí devoted his life to fighting for Cuban freedom from Spain and to keeping the tentacles of U.S. imperialism from creeping into Latin America. In his most famous essay, "Nuestra America" (Our America), first published in newspapers in Mexico City and New York in 1891, Martí expounded his views on the need for the peoples of the Americas to unify to prevent imperialist incursions.[28] The unity of the peoples of "nuestra America," Martí believed, was to come from their recognition of the fundamental distinction between those of Hispanic/Iberian heritage (i.e., peoples of Latin America) and those of British/Anglo heritage (i.e., the United States).

As if called upon to validate the point, the United States promptly stepped up and provided fodder for Latin American grievances against them. Like many Latin Americans at the turn of the century, Arielists were outraged at the stark imperialism of the United States after the "liberation" wars of 1898. This was closely followed by U.S. support of a revolution in Panama in 1903, during which the United States gained control of territory upon which they built the Panama Canal. Shortly thereafter, in December 1904, Theodore Roosevelt proclaimed his corollary to the Monroe Doctrine that explicitly allowed the United States to exert "international police power" to quell unrest in the Western Hemisphere.[29] In his poem "To Roosevelt," the noted Nicaraguan poet Rubén Darío captured the mood of much of Latin America after these events.

> But our America . . .
> [that] has lived since the earliest moments of its life
> in light, in fire, in fragrance, in love,
> America of the great Montezuma and Atahualpa,
> the fragrant America of Christopher Columbus,
> Catholic America, Spanish America . . . ;
> our America . . . lives, you men of Saxon eyes and barbarous soul.
> And it dreams. And it loves, and it vibrates, and it is the daughter
> of the Sun. Be careful. Long live Spanish America![30]

Arielists and other Latin American activists symbolized the struggle against authoritarian modernization that favored the imperialism and materialism of the United States. In Mexico, the the dictator Porfirio Díaz and his U.S.–friendly policies came to stand for that authoritarian modernity. U.S. foreign policy through the 1910s and early 1920s confirmed Mexican fears of U.S. authoritarian and expansionist designs in Mexico. President Woodrow Wilson's direct meddling in Mexican affairs culminated in the U.S. naval occupation of the Mexican port city of Veracruz in April 1914. Only two years later, in another unauthorized incursion into Mexican sovereignty, General Pershing led six thousand U.S. army troops through northern Mexico in search of Pancho Villa. Added to long memories of the U.S. invasion of Mexico City in the mid-nineteenth century and its conquest of nearly half of Mexico's landmass in 1848 and 1853, these events fueled fears of U.S. imperialist designs on Mexico.

Mexican postrevolutionary nationalists, most notably José Vasconcelos, Manuel Gamio, and Moisés Sáenz, in the 1920s and 1930s took up these anti-imperialist, Hispanocentric sentiments in their attempts to create a new, unified nation-state of Mexico.[31] Although they did not claim to be arielists, their perspectives often resonated with the anti-imperialist, even anti–U.S., strains of arielism and echoed its strong gen-dered-male bias.

As Sáenz explained so clearly on a visit to Chicago in 1926:

> Spaniards had gotten the soil; the Americans and Englishmen thought they had the subsoil. . . . When we finally had to do something against Diaz, we found ourselves facing the foreign powers once more. The Span-iards and the near-Spaniards had regained most of the workable land of Mexico. They were also using most of the available water supply. Fur-thermore, the Americans of the United States, the English, and the Dutch were pumping us dry of oil.[32]

The immediate problem for the revolutionaries and postrevolution-ary visionaries was how to take back Mexico, "to give the Mexican a place under the Mexican sun and to wrest from the foreign exploiter that which by right is ours."[33] Of course, the problem was more complex than simply taking the country back, for Mexicans still had "to integrate our people into a nation and to train them to use to better advantage their country and its resources."[34]

The principal postrevolutionary solution for integrating all Mexicans into a national collective was the educational system, and the *indio* be-came the primary medium for that tool. Official concern for the *indio* came as early as 1917, with the establishment of the Dirección de Antro-pología. The department was set up under the guidance of the prominent anthropologist and *indigenista* Manuel Gamio to study, document, and promote the Indian cultures of Mexico. Gamio's nationalist vision, as elaborated in his *Forjando Patria* (1916), was to learn about these peoples in order to bring them under the Mexican umbrella through the estab-lishment of social policies. By the early 1920s, however, he clashed with rising leaders, including José Vasconcelos, over the formation and work-ings of those policies.[35]

An attorney, social philosopher, and later minister of education under President Obregón, José Vasconcelos advocated his vision of *la raza cós-mica* as a way of incorporating the vast diversity of Mexico's peoples into the new nation-state of Mexico.[36] Through a public-education system, Vasconcelos believed that the country could incorporate the *indio* into the *mestizo* mainstream, thus creating *la raza cósmica*.[37] As minister of education (with Moíses Sáenz as the undersecretary), he oversaw the establishment of several thousand rural schools and an estimated two thousand libraries through which teachers sent into the countryside could work on the national mission: teaching the rural populations how to be Mexicans per his vision. This involved basic reading, writing, and arithmetic skills, along with Mexican history. Government printing offices published textbooks with the "official" history of Mexico, and now-famous muralists were employed to help bring that official history visually to the masses. All of "the fundamental tools [were given] in Spanish," since Vasconcelos believed that knowledge of the Spanish language was crucial to the incorporation of the *indio*.[38]

By some readings, the vision of *indigenismo* that Moisés Sáenz advocated even as he worked within the official organs of government was Pan-Americanist. "To him the Indians of his own country belonged to the same family as the Indians of the rest of our continent," wrote Concha Romero James in her preface to the republication of Sáenz's pamphlet, *The Indian, Citizen of America*.[39] It was ultimately his vision of the incorporation of the *indio* that triumphed during the Cardenismo years of the 1930s. It must be noted, however, that rhetorical nods to *indio* incorporation did not match the socio-economic and political realities of most *indios*. Recent resurgent *indio*-rights movements like those of the neo-Zapatistas in the late twentieth century underscore the ongoing nature of these struggles.

José Vasconcelos visited Chicago several times during the 1920s, and by 1929 a Clúb Pro-Vasconcelos had been formed to support his bid for the presidency of Mexico.[40] When he visited in June 1928, he took time to speak to Chicago's Mexican *colonias*. As a candidate for president in the upcoming Mexican elections, perhaps he used the occasion to reinforce his ties with the University of Chicago–allied business elites he had met in 1926 when he participated in the Harris Lectures series and to speak to potential constituents at the Sociedad Ignacio Zaragosa.[41]

Reflecting the urge to create and reinforce a glorious collective history, the Sociedad named itself after General Zaragosa who, along with General Benito Juárez, defeated the French at the Battle of Puebla on May 5, 1862. This social group of an estimated forty men and women seemed to function as a kind of mutual-aid society, though during 1928 it was reportedly undergoing a reorganization.[42] Apparently, however, they still were prominent enough to draw José Vasconcelos to speak to them. "'Mexicans, let us never forget or cease to show interest in our country,'" he urged.[43] As he continued his address, his agenda became clear: to keep Chicago's Mexicans within the purview of the Mexican state, to ensure that Mexico did not permanently lose these obviously productive and resourceful citizens. Undoubtedly he was aware of the anthropologist Manuel Gamio's research tracing the remittances Mexicans sent back to Mexico, and he must have calculated the financial implications of these wages for the Mexican economy.[44] Vasconcelos also revealed an awareness of the strong presence of prejudice and anti-Mexican sentiments, and he framed the Mexican condition in the United States with an analogy meant to offer comfort: "'We are but the children of Israel who are passing through our Egypt here in the United States doing the onerous labors, swallowing our pride, bracing up under the indignities heaped upon us here.'" In a version of "this too shall pass," Vasconcelos then advocated returning to Mexico and leaving "'this Egypt of ours.'"[45]

One of his earliest visits to Chicago, however, was shortly after publishing his treatise on "la raza cósmica." In the summer of 1926, he delivered three lectures at the noted Harris Foundation Lectures at the University of Chicago. Interestingly, two other familiar, prominent, and competing voices in Mexican nationalist politics, Manuel Gamio and Moíses Saénz, also presented three Harris Lectures that summer.[46] Each spoke eloquently about their understandings of the problems facing Mexico, and each carefully outlined his own vision of how to unify the nation-state.

As if in preparation for their visits, the most widely circulated Spanish-language newspaper in Chicago printed extracts from José Martí's "Nuestra America."[47] In the 1920s and 1930s, new generations of Latin Americans embraced Martí's views, and the editors of *México* were among them. The choice to publish selections from "Nuestra America" on the eve of the Harris Lecture series was clearly strategic. Gamio, Vasconcelos,

Fig. 5.1: Luis Lupián, Mexican consul in Chicago (right), Professor Moíses Sáenz, undersecretary of education (center), Armando C. Amador, vice consul in Chicago (left), 1926. Chicago Daily News negative DN-0081051, Chicago Daily News Collection, Chicago Historical Society.

and Saénz came to Chicago in their official capacities as representatives of President Plutarco Calles's Mexico. Speaking before audiences like those of the Harris Lectures, they appealed directly to major business leaders and investors who could bring economic capital and companies into Mexico. U.S. investment in Mexico represented exactly what Martí warned Latin American nations to eschew. Economic investment of this type could be tantamount to the incursion of U.S. economic imperialism into Mexico. In choosing the words of Martí, the editors meant to signal an anti-Calles stance and a warning against the policies of Calles's government—and by extension, those of its allies, including the Harris Lecturers.

These kinds of political divides lay at the heart of Mexican nationalist debates, and yet each proclaimed to be working toward creating the real Mexico, full of ideal Mexicans. At the same time, however, the increasingly negative consequences of "Mexican" identity in Chicago conjoined with Mexican nationalist rhetoric idealizing "the Mexican," and Chicago emerged as a kind of crucible within which these elements fused into Mexicanidad.

Mexicanidad in Chicago

LATIN AMERICANISM

Perhaps the Latin Americanist orientation of Chicago's Mexicans was also encouraged by the presence of Cubans, Puerto Ricans, Guatemalans, Nicaraguans, Colombians, and Brazilians within Chicago's Mexican *colonias*.[48] Although no data exists on the nativity of Latin Americans in Chicago by country of origin, a rough outline of the population emerges through analysis of a sampling of aggregate data in the 1930 census. Mexicans predominated in the Latin American population, but Central and South Americans formed a notable percentage.

Overall, Latin Americans were predominantly male, thus explaining to some degree rates of intermarriage. Other data drawn from naturalization papers adds a finer filter to the general demographic outline, and personal stories come to light. Consider, for example, Cubans like Angel Rodríguez, who lived in the Loop and worked as a sign painter, or Miguel Castillo, a cigar maker living on the Near West Side;[49] Puerto Ricans like Antonio Acosta, who lived with his Canadian-born wife, Gladys, in South Chicago;[50] or Guatemalans like Alfonso García, his Guatemalan-born wife Lutgarda, and their nine children (eight of whom were born in Guatemala), who worked as painters and lived on the Near West Side.[51] There were also notable numbers of Nicaraguans, possibly fleeing the

Table 5.1a: Distribution of Foreign-Born White Population: Latin America* in Chicago, 1930

Tract No.	Mexico M	Mexico W	Spain M	Spain W	Cuba M	Cuba W	Central & South America M	Central & South America W
20	13	3					10	6
30			22	1				
35							9	3
67	8	3						
68	5	6						
106							7	4
107							9	2
108							13	7
115	7	6						
117							8	5
119							9	2
124			12	0			8	2
129	6	4						
135	11	4	11	0				
288							7	4
316							11	5
318							7	3
319	10	6						
358	6	4						
392							5	5
399							5	6
405	7	3						
407							9	6
419	16	3						
420	18	0						
421	10	5						
422	5	8						
428	6	4						
441	6	4						
454	11	6	6	4				
517	14	0					31	0
524			20	12				
613	8	5						
633					8	7		
666	18	9						
670	9	1						
703	5	5						
712							9	2
782	9	4						
Totals	208	93	71	17	8	7	157	62

Data compiled from Burgess and Newcomb, *Census Data, 1930,* tables 2 and 3, Supplement, 26–31. (*in category "all other" in 1930 population census).

Note: All other aggregate census data, including "Color" and "Nativity," is not broken down beyond Native or Foreign-Born, and White, Negro, and "Other Races." M = Men, W = Women.

Table 5.1b: Distribution of Native-Born White Population of Foreign or Mixed Parentage: Latin America*in Chicago, 1930

Tract No.	Mexico M	Mexico W	Spain M	Spain W	Cuba M	Cuba W	Central & South America M	Central & South America W
115	5	5						
135	7	5						
275			7	5				
278			7	6				
287			11	3				
304			6	4				
318			5	8				
322			6	5				
339			5	9				
428	6	4						
429			8	4				
524			16	22				
666	9	8						
671	8	10						
711	7	8						
773							8	3
Totals:	42	40	71	66	0	0	8	3

Data compiled from Burgess and Newcomb, *Census Data, 1930*, tables 2 and 3, Supplement, 26–31. (* in category "all other" in 1930 population census).

Note: All other aggregate census data, including "Color" and "Nativity," is not broken down beyond Native or Foreign-Born, and White, Negro, and "Other Races." M = Men, W = Women.

Nicaraguan Civil War (1927–33) like Pedro José Gómez, a clerk living in Packingtown.[52] Colombians like Eduardo Bohorquez, a messenger, lived in Hyde Park, while Fernando Velásquez, an electrician, lived on the Near West Side.[53] There were even a few Brazilians, like the tailor Salvador Calvano, who lived in South Chicago, and Annibal Camillo Perreira, who was employed as a translator living on the outskirts of Packingtown.[54]

Nowhere were these nationalities a quorum, and they lived interspersed throughout areas of Mexican settlement. It is notable too that although Mexicans predominated in the Latino population, they were not the dominant group in any single neighborhood. In areas where they were concentrated, they were the majority in a few city blocks, and, though significant, they remained a minority group.[55]

While difficult to gauge actual degrees of interaction between these other Latin Americans and Chicago's Mexicans, there are a few suggestive examples. Julio I. Puente, for instance, was a Puerto Rican lawyer who came to Chicago in about 1914. By the mid-1920s, his caseload was

Table 5.2. Nativity of Foreign-Born Latin Americans in Chicago, 1930

Countries of Origin: Mexico, Spain, Cuba, Central and South America (aggregated)

Mexico	48%	Spain	14%
Central and		Cuba	2.4%
South America	35%		

Nativity of Foreign-Born Latin Americans in Chicago, 1930, by Sex

Mexico	69% Male	Spain	81% Male
Central and		Cuba	53% Male
South America	72% Male		

Compiled from data in Burgess and Newcomb, *Census Data, 1930*, tables 2 and 3, Supplement, 26–31.

"almost entirely the defense of Latin Americans charged with crime."[56] He worked with the Mexican consulate, handling Mexican criminal cases from all over the area. During the mid- and late 1920s, Puente also served as editor of *El Heraldo de las Americas*, a newspaper with a Pan-Americanist bent, sponsored by the Mexican consulate.[57]

By the late 1920s, even newspapers like *La Noticia Mundial* were founded with the express purpose of "establishing cooperation between all the Hispanic-Americans of Chicago." The paper sought the unity of "all the various Mexican societies welded into one single society," after which they could "proceed to the unification of the other brothers." Such cooperation and unification at heart was to combat prejudices they all faced; in the language of the day, "to make them stronger and more respected and . . . place them in a better light in the opinion of outsiders."[58]

Mexicans predominated in the Latin American population, but the presence of significant numbers of other Latin Americans potentially complicated moves toward a hemispheric Americanism, or Latin Americanism.[59] Moreover, this diversity simply added to the already heterogeneous Mexican population. Mexicans and other Latin Americans recognized the desirability of and the need for unity between them. This was especially pressing when they recognized that "Americans almost never distinguish between us. . . . [T]o them . . . it is all the same whether one is Mexican or Spanish, Chilean or Nicaraguan, Argentinian or Salvadoran." The obviously injurious slight motivated some to call for unity within *la raza*. The same editor continued: "[L]et us then redeem our *raza*. . . . Wouldn't it be better for these groups, now completely disunited to join in forming one . . . strong and powerful, which could say much for our Indo-Spanish race in this city?"[60] This use of *la raza* only roughly translates into English. The closest English-language usage is that of contemporary African American newspapers like the *Chicago Defender*, which referred to African Americans as "the Race." In common usage, African American women and men, then, were "Race women" and "Race men," though no equally gendered referents were used in Spanish.

The strategy of uniting to present a better face to Chicagoans at large functioned as coded language for uniting to combat prejudice. This was especially evident in Mexican calls to unify themselves within the city. Many contemporaries, however, including social workers and academics, misunderstood these calls for unity as indications of tremendous social disorganization—which neatly explained various pathologies ranging from juvenile delinquency to overcrowded housing. Even well-meaning allies betrayed their biases as they looked for those they could recognize as community leaders and found only potential. "If some way could be found of making use of [those capable of leadership], they could contribute much to the betterment of their countrymen."[61]

When read against a larger Mexican and Latin American backdrop, however, Mexican calls for unity take on a much richer and more complicated texture. No longer can they be misconstrued as attempts to "fix" social pathologies and make their people more assimilable. Mexican calls for unity in Chicago operated on two levels: they were reminiscent of Mexican nationalist rhetoric seeking to unify the nation-state; however, they were also truly concerned with unifying the Mexican population in Chicago, not simply out of nationalist leanings but also to fight against rising anti-Mexican prejudices and discrimination. In this sense, Mexicans in Chicago wielded the tools of Mexican nationalism to combat local conditions.

UNITY

As being Mexican carried with it an increasing liability, Mexicans sought ways to redress the inequities. However, the overwhelming majority did not seek U.S. citizenship, for they did not see citizenship as a means toward that redemption. Señor Alonzo summarized the issue: "If you carry naturalization papers in your pocket . . . you may hold your head up and say to yourself, 'Now I am as good as anybody.' But that won't prevent an American from kicking you and saying, 'Get out of here, you damned Mexican!'"[62] Clearly, naturalization papers were not sufficient to protect one from being branded "Mexican" and suffering the discriminatory consequences of that label. As Manuel Bueno, a Mexican in Packingtown, observed, "Even if we do become citizens here, we always remain Mexicans."[63]

Mexicans in Chicago found that they were treated as "Mexicans" regardless of their legal status. Thus, their primary task was to "make the colony understand our great need of remedying our collective status."[64] Those remedies came in the form of appeals to pull together. Justification for such appeals to Mexican unity included concerns for future generations: "Unite to work for the good of our children."[65] During 1924 and 1925, several people worked to unite existing Mexican civic and social groups into a Confederación de Sociedades Mexicanas de los Estados Unidos Americanos (Confederation of Mexican Societies of the United States).[66] The organization included groups from several areas outside Chicago, including Indiana Harbor, Joliet, and Waukegan.[67] The group was short-lived and dissolved a little over a year later.[68] While it existed, however, it focused on "assisting Mexicans to meet problems arising in the[ir] new environment" including "combatting public social discrimination against Mexicans."[69]

By the mid-1930s formalized groups sprouted, organized specifically to unify the Mexican *colonia* to combat anti-Mexican prejudice. A group of Mexicans from Packingtown, for instance, formed the Association for the Unification and Defense of the Mexican Colony around 1933.[70] Throughout much of the 1930s, many in the greater community wanted to create a centralized location that would fill the needs of all Mexicans in Chicago. By the late 1930s, yet more voices rallied to try to build a Casa del Mexicano. Sadly, such a place never emerged. In 1943, new moves surfaced to push for the Casa, and Pro–Casa del Mexicano committees were formed at the behest of the Mexican consulate.[71] Even then, the motivations were clear: to give "good reputation to the progressive spirit and unity of those *colonias*."[72]

Racial prejudice against Mexicans in Chicago worked in two contradictory ways. It separated people from each other depending on the extent to which one carried various markers of "Mexican" identity, such as skin color, proficiency with English, dress, economic status, work habits, or cultural practices, all of which fed into creating one's "reputation." The whole notion of passing grew out of this, whether Mexicans were passing as Spaniards or at least not Mexicans.

Racial prejudice also worked to unify Mexicans as they found themselves tagged "Mexican." In a perverse way, the effect of being branded pejoratively—despite any attempts to separate themselves—provided Mexicans with a unifying weapon that they could brandish against those people and institutions that discriminated against them. The net effect of this brand of prejudice was to homogenize Mexicans in the eyes of these same institutions and people. Mexicans in effect became interchangeable.

Manuel Bravo's experience getting work points to one such example of the anonymity that racial prejudice effectively created for Mexicans in the eyes of their employers.

Bravo described a practice common among Mexican workers in the area by which one would fill out job applications and take physical exams posing as someone else.[73] In Manuel's case, it allowed him to pass a physical exam to work in the steel mills that he would have failed otherwise because of a bad eye. In other cases, it created an informal way to build in flexibility not allowed by the employer (and still not won by nascent steel unions). Essentially this practice allowed men to have sick leave, vacation time, and holiday leave while being able to return to their jobs. And in other cases, according to Bravo, men were able to gain jobs that they otherwise would not have gotten because of their limited English. "Being Mexican" in these instances actually worked favorably for them.

These innovative solutions to the conditions under which they labored also diluted the strength of labor's appeal to the Mexican worker. Not only did they know this kind of flexibility was not yet available through unions, but Mexicans also knew there was racial prejudice against them.[74] As one Mexican explained, "'The Mexicans don't like the unions very well; they don't like the high fees, and then after they are members they feel that because of *distinción* they are not sure of a job even if they have a union card.'"[75] In this case, *distinción* carried significant meaning, referring to the prejudice and discrimination Mexicans experienced from within the unions themselves.[76]

"There was not a lot of solidarity among the Mexicans, at least that's what Angelo Soto used to complain about. He didn't think most Mexicans were interested," Sidney Levin explained.[77] After all, if conditions became intolerable, they could choose the common option of simply leaving. Their mobility became a means of changing the situations under which they toiled. Such mobility also undercut whatever solidarity or unity such workers might have felt together. This was coupled with employer strategies that sought to isolate workers from each other to diffuse unity. While historians like Lizabeth Cohen have argued that such strategies created cross-ethnic coalitions, for most Mexican workers they fed into disaffection with the U.S. labor movement.[78]

Counter to predominant labor historiography, the few Mexicans who joined labor unions explained that they did so not primarily to better their wages and working conditions but rather to combat the prejudice and discrimination they faced in the workplace.[79] Their fights for improved wages and working conditions thus became symptoms of much larger issues and not their primary motivation. Angelo Soto, for instance, was one such Mexican who joined the steel workers union in South Chicago because he never moved up in the work he did. He knew this was a form of discrimination against him as a Mexican, and he "saw the Union as a way of combating" this prejudice.[80] This insight also throws into question the idea that Mexicans joined unions out of some idealized kind of cross-ethnic coalition building.[81] From the Mexican perspective, their choices were simply pragmatic. As Jack García, a steel worker in South Chicago, explained, "They used to have what they called picket lines, asking everybody if they joined the union, did you join the union . . . so finally, to overcome the bothersome things, you know, I joined the union."[82]

Even those assumed by historians to have been active labor leaders who really believed in the cause explained their involvement in entirely casual, almost accidental ways. Max Guzmán, for instance, marched at the head of the strike line in the Little Steel Strike of 1937, even carrying the American flag as the strikers began to be attacked and killed by the police outside the gates of Republic Steel. He was clubbed severely, thrown into a paddy wagon, and hauled off to jail. When asked years later how he came to be involved in the strike, he explained that he was just coming out of the gates getting off his night shift. "I happened to come out, out in the morning . . . there was no, no picket line or nothing there." He met up with some strike leaders, who handed him the flag, "and they told us, we march from 113th . . . to 118th."[83]

Thus, the lack of Mexican solidarity, whether in unions or not, contributed to prejudices against them and to the collective branding of "Mexican" with its attendant pejorative connotations and real discriminatory repercussions. As the editors of *México* remarked, "Racial prejudices exist in which we Mexicans are always unequally matched."[84] Unity did gel, however, around commonly experienced discrimination, and it coalesced into pride when folded into Mexicanidad.

THE BELOVED COUNTRY

Mexicanidad functioned as an ethnic and racial identity, a collectively imagined and experienced way of "being Mexican in Chicago."[85] As in other areas in the U.S. Southwest, immigrant identification with *lo mexicano* "helped bridge *patria chica* [small fatherland] allegiances to the home village and class divisions."[86] In Chicago, however, against a Latin American and Euro-ethnic backdrop, pride in being "Mexican" at once acknowledged racialized negativity and at the same time celebrated "being Mexican" through a nostalgic tradition that empowered and unified.

Valorizing heroes of a past that was imagined to be collective included annual celebrations of Mexican independence from Spain in 1810. At such a celebration in 1924—marking the 114th anniversary—sponsored by the Mexican Fraternal Society of Chicago, festivities began before an altar to the *patria* displaying "pictures of the Father [Hidalgo]" and the "Heroes of Independence."[87] The program included an address and "a splendid dance which lasted until three in the morning."[88] The fiesta was also attended by non-Mexicans, which served an ulterior motive: to demonstrate Mexican unity and thereby blunt criticism of the social disorganization of the Mexican communities. "The American public . . . noted the solidarity of the Mexicans and the love which is hidden in their hearts for the[ir] beloved country."[89]

Two years later, celebrating the 116th anniversary of Mexican independence from Spain, *México* dedicated an issue "to the memory of the *patria,* longing for peace and prosperity."[90] Calling Mexico the *tierra azteca* (land of the Aztecs), the paper ran a front-page picture of Don Miguel Hidalgo y Costilla, explaining that he was "the immortal priest of the people and father of the independence of Mexico."[91] It is interesting to speculate on the underlying message being sent, knowing that the Cristero conflicts were erupting full-force by 1926.

During Plutarco Elías Calles's anti-Catholic presidency, statements valorizing a priest of any kind could have been read as political commentary with the express purpose of showing support for the church.[92] In an attempt to enforce the secular articles of the 1917 Constitution, Calles had attempted to limit the power of the church by banning religious schools, outlawing monastic orders, preventing religious organizations from holding property, and forbidding clergy from voting or wearing religious dress.[93] Church authorities responded by ending religious instruction and halting their public services from 1926 until 1929. For three years, there was civil unrest and violence on all sides. Fighting primarily in central and western Mexico, especially Jalisco and Guanajuato, the Cristeros fought to reinstate the powers of the church, the clergy, and to open schools of faith. Many also fought not simply out of religious conviction but because they did not support the Calles government. By 1929, mediated by the United States, a truce of sorts was worked out before federal troops could decimate the remaining Cristeros.[94]

Chicago's Mexicans were aware of the Cristero rebellions: much of the violence was concentrated in states from which many of them came, including Jalisco and Michoacán. News accounts described in detail the violence, and several firsthand accounts must have traveled via the population of newly arriving immigrants. In 1928, a group of Cristero sympathizers in Chicago formed the Unión Nationalista Mexicana.[95] Local religious leaders also forayed into events by expressing their own views publicly. Father Tort, the Catholic priest who tended to Mexicans on the Near West Side and in South Chicago, viewed the conflicts as anti-Catholic persecutions on the part of an illegitimate government. He explained, "President Calles of Mexico is nothing but a rebel, a bandit, that has secured control of the government and is using his power to persecute the Catholics."[96]

Antonio Pérez of the Mexican Methodist church in South Chicago offered a local Protestant perspective: "Most of the trouble has been the result of the historical union of church and state."[97] By this view, the conflicts were the result of necessary albeit painful moves to secularize the nation-state of Mexico. It is interesting to consider that Pérez himself may have been converted to Protestantism by the missionaries that President Alvaro Obregón invited into Mexico during the early 1920s in an effort to counter the power of the Catholic church.

A similar complexity existed on the ground in Chicago. The active presence of several Protestant and non-Catholic organizations working among Chicago's Mexicans must also have sharpened the splits between Catholic and non-Catholic Mexicans and, by extention, the ideological splits between supporters of the federal government and of the Cristeros.[98] The Sociedad Hispano-Americana of Chicago held a Baptist affiliation and was criticized by the editors of Corréo Mexicano, a Catholic-friendly newspaper, for mismanagement of funds.[99] The members of this group reportedly also affiliated themselves with the Cruz Azul in Chicago and, according to the newspaper, led to the destruction of the Cruz Azul because of similarly shady financial proceedings. The Mexican Masonic Lodge arose in 1928, reportedly in direct response to the pro-Cristero Unión Nationalista Mexicana. To complicate the religious mix further, there were at least three spiritualist societies (possibly Seventh-Day Adventists) at Hull-House (1927), in South Chicago (1928), and in Packingtown (1929).[100]

A consulate-sponsored newspaper geared toward Mexican youth, El Heraldo Juvenil, echoed Pérez's understanding of events in Mexico: "The clergy of Mexico has . . . at all times . . . coveted the domination of national politics and control of the government. . . . Rome has not hesitated to form a political party and meddle directly in the national affairs."[101] This language also mimicked the official Calles position, adding to evidence of official sanctioning if not sponsorship of this publication.

Regardless of the political sentiments expressed, commemorations of major historical events and actors helped to build and solidify a commonly agreed-upon heritage among Chicago's Mexicans. Such a collectively imagined history necessarily included major Catholic figures like Father Hidalgo. Pre-Hispanic threads also ran through the texture of this evolving history. Appeals to an imagined Aztec past, for instance, included the naming of popular local sports clubs, including Clúb Anáhuac (after the Aztec name for the Valley of Mexico where Mexico City is located) and Clúb Atlético Cuauhtémoc (after the last ruler of the Aztec empire [1520–21]).[102] A few Mexicans even wrote stories about the spirit of Quetzalcóatl and read them at public gatherings.[103] In the 1930s, even as Cardenismo took root in Mexico, Chicago's Mexicans celebrated Cinco de Mayo, publishing celebratory histories of the Battle of Puebla while groups from a variety of mutual-aid societies organized parades and dances.[104] Spurred on by Mexican consuls, Mexicans organized feasts to honor Benito Juárez and invited speakers to "relate the accomplishments of the Indian of Guelatao."[105] The "Mexican Village" at the 1933 World's Fair in Chicago offered another opportunity to construct a collective tradition and to display "the typical Mexican." The Mexican consulate, for example, recruited many local Mexican women and men to be in the display, performing "traditional" tasks like making tortillas while dressed in "trajes typicos mexicanos" (typical Mexican outfits) against a backdrop of photographs of Mexico.[106] Economic motivations must have fueled the creation of the display, for the Commerce Department of Mexico's Secretary of Foreign Relations office organized the Villa Mexicana.

Local Spanish-language newspapers also commemorated the four hundredth anniversary of the appearance of the Virgen de Guadalupe and included brief historical accounts of her apparition to Juan Diego.[107] Even into the 1940s, appeals to a pre-Hispanic heritage continued, including a popular theater production called *La Virgen Morena, El Milagro de Tepeyác.* Performances were at the Globe Theater on the Near West Side in early April 1943, followed a week later in South Chicago at Theater Joy.[108] The play recounted the story of the apparition of the Virgen de Guadalupe, the patron saint of Mexico, to the baptized Aztec peasant Juan Diego on the sacred hill of Tepeyác in 1531. The hill of Tepeyác had been sacred in pre-Columbian times and was the location of the temple of Tonantzín, also a virgin goddess like La Virgen de Guadalupe. The Virgen Morena, or the Brown Virgin, was a way of signifying the Virgen as looking like and being "of the people," reinforced, of course, by the common belief that she spoke to Juan Diego in his native Indian language. The Virgen appeared to request that a church be built there to replace the temple that the Spaniards had destroyed.[109] Allegorically, this often played as the triumph of Mexico's pre-Hispanic heritage over that of the conquerors and a celebration of the *indio*. Even in their appeal to and use of "tradition," Mexicans understood its cohesive power.

In 1935, representatives from several Mexican groups and social societies, along with many individual Mexicans and the Mexican consul, Eugenio Prequeira, worked together to form the Comité Pro-Mexico (the Pro-Mexico Committee), a confederation that apparently existed for several years.[110] Ironically, the initial purpose of the Pro-Mexico Committee was "to counteract the campaign against our country" that reportedly was run not by Anglos or other Chicago ethnic groups, but by a group of Mexicans. The majority of these Mexicans who were outspokenly critical of Mexico were supposedly "women directed by Spanish priests."[111] While such reports may have been true, they also betray the gendered spaces in which Chicago's Mexicans operated—the churches were populated mostly by women parishioners. The historian Sarah Deutsch has discovered similar church demographics among Irish Catholic working-class women in Boston. For them, the church, "although unequivocally male-dominated, provided a refuge, a site of organizing and female activism, and a welter of mixed messages."[112] Little evidence is available to determine whether such activism even existed on the part of Chicago's Mexican Catholic women. Chicago's Mexican women were understood in these accounts not to have opinions and thoughts of their own but were instead believed to be pawns of the all-powerful Spanish priests. Apparently the dispute centered around the establishment of schools for Mexican children, but the consulate records never stated explicitly what were the sources of conflict. Perhaps it came out of the Cardenas government's version of attempting to maintain a separation between church and state, even in "Mexico de afuera" (the Mexico outside of Mexico).

As it matured, the Comité Pro-Mexico fought against more generalized derogatory stereotyping of Mexicans in Chicago and served "to unify the *colonia Mexicana* in Chicago and to remind it of its civic duties."[113] These reminders of their civic duties along with consular concern with *Mexico de afuera* spoke vividly of the degree to which successive Mexican governments worked not to lose their nationals. The tremendous irony, of course, is that most of these people would not have been noticed much by government structures at any level, beyond perhaps the local, had they stayed in Mexico. Once outside of Mexico in the United States, however, Mexican citizens represented a vibrant, productive, and therefore valuable citizenry that the Mexican nation-state targeted with resources and support. Thus Mexican consuls, as the official representatives of the Mexican national state, concerned themselves with reinforcing these people's Mexicanness in a variety of ways.

MEXICO'S CONSULS IN CHICAGO

Like the postrevolutionary nationalists in Mexico, the Mexican consulate in Chicago relied on unity as its principal organizational theme, and they labored during the 1920s and 1930s to unify Mexicans throughout Chicagoland. Working through the Pro-Mexico Committee, for instance, the consulate could promote cooperation, which in turn aided in "remind[ing the Mexican *colonia*] of its civic duties" to Mexico. Indeed, as early as 1925 the Mexican consul was working "to achieve some sort of federation of the local groups, but amid much oratory, nothing was done."[114]

Occasionally arrangements were made for Mexican presidential candidates to visit Chicago. In late 1929, president-elect Pascual Ortíz Rubio spoke to a large crowd of Mexicans at the Hotel Blackstone in downtown Chicago.[115] He drew "enthusiastic applause . . . when he said that one of the objects of his administration would be to help establish such conditions in Mexico that the emigrants might return to their own country without economic sacrifice."[116] Again, the agenda was clear: to keep Mexicans within the national fold even as they lived and worked outside the nation-state. Notably, he came as the president-elect and not as a presidential candidate (as did José Vasconcelos, whom he defeated), a subtle yet telling detail that suggests the relative political weakness of Mexicans living in *Mexico de afuera*. Yet, simply having the president-elect come to visit must have bolstered the political muscle and profile of Chicago's Mexicans, while supporting those who would not "change flags."

As seen through its participation in the fiestas, the Pro-Mexico Committee, and other examples, the consulate centered its high-profile activities around social and cultural events in Chicago. The consul and his local allies, especially businessmen and the editors of a few of the newspapers, used political events and knowledge of political conditions in Mexico to maintain ties with Mexico and among Mexicans. Accordingly, Spanish-language newspapers announced, and at times sponsored, *fiestas patrias,* parades, and theatrical productions about political conditions in Mexico.[117]

Beyond their concerns with social and cultural events to promote Mexico and positive images of "Mexicanness," the Mexican consulate in Chicago did take an active part in mediating conditions for Mexican nationals. Clearly, the extent of consular visibility within the community must have changed with the succession of men who occupied the post.

While information on these men is slim, hints of their perspectives and sympathies are revealed in what little evidence remains of their activities among the Mexican population of Chicago.

Although a succession of men rotated through the Mexican presidency during this period, the directives to the consuls and the attendant bureaucracies changed only superficially.[118] Primarily, the consul was charged with three duties: facilitating business and commerce between the United States and Mexico, providing protection to Mexicans living and working in the area, and defending the good name of the Republic of Mexico.[119] In practice, these duties often conflicted. The interests of Mexican workers, for instance, often collided with those of business and commerce. Nevertheless, a few of Chicago's consuls worked doggedly to resolve wage disputes between Mexican workers and American employers.[120] In spite of this, many Mexicans tended to view their consul with suspicion. In part, their distrust grew from the simple fact that the consul represented an authoritative government that they had known always to be corrupt and in which they held little direct representation. In addition, the frequency with which Mexico changed presidents, especially during the 1920s, meant that alliances with the consulate were usually short, and therefore people did not work as vigorously to build or maintain those ties. Moreover, the instability of the Mexican nation-state only confirmed the trepidation with which many Mexicans approached their government. After all, connections to one consul or government could be costly politically during sudden shifts in which opponents gained power.

The mobility of Mexican migrants into and out of Chicago and throughout the United States and Mexico added to their detachment from the consulate in Chicago. A consul's active involvement with the U.S. and Mexican governments to expedite and promote the repatriation campaigns of the 1920s and 1930s did not make him any more popular with Chicago's Mexicans.[121] Yet many saw no contradiction in going to the consul when they were in trouble or needed his help. This was especially true when Mexicans came to him to perform what they believed to be his official duties. These ranged from cultural events like sponsoring (and funding) *fiestas patrias* to intervening with negligent employers on behalf of Mexican workers. The difficulties the consulate must have had with carrying out its mandate were often unseen by those who called on the office for aid. Indeed, Mexicans often perceived a consul's inability to free jailed compatriots or to remedy other kinds of wrongs as inaction or indifference.

The case of Serapio Magaña, for example, seemed to illustrate the indifference of the consul to the plight of his people in Chicago.[122] On

November 23, 1929, Magaña was killed while crossing the tracks of the Chicago and Northwestern Railroad in an automobile. Since he had been an employee of that railroad, the company remitted $750 to the Mexican consulate "to help the family of the deceased." The Mexican consul, Rafael Aveleyra, notified the Foreign Relations Office in Mexico City, who then notified Magaña's sons. Twice during 1930, his adult sons wrote in vain to the Mexican consulate in Chicago requesting that the money be sent to them. Finally, on April 21, 1931, they wrote the Foreign Relations Office directly, lodging complaints about the inattention of the consul in Chicago. A month later, the Foreign Relations Office notified the sons their money awaited them at their local post office. To Andrés, Arcadio, and Antonio Magaña, it appeared that the consul's negligence and indifference toward them had been remedied by the officials in Mexico City. In fact, however, throughout 1930 the consul was arguing the case to the Foreign Relations Office in an attempt to garner support against the railroad company. Aveleyra was convinced Magaña's death was the fault of the railroad and worked to force the company to admit responsibility— and perhaps to provide further compensation to the family. Aveleyra had apparently chosen one consular duty over the other: to protect the people in his jurisdiction at the risk of hindering commercial relations with the railroad company. With their appeals directly to Mexico City and the quick resolution that followed, the Magaña sons unknowingly negated nearly a year's worth of Aveleyra's work on their behalf against the railroad company. The payout made to the sons ended the matter, and there were no recriminations for the railroad company whatsoever. However inaccurate, the appearance of consular apathy among the people of Chicago in these kinds of instances curtailed some of the power he could have wielded with and for them.

In another case, the efforts of Luis Lupián, the Mexican consul from about 1924 to about 1926, on behalf of the Mexican population were more visible. The case did not put him in conflict with business interests but rather with the South Chicago police. In the case recounted by Rafael Guardado Valadez in an earlier chapter, the police arrested a whole group of Mexicans who apparently were squatting on railroad property, living in a building on the railroad bridge over Baltimore Street.[123] Most apparently were employed by the Rock Island Railway. While in custody, one woman died of large lump that appeared on her left side. Dr. Alejandro Treviño somehow heard about her. As he worked for the Mexican consulate, he was able to get that office involved in investigating her death. South Chicago police blamed the woman's death on Mexican male brutality. In the end, however, Treviño proved that she had died of unnatural causes while in prison—the likely scenario being that she died of injuries sustained at the hands of the police, not of her fellow inmates, as claimed by the police. Subsequently, the doctor through the consulate secured the release of the other Mexicans. Though the incident does not seem to have been publicized, nor did the police incur any liability, Guardado knew Doctor Treviño and heard about it through him. Given that this account is drawn largely from the perspective of the doctor, it is impossible to tell whether the consul got the recognition he was due for his intervention with the South Chicago police. Clearly, however, the doctor could not have secured the release of all the prisoners without such help, and the South Chicago police would not have responded without being under the gaze of an independent nation-state.

Just as Mexicans held expectations of their consulate, so too did the consulate and its allies expect Mexicans to comport themselves as true patriots. As one local consulate-sponsored newspaper proclaimed, "True patriotism is highly constructive; it should be apparent in our tendency to improve ourselves in all respects, . . . to be more useful to our families and to our country." As true Mexicans, they were expected to have strong clubs and societies (back to the trope of unity), to have "irreproachable conduct, public and private," and to develop "business[es] which increase the wealth and the prestige of our country."[124] It was no accident that this enumeration of the duties of the true patriot mirrored the official mission of the Mexican consulate.

"TRUE" MEXICO, MEXICANIDAD

Of course, other views on the "true Mexico" existed in Chicago. Ignacio Elizalde, for instance, "a quick, nervous, bald-headed white Mexican . . . friendly and talkative," bemoaned that North Americans "did not appreciate the true Mexico."[125] Betraying clear class and race biases, he explained that this was because "North American[s] saw only the crude Mexicans, los rudos, los Indios." His perspective is interesting in light of the trajectory of *indigensimo* and even of *mestisaje* occurring in Mexico. Elizalde was clearly not an *indigenista,* nor did he seem to believe in the centrality of *mestisaje* to the Mexican state. Neither was he the "typical Mexican" as racialized in Chicago, given his light skin and education. As one contemporary noted, "The better looking of the race usually are not taken for Mexicans by the passerby, and the nationality gets no credit for the proportion of fairer semblance."[126] Again, being Mexican carried with it certain markers in physiognomy and comportment—white skin, fair complexion, and education somehow didn't signal "Mexican" to a non-

Mexican, and by implication, "Mexican" really meant dark complexion with little or no education.

In attempting to depict the "real Mexican," another Mexican expressed views that echoed those of Elizalde. "'The real Mexican is polite and courteous and tries to learn all that is good and will benefit him. In Mexico a lot of the people that are here were either servants or mountain Indians. There are many *peones* from the haciendas here too. There they were uncultured and savage. Here they dress like civilized people and eat well but do not pick up any education or manners.'"[127] Clearly, the fear among these men was that in Chicago they would be lumped together with these "lesser" peoples into one derogatory category called "Mexican." They were concerned that non-Mexicans would not understand or even notice what to them were vast differences in their qualities as national representatives of Mexico. As one man said, "'I am not ashamed of being a Mexican. But I am not proud of the Mexicans in Chicago. They are mostly Indians of the lower uneducated classes of peones.'"[128] These views offer a direct window into the complexity of perspectives that existed among Chicago's Mexicans and also neatly capture the difficulties facing those who might aim for solidarity across these differences. As if in dialogue with them, another Mexican man "of middle class and with some education," explained, "'[I]f I were a true Mexican, I would not be here [in the United States].'"[129]

Even though Mexicans spoke this way of each other, they increasingly presented a more unified front when attacked from outside the *colonias*, particularly by racial prejudice. Time and again, the prominent voices of Chicago's Mexican *colonias*, like newspaper editors and publishers, resorted to pre-Hispanic glories to counter anti-Mexican sentiments. When the *Chicago Tribune*, for example, published an article in 1928 by the physician Dr. Benjamin Goldberg that declared Mexican immigrants "a menace to the health of the American people," the editors of *México* responded pointedly.[130] Drawing on *indigenista* leanings, they reminded all their readers of the achievements of the Aztecs, the Toltecs, and the Maya as proof of the high civilization of the Mexican people and of their desirability. Quoting a writer for the *Saturday Evening Post*, the editors went on to note, "[T]he cultural past of Mexico and of Central America is an object of pride for the entire human race . . . [and has] so much to offer us that we should not dare to underestimate them." Despite the affirmative tone of the *Post* writer, the editors of *México* concluded their column by observing that "many treat us [Mexicans] as slaves."[131]

Evidence suggests that Chicago's Mexicans were interested in celebrating their Mexican identities even in the face of rising discrimination against them. By the late 1920s, they used the term "de-Mexicanization" to refer to negative changes they saw among their populations in Chicago.[132] Nostalgic conservative nationalist sentiments became especially transparent when dealing with children, the future generations of Mexicans in Chicago. Children who had little or no experience of Mexico itself were told stories and given descriptions of a romantic place frozen in time, frozen the moment their parents left. The Grabozo children, for instance, without having been to Mexico, were able to paint a "surprisingly graphic picture" of the country that emphasized the colors and romance, "the lovely flowers and fruit orchards," and "the spirits with whom their grandfather convers[ed]."[133] Chicago's Mexicans created formal and informal institutional structures to keep their children's Mexican heritage by teaching them the Spanish language, Mexican history, and Mexican cultural and social practices. One man ran a school in a vacant storefront, where (as described by an Irish woman) "the children [were] taught Mexican."[134] As one newspaper editorial explained, these schools were necessary "for the little Mexicans who are obliged to receive their education in the schools of the United States."[135] The Sociedad de Miguel Hidalgo y Costilla, a mutual-aid society whose name evoked romantic elements of a shared history, even formed an orphans committee in April 1933, requesting Mexicans to adopt these children so that they may grow up knowing their people.[136] By raising their children within the Mexican community and by teaching them to become good Mexicans, Chicago's Mexicans saw themselves as making "a glorious monument to our country in the innocent and blessed hearts of our little Mexicans."[137]

Fears of "de-Mexicanization" extended to mutations in food dishes collectively imagined to be national dishes. One Mexican restaurant famous for its food reportedly served tamales "in waxed paper, made of wheat flour and with a 'pickle' in place of the traditional pork." A customer wrote to *El Heraldo* that "his outrage drips from the page at this bastardization of the tamale, 'whose history dates back a hundred years before Christ.'" "What," the customer continued, "would our ancestors say if they saw the abused [sic] that had been committed upon the tamale?"[138]

Elements of a collectively imagined history could also be frozen in time as familiar cultural markers. In this sense, memory became another tool through which Mexicanidad was constructed in Chicago, for Mexicans drew from their memories of Mexico and their knowledge of history, beliefs, and practices in Mexico to hold the line against de-

Mexicanization. "'It is not as happy and gay a life here as in Mexico,'" recalled a Mexican man. "'They have no *fiestas* or *serenatas* and no places for *paseos* in the evening. . . . Life in Mexico is much easier . . . there you are not in constant dread of your employer.'"[139] Another noted, "'It is very cold here in the winter. I seldom go out. In the summer it is too hot and I seldom go out. The life here is very cheerless in contrast to Mexico. . . . I miss the *paseos* and *serenatas* of Mexico. I miss the *fiestas* and the good times."[140]

Remembered places and longed-for locations also were frozen in the names of restaurants, barbershops, and billiard halls. El Chapultepec was a South Chicago restaurant and pool hall whose name evoked the beautiful central park in Mexico City where the Aztec emperor had his home. There was also a poolroom/barbershop near Hull-House with this name and a restaurant in Packingtown named El Chapultepec. Bello Jalisco (Beautiful Jalisco) was a restaurant on the Near West Side, and there was a similarly named restaurant in Packingtown. El Azteca was a South Chicago restaurant, and El Cinco de Mayo was a poolroom/barbershop on the Near West Side.[141]

Conclusion

The appropriation of historical elements in such simple ways helped to bolster the belief in a common heritage and to offer some measure of pride in this frozen, nostalgic history. Indeed, elements of pre-Columbian history and of nineteenth-century national heroes blended to provide Mexicans in Chicago with a shared sense of heritage. Even as they sought ways to take pride in "being Mexican," they continually faced anti-Mexican prejudice and discrimination. Thus their identity as Mexicans in Chicago, their Mexicanidad, necessarily contained the negative and positive aspects of "being Mexicans in Chicago."

Pride in their Mexicanidad provided comfort and an empowering belief in themselves as Mexicans, which helped to counter growing prejudices many faced by virtue of being Mexican. To those Mexican nationals living in Chicago who refused to change flags and who did not see changing citizenship as effecting any real change, Mexicanidad provided a means of coherence. It was their growing sense of national identity that emboldened many and provided the seeds for collective action, whether through fiestas, sports clubs, or parades. And its Latin Americanist bent allowed some Mexicans to actively claim their American identity by virtue of continental, or hemispheric, citizenship, not U.S. citizenship.

For, as is clearly the case with Mexicans in Chicago, lack of U.S.

citizenship—and lack of desire to become U.S. citizens—did not indicate a fundamental indifference to their lives in Chicago, as social workers and others had thought. They struggled to lay claim to their American identity and to maintain their Mexican citizenship even while seeking lives outside the Mexican nation-state. The active involvement of the Mexican state (in the form of sponsored visits like the Harris Lectures, presidential tours, or consular work) and the prevalence of Mexican revolutionary/nationalist rhetoric all fed into Mexican determinations not to change flags. Indeed, in an ironic testament to the powers of nationalist sentiments, Chicago's Mexicans became Mexicans not while in Mexico but rather once outside of the bounds of the nation-state of Mexico.

Mexican attempts to maintain their continental citizenship while constructing their Mexicanidad, however, were stunted by the weight of insular Eurocentric forces of Americanization and by deep economic hardship. As economic conditions worsened for everyone in Chicago during the early 1930s, Mexicans experienced ever-more profound discrimination. They found themselves passed over for work in favor of European Americans, singled out as "Mexicans" and not "Americans" by relief workers, even formally segregated racially as "Mexicans" on the federal census of 1930.[142] As the early phases of voluntary repatriations gave way to more forced deportations, the Mexican population in Chicago was cut by at least one-quarter, dwindling to less than sixteen thousand in 1940 from up to twenty-five thousand at the start of the Depression.[143] Ultimately, Mexican visions of themselves as hemispheric Americans dimmed under the burdens of state and federal infrastructure that increasingly solidified the "barrier of prejudices" against which they struggled.[144]

The economic depression and its attendant social and political consequences erected a more effective barrier to any transnational or continental vision than the creation of the Border Patrol had nearly a decade earlier, as it stymied the flow of people, culture, and ideas. While Mexicans in Chicago perceived themselves still to be involved actively with Mexico in shaping a collective Mexicanidad, the Depression-era constraints of transnational migrations ensured that the Mexican nationalist project under Cárdenas went on without them. The Mexicans who stayed in Chicago remained largely cut off from these movements. Yet they still wielded the tools of Mexican nationalism and a nostalgic past as they turned their energies to fighting this barrier of prejudice and continued to work at unifying the Mexicans in Chicago. Along the way, they became Mexicans. That is, their efforts at constructing a collective sense of group identification, Mexicanidad, coalesced with externally defined constraints founded in prejudicial and negative characterizations of "Mexican." Ultimately, "Mexican" in Chicago by the end of the 1930s came to embody the results of positive internal forces of identification, including responses to racial discrimination and the more negative external processes that infused racialized, prejudicial meaning. Together, these elements provided rich territory upon which the Mexicans of the 1940s built to confront a changing world.

As the 1930s came to a close and world war loomed on the horizon, the terrains of national identification once again shifted. Issues of citizenship, national security, and serving one's country reordered the ways Mexicans could and did participate economically, politically, and socially in Chicago. Young Mexicans from Chicago like Manuel Pérez Jr. and Jesse Escalante went off to war to fight in the U.S. armed services. Escalante returned; Pérez did not. After the war, a local American Legion Post in the Near West Side was named after him: the Manuel Pérez American Legion Post 1017.[145] Local civic groups organized in the mid-1940s to create the Mexican Civic Committee, and Mexicans established themselves as an emerging political and social presence. The next decades saw the triumph of the "Mexican economic miracle" as Mexico prospered in the 1950s. The influx of a vast Puerto Rican migration into Chicago coupled with various "urban renewal" projects that changed the geographic and demographic landscapes of the city dramatically. These changes and others provided the children of Chicago's first Mexican communities new opportunities, promises, and challenges in the crucible of Mexican Chicago.

NOTES

Introduction

1. This trope entered common usage after Israel Zangwill's wildly popular play *The Melting Pot* opened on Broadway in New York City in 1908.

2. See Jacobson, *Whiteness*; Ngai, *Impossible*; and Ngai, "Architecture."

3. On Asian exclusions in Mexico, see Rénique, "Race." See also Wade, *Race and Ethnicity*; and Wade, *Blackness*.

4. Wade, "Race and Nation," 265.

5. On "distant" and "proximate" race mixing, see Martínez-Echazábal, "Mestizaje."

6. Stutzman, "El Mestizaje."

7. On Italians and whiteness, see Guglielmo, *White on Arrival*.

8. This conclusion is based on my research in the 1920 and 1930 manuscript censuses for the City of Chicago.

9. Gutiérrez, *Walls and Mirrors*.

10. Omi and Winant, *Racial Formation*; Hodes, "Mercurial Nature," 84.

11. I draw here from Hall, "Signification"; and Hall, "Cultural Identity."

12. Lisa Lowe uses a similar strategy in her use of "heterogeneity" and "multiplicity" to understand Asians in the United States. See Lowe, *Immigrant Acts*, 67.

13. Hall, "Cultural Identity," 225.

14. On Texas, see especially Foley, *White Scourge*; Montejano, *Anglos and Mexicans*; De León, *Ethnicity in the Sunbelt*; and Orozco, "Origins." On other parts of the U.S. Southwest, see especially Stern, *Eugenic Nation*; Montoya, *Translating Property*; Guerin-Gonzáles, *Mexican Workers*; Gutiérrez, *Walls and Mirrors*; Sánchez, *Becoming*; and Almaguer, *Racial*.

15. Taylor, *Mexican Labor*.

16. Reisler, *By the Sweat*; McWilliams, *Factories*; and McWilliams, *North*.

17. See Reisler, *By the Sweat*, chap. 5, 96–126.

18. Cárdenas, "Desarraigados"; Handlin, *Uprooted*.

19. Valdés, *Barrios*; Valdés, *Al Norte*; Vargas, *Proletarians*; García, *Mexicans*.

20. Sánchez, *Becoming*; Gutiérrez, *Walls and Mirrors*.

21. Ruiz, *Cannery Women*; and Ruiz, *From Out of the Shadows*.

22. Ruiz and Sánchez Korrol, *Latina Legacies*.

23. See, for example, Nelli, *Italians*; and Pacyga, *Polish Immigrants*.

24. Slayton, *Back of the Yards*; Barrett, *Work and Community*; Cohen, *Making*.

25. On the significance of the one-drop rule in discussions of whiteness, see Fields, "Whiteness," 50.

26. Vasconcelos, *La raza cósmica.* For a broader discussion, see Miller, *Rise and Fall;* Alonso, "Conforming"; Stern, "Eugenics"; and Knight, "Racism." See also chapter 5 of this volume and Arredondo, "Cartographies."

27. See Menchaca, *Recovering History;* Dawson, *Indian and Nation;* and Stepan, *"Hour of Eugenics."*

28. Barrett and Roediger, "Inbetween Peoples." On the connections between whiteness and Americanness, see King, *Making Americans.*

29. On whiteness or white racial identity as a component of American identity, see Horsman, *Race and Manifest Destiny;* Saxton, *Rise and Fall;* Roediger, *Wages of Whiteness;* and Foley, *White Scourge.* Matthew Frye Jacobson continues the historiography linking whiteness to Americanness, though he makes the distinction between American (as nationality) and Caucasian (as race). Jacobson, *Whiteness;* Roediger, *Colored White.* On whiteness as related to the Italians of Chicago, see Guglielmo, *White on Arrival.*

30. Stoler, "Racial Histories"; Holt, "Marking."

31. For another discussion of Mexico Lindo, see Rosales, *¡Pobre Raza!*

Chapter 1: Al Norte

1. Standard narratives of Mexican migration to Chicago and the Midwest can be found in works covering most of the twentieth century. See Taylor, *Mexican Labor;* and Valdés, *Al Norte.* Zaragosa Vargas's work on Mexicans in Detroit suggests that men of all skill levels and economic backgrounds migrated. This also appears to be the case in Chicago. Vargas, *Proletarians.* For an older, though still useful, study on where Mexicans in Chicago came from, see Rosales, "Regional Origins."

2. Immigration restrictions and deportation programs would help to equalize/stabilize sex ratios of Mexicans in Chicago, but even into the 1930s numbers remained uneven. On repatriation programs in the U.S. generally, see Hoffman, *Unwanted Mexicans.* On regional impacts of these programs and of federal legislation, see Bogardus, "Mexican Repatriates"; Kiser and Kiser, *Mexican Workers;* and Kerr, "Chicano Experience." Some historians have suggested that curtailed immigration allowed the Americanization process to take hold in the 1930s. See Cárdenas, "Desarraigados"; and García, "Making."

3. "Protesta El Consul Mexicano en Chicago," August 2, 1919, 16-9-160, Archivo Histórico de la Secretaria de Relaciónes Exteriores. Carter Harrison II was the son of the former Chicago mayor Carter Harrison I. Carter Harrison I served four consecutive terms between 1879 and 1887, then began a fifth term in 1893. His son served two terms, 1897–1905 and 1911–15. Unless otherwise noted, all translations are my own.

4. The Mexican consul also contacted the city comptroller, who agreed to speak with Mr. Holstein, the chief of the city's Department of Law. In cooperation with Mr. Jones, "corporation counsel," they decided to paint over the word "barbarous." When the consul surveyed the movie theaters, however, he discovered that no action had been taken. After follow-up protests, a few of the posters were modified. Ibid.

5. Turner, *Barbarous Mexico*. The first edition was published in 1911 by Kerr and Company in Chicago.

6. The *ejidatario* was a resident or worker on the *ejido*, the communally owned and operated land that lay at the heart of Mexico's revolutionary attempts at land redistribution. *Peón* in this usage refers to the landless, unskilled rural peasant of the prerevolutionary period in the late nineteenth century. Though dated (and in fact, nearly contemporary with the events) and presenting a romanticized version of Mexico, see Simpson, *Ejido*. See also Hall, "Alvaro Obregón"; and Hall and Coerver, *Revolution*.

7. On social change in Mexico during this period, see Rodríguez, *Revolutionary Process*. Other studies focus on more contemporary periods but include significant historical material. On southern Mexico and Oaxaca, the original stronghold of the revolutionary figure Emiliano Zapata, see Murphy and Stepick, *Social Inequality*. On Zacatecas primarily, see Jones, *Ambivalent Journey*.

8. For the particulars of his nationalist ideologies, see Vasconcelos, *Mexican Ulysses*. For a general history of Mexico, see Meyer and Sherman, *Course of Mexican History*.

9. See, for example, Ruíz, *Breve Historia*.

10. Vaughan, *Cultural Politics*. The success of these schools was mixed. Generally, girls and women remained severely undereducated in Mexico throughout this period.

11. Weber, *Dark Sweat*, 8.

12. Ibid., 8–9. In Chicago there is little evidence of the strong personal alliances that existed between labor activists and union leaders of Mexico and California. Because of this, the distance to the border, racial prejudice, and the realities impacting travel and migration to Chicago, I hesitate to call these workers "sin fronteras" in the same sense that Weber does the cotton workers in California. See ibid., chap. 2.

13. Tutino, *From Insurrection*; Katz, *Secret War*; Katz, *Riot, Rebellion, and Revolution*. On revolutionary conflicts in northern Mexico, see Stout, *Border Conflict*.

14. I relate typical examples of accounts and interviews of revolution and migration that run throughout the archival papers of contemporary researchers like Paul S. Taylor, Manuel Gamio, Robert Park, Ernest W. Burgess, Robert Redfield, and their students. See the bibliography for full citation of these collections. It is important to note that women were instrumental to the revolution in myriad ways, including serving as soldiers. See Salas, *Soldaderas*, esp. chaps. 4 and 5; Macias, *Against All Odds*; Soto, *Emergence*; and Ruiz, *From Out of the Shadows*, esp. chap. 1.

15. Ignacio Elizalde interview, February 14, 1925, Robert Redfield Papers.

16. Gamio, *Mexican Immigration*; Cardoso, *Mexican Emigration*.

17. I. M. Valle interview, February 14, 1925, Robert Redfield Papers. Valle stated that he was from a small town in Jalico near Ototonilco. His store was the Rialto Music Shop, located at 330 South State Street. He reported selling many *corrido* records, dance records, and what he called "sentimental songs" to his Mexican customers. Unfortunately, the interview is sketchy and does not indicate dates of migration and residence in Chicago, nor does it reveal any background information on how he lived or worked before serving in the military.

18. Many of the conservative elites and the locally wealthy cronies of the Porfiriato escaped the revolution and set up expatriate support networks for the Mexican nationalists from San Antonio and Los Angeles. Many of these people expected to return to Mexico and resume their positions of power after the revolutionary fervor died down. On San Antonio, see García, *Rise*. On Los Angeles, see Sánchez, *Becoming*. On the Mexican government's use of their consuls in promoting Mexican nationalism in Los Angeles, see González, *Mexican Consuls*, esp. chaps. 1 and 2.

19. Unidentified Drugstore Clerk interview, April 16, 1925, Robert Redfield Papers. The interview does not note any specific dates or make clear whether the clerk was drafted or volunteered. The tone of his account suggests that if he did volunteer, he did so under duress. That he went first to San Antonio raises interesting, though currently unanswerable, questions about the connections between the expatriate communities in San Antonio and Chicago.

20. Quoted in Jones, "Conditions," 79.

21. Correa, *Movimientos*.

22. On the early revolutionary unrest in Guanajuato specifically, see Blanco, *Revolución*.

23. Interview with unidentified Mexican man, 1924, Field Notes, Robert Redfield Papers.

24. Meyer and Sherman, *Course of Mexican History*, 587.

25. Kerr, "Chicano Experience," 56.

26. See, for example, "The Catholic Church and the Mexican Government," *México* (Chicago), September 25, 1926. The authors of the articles in Chicago were supportive of Calles, which suggests, at least, that the publishing "elite" in Chicago were probably not the conservative wealthy Catholics displaced in the Cristero Rebellions.

27. Gamio, *Mexican Immigration*, 13–21.

28. On the presidency and continued power of Calles, see Richard, *Vida y Temperamento*; and Castro, *En la Presidencia*.

29. Peter Reich's work on the period between the settlement of the Cristero conflicts and the renewed tolerance for religion in the 1940s suggests that in spite of official intolerance, the government and the church actually worked together in cooperative ways. See Reich, *Mexico's Hidden Revolution*. Classic works on the Cristero revolts include Meyer, *Cristero Rebellion*; and Bailey, *¡Viva Cristo Rey!* On the Cristiada in Jalisco, see Tuck, *Holy War*. See also Lecuona, *Constitucionalistas*. On the Cristero rebellions in Michoacán, see Purnell, *Popular Movements*.

30. Vaughan, *Cultural Politics*.

31. Becker, *Setting*. Cárdenas served first as governor of his home state of Michoacán from 1928–32, then as president of Mexico from 1934–40. He was the father of the Jefe de govierno (akin to mayor) of the Federal District of Mexico City (1997–99) and presidential candidate in 1994 and 2000, Cuauhtémoc Cárdenas.

32. Padua, *Educación*.

33. Meyer and Sherman, *Course of Mexican History*, 600. For regional statistics on land use in the central Cristero state of Jalisco, see Arias and Rivas, *Estadística*. On rural migrations primarily to the United States in a more recent period in the history of Jalisco, see Alejandre, *Migración*; and Girón, *Sólo Dios*.

34. Meyer and Sherman, *Course of Mexican History*, 609. See also Gamio, *Mexican Immigration*, 34.

35. Although he focuses more on the effects of the U.S. repatriation of Mexicans on Mexican nationalism in Mexico, Dennis Nodín Valdés offers some insight for considering Mexican nationalism in Chicago during this period. See Valdés, "Mexican Revolutionary." On the issue of regionalism in Mexican nationalism, see Lomnitz-Adler, *Exits*.

36. Mark Reisler argues that the intensive lobbying of industry to exempt Mexicans from the restrictive immigration legislations of 1921 and 1924 increased the demand for Mexican labor in the United States. See Reisler, "Mexican Immigrant."

37. As yet, we have no comprehensive study of the relationships between the Cristero wars and Mexican immigration to Chicago or to the United States more generally. Manuel Gamio began to sketch out this kind of information nearly eighty years ago. See Gamio, *Mexican Immigration*, chap. 2.

38. As Vicki L. Ruiz points out, precise population and immigration figures for Mexicans in the United States between 1900 and 1930 do not exist. Contemporary estimates and census figures are complicated by several factors, including inability to separate those born in the United States and those born in Mexico. The census category of "Mexican" that appeared in 1930 did not make this distinction, and to complicate matters further, the category disappeared again in the 1940 census. Current historians calculate a range of estimates as to the numbers of Mexicans migrating to the United States between 1910 and 1930. Ricardo Romo and Albert Camarillo rely on there being about one million; George Sánchez and David Gutíerrez estimate around 1.5 million. See Ruiz, *From Out of the Shadows*, 162; Romo, *East Los Angeles*, 42, 61; Camarillo, *Chicanos*, 200–201; Sánchez, *Becoming*, 18; and Gutiérrez, *Walls and Mirrors*.

39. Montejano, *Anglos and Mexicans*, esp. pt. 3; Foley, *White Scourge*, esp. chap. 2; Sánchez, *Becoming*.

40. In part, this pattern helps to explain why nearly all of the small number of studies of Mexicans focus on the region and few on the cities themselves. See Reisler, *By the Sweat*; Rosales, "Mexican Immigration"; Valdés, *Al Norte*; and García, *Mexicans*. Zaragosa Vargas frames the centrality of Detroit, though his work is broadly regional. Dennis Valdés locates his second study in St. Paul, Minnesota, though it too hangs in a regional frame. Vargas, *Proletarians*; Valdés, *Barrios Norteños*.

41. Cardoso, *Mexican Emigration*, 9–11.

42. Garcilazo, "*Traqueros*," 70.

43. Taylor, *Mexican Labor*, 28. Although the total workforce grew to 1,178 by 1915, Mexicans comprised less than half the 1910 total. See also Garcilazo, "*Traqueros*," esp. chap. 2 on the immigration and labor-recruitment experiences of *traqueros* throughout the Southwest and Midwest.

44. Valdés, *Barrios Norteños*. See also Valdés, "Betabeleros"; and Wilson, "Historical Development."

45. Workers were recruited from border towns like El Paso and Laredo and from areas further inland like Chihuahua and Zacatecas. Taylor, *Mexican Labor*, 33–34.

46. Kerr, "Chicano Experience," chap. 2; Taylor, *Mexican Labor*, chap. 1.

47. Rosáles, "Regional Origins," 187. See also Rosáles, "Mexican Immigration." Anita Edgar Jones suggests that 61 percent of the 1,151 Mexicans registered with the Immigrants' Protective League in 1927 were from Michoacán, Guanajuato, Jalisco, and Zacatecas. Jones, "Conditions."

48. Mendoza, "Creation"; Garcilazo, *"Traqueros"*; Leftwich, "Migratory Harvest"; Laird, "Argentine, Kansas"; Palmer, "Building."

49. The most recent synthesis of research on Mexicans in the Midwest is García, *Mexicans.* His earliest published work is García, "History." See also García's dated but still useful state-of-the-discipline article, "Midwest Mexicanos"; Cárdenas, "Desarrigados"; and Weeks and Benítez, "Cultural Demography."

50. "Life History of Ladislao Duran," Robert Redfield Papers.

51. Very likely, he was one of the many Mexican cotton workers highlighted in Neil Foley's study of east Texas. Foley, *White Scourge.*

52. Jones "Conditions," 78.

53. Data gleaned from Juan Manuel Gómez, Declaration of Intention No. 69270, Petition for Naturalization No. 141606, National Archives and Records Administration (herafter NARA).

54. Dennis Valdéz cites many contemporary sources concerned with the problems of Mexican child labor in the beet fields. See, for instance, Armentrout, Brown, and Gibbon, *Child Labor;* and Johnson, "Wages."

55. American Beet Sugar Company, *El Cultivo de Betabel: Manual Para los Trabajadores* (1929), Paul S. Taylor Papers.

56. Ruth Camblón interview, November 29, 1924, Robert Redfield Papers. On Mexicans in cotton-field work, see Foley, *White Scourge.*

57. Jones, "Mexican Colonies," 589.

58. Ibid.

59. American Beet Sugar Company, "A Nuestros Trabajadores," August 19, 1926, Paul S. Taylor Papers.

60. Jones, "Conditions," 83.

61. Story constructed from excerpts of United Charities case notes given to Robert Redfield, November 1924, Robert Redfield Papers. Redfield's notes indicate that Mrs. Mendoza and Mrs. Juariga were pregnant in November 1924; both were delivered by their husbands without midwives (who would have cost fifteen dollars for each birth).

62. Mr. Belcher Interview, November 19, 1924, Robert Redfield Papers. The factory was at 711 West Harrison.

63. Jeff Garcilazo discusses a similar phenomenon, couched in terms of "casual labor" and "common labor," that rendered Mexican rail workers invisible and interchangeable. Garcilazo, *"Traqueros,"* 4–7 and chap. 2.

64. Jones, "Mexican Colonies," 591.

65. Ibid.

66. Jones, "Conditions," 78.

67. Salvador Zavala Interview, October 31, 1924, Robert Redfield Papers. Zavala's father "owned some property" and bought and sold corn in their hometown of Xasipítio, Guanajuato, about eighty miles from the state capital of Guanajuato. Salvador had left school to come to Chicago.

68. Salvador Zavala interview, October 31, 1924, Redfield Journal 1924–25, box 59, p. 21, Robert Redfield Papers.

69. He was arrested and killed at an "alleged disorderly house" at 9170 Houston Avenue in South Chicago. Chicago Police Dept. Homicide Report Index, 1870–1930, vol. 4, p. 170A, Illinois Regional Archive Depository.

70. Registration included birthplace, age, marital status, and occupation. "Matriculas. Departamento Consular, 1929–30," IV-102-029, Archivo Histórico de la Secretaria de Relaciónes Exteriories. There is some evidence that another of Salvador's five brothers, Eduardo, also came to Chicago with his wife (María Soledad Herrejon Vda. de Zavala) and registered the births of two sons in Chicago with the Mexican consulate. However, the registrations only indicate that this Zavala was born outside of Guanajuato, so it is not clear whether this was another Zavala brother from Xasipítio. Moreover, María registered her name as "Vda," indicating *viuda* (widow) of Zavala. Perhaps Eduardo died before the family registered the children?

71. Mr. Gutiérrez interview, April 16, 1925, Robert Redfield Papers.

72. Weber, "Anglo Views."

73. The Mexican foreign secretary's office issued a directive in 1930 to this effect. See "Dirección General de Aduanas, Informe sobre mujeres que viajan solas," April 3, 1930, IV-169-17, Archivo Histórico de la Secretaria de Relaciónes Exteriores. On the mobility of women during armed conflicts in Mexico, see Salas, *Soldaderas.* On women's mobility into and within Chicago, see Meyerowitz, *Women Adrift.*

74. Fortunata Ramos, Petition for Naturalization No. 198069, NARA.

75. Jones, "Conditions"; Manuel Bueno, "The Mexican in Chicago" (1924), Ernest W. Burgess Papers; Houghteling, *Income.*

76. Manuel Bueno, "The Mexican in Chicago" (1924), Ernest W. Burgess Papers. The study did not, however, determine how many of these were married or single men. Nor did it indicate whether those with families in Chicago were married or single.

77. U.S. Bureau of the Census, *Abstract of the Fifteenth Census;* Burgess and Newcomb, *Census Data, 1930.*

78. As Kathleen Neils Conzen has suggested, if there were twenty thousand Mexicans in Chicago in 1930, given the high levels of turnover, it would be interesting to consider how many different Mexicans may have experienced life in Chicago during the 1920s (personal communication with the author, 1997). Unfortunately, the scarcity of data does not currently allow for this kind of analysis.

79. Burgess and Newcomb, *Census Data, 1930,* comparing their 1933 edition based on the 1930 census and their 1934 edition based on new research. The population of Cook County in 1910: 2,405,233; 1920: 3,053,017; 1930: 3,982,123; 1940: 4,063,342. U.S. Bureau of the Census, *Population Abstract.* Again, confusion created by the 1930 census category of "Mexican" and the lack of information on foreign-born as opposed to U.S.–born Mexicans also prevents determining what percentage of the Mexican population in Chicago (foreign-born or "native") was female. The Consul of Mexico stationed in Chicago estimated upwards of forty-five thousand Mexicans in his jurisdiction (Milwaukee to Gary, Indiana, across to Rockford, Illinois). Interview with Mexican Consul in Chicago, September 30, 1926, box 3, folder 14, Manuel Gamio Papers.

80. Luis Lupián Interview, July 21, 1926, box 3, folder 11, Manuel Gamio Papers.

81. Ibid.

82. George C. Kiser and Mary W. Kiser indicate that repatriations, voluntary and forced, occurred in the early 1920s as well as the more commonly known deportations of the 1930s. See Kiser and Kiser, *Mexican Workers*. On the deportation of Mexicans during the 1930s, see Hoffman, *Unwanted Mexicans;* Balderrama and Rodríguez, *Decade of Betrayal*. On repatriations in the Midwest in particular, see Reisler, *By the Sweat;* Betten and Mohl, "From Discrimination to Repatriation"; and Simon, "Mexican Repatriation."

83. Perhaps this distrust of official institutions was related to their experiences with crumbling and corrupt governmental and political structures in Mexico during the revolutionary years. Perhaps it was also tied to more localized political cultures and ideologies. See Lomnitz-Adler, *Exits;* Joseph and Nugent, *Everyday Forms*.

84. Hughes, *Illinois Persons*.

85. George Edson, "Mexicans in Chicago" (1926), Bureau of Labor Statistics, U.S. Dept. of Labor, Paul S. Taylor Papers.

86. Reisler, *By the Sweat;* Betten and Mohl, "From Discrimination to Repatriation"; Simon, "Mexican Repatriation."

87. This does raise the question, as yet unanswered, of what percentage of these men actually registered with the consulate and why they registered. My research indicates that some believed that registration would help to protect them from discrimination and forcible deportation. Those who owned small businesses also seemed to hope that the consulate would offer some protection. Perhaps this indicates that a more conservative element of the single-male population was registering.

88. In fact, none of the studies on the single Mexican male population in Chicago systematically looked at the ages of these men, which is surprising given the attention paid to civic order, juvenile delinquency, and reform during this period. See Baur, "Delinquency"; Tanenhaus, *Juvenile Justice;* and Willrich, *City of Courts*.

89. "Departamento de Asuntos Comerciales y de Protección, 1929: Matriculas, Chicago," IV-102-29, Archivo Histórico de la Secretaria de Relaciónes Exteriores; "Departamento de Asuntos Comerciales y de Protección, 1935: Matriculas, Chicago," IV-102-29, Archivo Histórico de la Secretaria de Relaciónes Exteriores. Of course, it is difficult to draw any definite conclusions from these observations because of the element of self-selection involved in those who opted to register with the consulate. Nevertheless, it continues to be significant to the Mexican experience in Chicago during this period that so many "older" single men remained in the population even during the 1930s.

90. Ramiro Estrada, Declaration of Intention No. 77554, Petition for Naturalization No. 11491, NARA.

91. Gonzalo Sánchez Velásquez, Declaration of Intention No. 139178, Petition for Naturalization No. 224422, NARA.

92. Librado Ramírez, Declaration of Intention No. 139421, Petition for Naturalization No. 230047, NARA.

93. Also recorded in the birth records were the names of the father, his country of origin, and the mother's name. All of the fathers recorded in this sample year were from Mexico. While the mothers registered their full maiden names and all

had Spanish names, there was no indication of their country of origin. "Registro de Nacimientos en Chicago" (1929), IV-271-69, Archivo Histórico de la Secretaria de Relaciónes Exteriores.

94. Elena Salcedo de Gutiérrez, Declaration of Intention No. 132293, Petition for Naturalization No. 200010, NARA.

95. This kin group's registered births and locations of those births indicate that Consuelo's immediate family had been in Chicago fairly regularly at least from 1925.

96. "Registro de Nacimientos en Chicago" (1929), IV-271-69, Archivo Histórico de la Secretaria de Relaciónes Exteriores.

97. The consul records indicate Viviano was born in December 1926, but this would have been nearly impossible, since his older brother was supposedly born in June 1926. It is more likely that Viviano was born in December 1927, and I have indicated this in table 1.2. Either way, two sons were born to the family during that three-year span.

98. Hughes, *Illinois Persons*, 15.

99. Declaration of Intention No. 115119, Petition for Naturalization No. 178708, NARA. Guadalupe's first wife also died, though the records do not state either when or why.

100. Antonio Iniguez, Petition for Naturalization No. 179724, NARA.

101. Valdés, *Al Norte*. Valdés suggests that the rural-urban connections between the beet fields and large urban centers like Chicago and Detroit were symbiotic. The fields provided work when times were tight in the cities, while the cities provided beet workers shelter and job opportunities over the winter. A more systematic study of these patterns would significantly strengthen Valdés's point.

102. Jones, "Conditions," 84.

Chapter 2: Mexican Chicago

1. The terms "white" and "black" were in current usage in Chicago during this era. "Colored" and "Negro" were also employed interchangeably with "black." Unless the speaker, writer, or document employs another term, I use "Black" throughout most of this book. I do so with an awareness, however, of the constructedness of this term as well as the varieties of people who could be categorized or treated as "Black."

2. Cook County (Ill.) Coroner, *Race Riots*, 20. The Chicago Commission on Race Relations Report described Eugene Williams as "a Negro boy of seventeen." *Report of the Chicago Commission on Race Relations* (1922), City of Chicago, Special Collections, Regenstein Library, University of Chicago.

3. Ibid., 20.

4. Numbers quoted are from ibid., 31–32. Race riots exploded in many places in the United States during the "red summer" of 1919, including Charleston, South Carolina (May), Longview and Gregg Counties, Texas (July), and Washington, D.C. (July 19–23). For a classic narrative of Chicago's red summer, see Tuttle, *Race Riots*.

5. *Chicago Tribune*, July 27, 1919, through August 3, 1919; *Chicago Defender*, July 27, 1919, through August 3, 1919; Cook County (Ill.) Coroner, *Race Riots*;

Report of the Chicago Commission on Race Relations (1922), City of Chicago, Special Collections, Regenstein Library, University of Chicago.

6. U.S. State Department Records, Record Group 59, folder 311.121, record 71, U.S. National Archives.

7. Cook County (Ill.) Coroner, *Race Riots,* 31–32. Ironically, José's last name means "white" in Spanish.

8. Vice Consul's Report for June 1919, 17-14-146, Archivo Histórico de la Secretaria de Relaciónes Exteriores. The report is dated June, but it contains information pertaining to activities throughout the summer.

9. Holt, "Explaining Racism," 117–18.

10. See, for example, Spinney, *City of Big Shoulders,* esp. 171–74; Horowitz, *"Negro and White";* and Halpern, *Down on the Killing Floor.* In a front-page story on the NAACP's statement about the riots in Chicago, the *Cleveland Advocate* (a Black newspaper) briefly mentioned whites being indicted for killing a Mexican who they mistook for a Black man, but only as a set-up for the unjustness of thirty Blacks being indicted for their roles in the rioting. The headline read, "Chicago Has Outdone Mississippi in Unjust Treatment." No other mention or discussion of the Mexican followed. See the *Cleveland Advocate,* August 16, 1919, 1. The phrasing and concept of "ethno-racial" I have borrowed from Neil Foley. He argues that Mexicans in Texas hovered in the ethno-racial borderlands between whiteness and blackness. Foley, *White Scourge.*

11. Holt, "Marking."

12. The largest of the Polish neighborhoods stretched along Milwaukee Avenue. Poles also settled in the Bridgeport area. Pacyga, *Polish Immigrants;* Kantowicz, *Polish-American Politics.* For an interesting study on the housing and architecture of these neighborhoods, see Biggott, *From Cottage to Bungalow,* esp. chap. 4. On the migration of Poles to Chicago, see Erdmans, *Opposite Poles.*

13. I have surveyed the recently released 1930 Manuscript Census for the Chicago areas of the Near West Side, Packingtown (broadly defined), and South Chicago. Occasionally Mexicans predominated in specific city blocks, but those blocks were always sandwiched between residents of many other groups.

14. Mexican settlements in Chicago largely developed around specific local employers and among particular ethnic groups, which might suggest the development of distinctive neighborhood characteristics. Kerr makes this argument about the three major areas of Mexican settlement. I agree with her that this occurred by the 1950s, but not by 1939. See Kerr, "Chicano Experience." However, during the 1920s, Mexican migration patterns, the revolutionary context out of which they emerged, and their motivations for leaving Mexico all contributed to a dynamic and mobile group of people who lacked strong commitments toward settling down long-term in Chicago. During the economic crunch and deportations of the 1930s, this ambivalence remained, as Mexicans found their lives in Chicago shaped by much stronger pressures.

15. Kerr, "Chicano Experience," chap. 1; McCarthy, "Which Christ," 253–56.

16. Bird Memorial was located at 9135 Brandon Avenue; Friendship Center was nearby at 9124 Houston Avenue. See Kerr, "Chicano Experience," chap. 1; McCarthy, "Which Christ," 138–40.

17. For a more extensive discussion of settlement-house work and the social workers who worked with Mexicans, see chapter 3.

18. Ganz and Strobel, *Pots of Promise.*

19. Unnamed Spanish-language newspaper, June 2, 1938, trans. Nicolás Hernández, box 40, folder I M/IV, WPA Foreign Language Press Survey Papers.

20. Martínez, "Bordering."

21. Jones, "Conditions," 92.

22. Ibid., 90.

23. Ibid., 51.

24. Miss Garvey interview, Journal, November 3, 1924, pp. 31–32; and Miss Stanton interview, Journal, October 20, 1924, p. 16, Robert Redfield Papers. Miss Garvey was Irish-born and a devout Catholic. There is no indication how long this small mission lasted, particularly as it was not officially recognized, as noted by Redfield and later confirmed by McCarthy, "Which Christ," 257–59.

25. Jones, "Conditions," 91–92; Kerr, "Chicano Experience," chap. 1; McCarthy, "Which Christ," 204–14.

26. Mexicans had been excluded from local Polish and Slovakian parishes. The chapel was founded by Spanish Claretian priests and later staffed in 1929 by Cordi-Marian sisters who were ejected from Mexico during the anticlerical purges of the Cristeros. See Kerr, "Chicano Experience," 56. See also McCarthy, "Which Christ," 208–9.

27. Jones, "Conditions," 42–44; Houghteling, *Income;* Taylor, *Mexican Labor,* 181–86, 260–62.

28. Redfield Comments on Quintero Family interview, November 1924, Robert Redfield Papers.

29. Quintero Family interview, November 1924, Robert Redfield Papers.

30. "Life History of Ladislao Durán," Robert Redfield Papers.

31. Jones, "Mexican Colonies," 596.

32. Robert Jones, "The Religious Life of the Mexican in Chicago," n.d. (data from 1928), Robert Redfield Papers; Kerr, "Chicano Experience," chap. 3.

33. Jones, "Conditions," 42.

34. Pacyga and Skerrett, *Chicago,* 199.

35. Anita Jones surveyed enrollments at the elementary schools in the area: 143 at St. Francis, 105 at Dante, 97 at Foster, 88 at Goodrich, 87 at Dore, 76 at Garfield, 62 at Jackson, and 14 at Guardian Angels. Jones, "Mexican Colonies," 582–83.

36. Robert Jones, "The Religious Life of Mexicans in Chicago," n.d. (data from 1928), Robert Redfield Papers.

37. Jones, "Conditions," 121.

38. Field Notes, Journal 1924–25, Robert Redfield Papers. The Jews had settled in Brighton Park in the 1890s, the Poles in the first decade of the twentieth century. See Pacyga and Skerrett, *Chicago;* Holli and Jones, *Ethnic Frontier.*

39. Robert Jones, "The Religious Life of Mexicans in Chicago," n.d. (data from 1928), Robert Redfield Papers. The Crane Company (at 4100 South Kedzie) employed an estimated 450 to 500 Mexicans in the manufacturing of plumbing supplies. Most worked in the foundry, mill room, or on the track gang. In the foundry, they earned wages of forty-nine cents per hour; after a month they were often given raises to fifty-four cents per hour. In the Santa Fe roundhouse, Mexican men worked as fire-knockers, blacksmith helpers, and wipers on the day shifts. On the night shifts, they were boiler-washers and pitmen. The highest-paid jobs

were the stationary fireman (one Mexican in 1929) at fifty-five cents an hour; lowest were the pitmen at forty-one cents per hour. George Edson, "Mexicans in Chicago" (1926), Bureau of Labor Statistics, U.S. Dept. of Labor, Paul S. Taylor Papers.

40. Jones, "Conditions," 121.

41. Field Notes, Journal 1924–25, Robert Redfield Papers.

42. Mrs. McAvoy interview, November 16, 1924, Robert Redfield Papers. It is unclear from the interview whether she charged Mena rent for the storefront schoolroom, but from the tone of the conversation, it sounded as though she did not and only allowed him to use the space until she could find a merchant to rent it.

43. Field Notes, Journal 1924–25, Robert Redfield Papers.

44. This was often referred to on maps of the time as Corwith Yards and fell roughly in the greater Packingtown area. For a study on the *traqueros* (trackworkers) who lived in boxcar colonies traveling through the nation's midsection, see Garcilazo, "*Traqueros.*"

45. Ibid.

46. Field Notes, Journal 1924–25, Robert Redfield Papers.

47. Alexander Street ran west to east between Twenty-second and West Twenty-third. It is six blocks east of Halsted, one block west of LaSalle, and thirteen blocks north of Armour Square. Description from Miss Garvey interview, 1925, Journal, Robert Redfield Papers.

48. Miss Garvey interview, January 10, 1925, Journal, Robert Redfield Papers.

49. Ibid.

50. Jones, "Conditions," 118–21.

51. For a discussion on the multiple functions pool halls served for Mexicans throughout the Midwest, see García, *Mexicans;* and Valdés, *Barrios.*

52. Robert Jones, "The Religious Life of Mexicans in Chicago," n.d. (data from 1928), Robert Redfield Papers.

53. Interview, Unnamed Mexican Man, 1928, by Paul S. Taylor, box 1, Paul S. Taylor Papers.

54. Quoted in Taylor, *Mexican Labor,* 221.

55. Interview with Sr. Carlos Pérez López, clerk in men's clothing store, in South Chicago, June 27, 1926, box 2, folder 13, Manuel Gamio Papers. Ironically, during the late 1920s and early 1930s, a sizable population of Polish agricultural workers from Varsonia, Poland, sought refuge in Mexico. The Mexican consul in Poland argued for the Mexican government to help these industrious souls with land grants as had Brazil and Peru. The final decision allowed the Poles to immigrate and settle in unpopulated areas, but no land would be given outright. The letters do not indicate if these families were Jewish, but the consul in Varsonia did point out that 990 of the 1,047 visas he issued in the previous five years were for Jews. Given events in Europe, it is possible that these were Jewish families fleeing rising anti-Semitism. See the series of letters between Mexican consuls in Poland and Mexico, Departamento Consular, 1931: "Inmigración," IV-395-50, Archivo Histórico de la Secretaria de Relaciónes Exteriores.

56. *México* (Chicago), September 11, 1926, 4.

57. Manuel Bueno, "The Mexican in Chicago" (1924), Ernest W. Burgess Papers.

58. *México* (Chicago), January 8, 1927, box 1, Paul S. Taylor Papers.

59. Taylor, *Mexican Labor*, 222. See also Slayton, *Back of the Yards*, 35–37.

60. Quoted in Taylor, *Mexican Labor*, 222.

61. Field Notes, November 1, 1924, Robert Redfield Papers.

62. Jones, "Mexican Colonies"; Kerr, "Chicano Experience." On the Irish, see McCaffrey, Skerrett, Funchion, and Fanning, *Irish in Chicago.*

63. Taylor, *Mexican Labor*, 223. Gross Street was renamed McDowell Street in the late 1930s in honor of Mary McDowell, who headed the University of Chicago Settlement House for many years.

64. Davis Square Park (established 1907) is at Forty-fifth and Marshfield; Cornell Square Park (established 1905), the second park in the area, is at West Fifty-first and Wood. Both had field houses, locker rooms, showers, game rooms, educational classes, outdoor swimming pools, and athletic fields.

65. Jones, "Conditions," 51. A park employee estimated that Mexicans took a total of about five thousand baths per month in the winter and more in the summer.

66. See, for instance, Jacobson, *Whiteness*, esp. chaps. 2 and 3.

67. Taylor, *Mexican Labor*, 222.

68. Jewish Real Estate Officer interview, November 16, 1924, Robert Redfield Papers.

69. Ibid.

70. Taylor, *Mexican Labor*, 225.

71. I discuss the issue of language and its ties to class among Chicago's Mexicans in chapter 4.

72. Tuttle, *Race Riot.*

73. Jones, "Conditions," 121–22.

74. Unidentified desk sergent interview, South Chicago Police Station, January 10, 1925, Robert Redfield Papers.

75. Illinois Steel recruited a group of Mexicans in 1923 from Fort Worth, Texas. See Jones, "Mexican Colonies," 585.

76. George Edson, "Mexicans in Chicago" (1926), Bureau of Labor Statistics, U.S. Dept. of Labor, Paul S. Taylor Papers. Raymond Nelson of the Chicago Congregational Ministry also conducted interviews and research on the area. The estimates of the number of Mexicans in South Chicago he collected include Father Tort, a priest at the Mexican Catholic church in South Chicago: eight thousand; Mr. A. Reed, the industrial secretary of the South Chicago YMCA: five thousand; Reverend O'Neil, the pastor of the Mexican Methodist church: four thousand. Raymond Nelson, "The Mexican in South Chicago," box 1, folder "Mexican Life in Chicago," p. 7, Paul S. Taylor Papers.

77. On the details of the establishment and growth of Bird Memorial, see McCarthy, "Which Christ," 136–38.

78. Raymond Nelson, "The Mexican in South Chicago," box 1, folder "Mexican Life in Chicago," pp. 30–32, Paul S. Taylor Papers; Jones, "Conditions," 52, 106. See also Jones, "Mexican Colonies."

79. Field Notes, April 1925, Robert Redfield Papers.

80. Jones, "Conditions," 119.

81. Ibid. I have found no evidence of why the restaurant moved. Perhaps it was a bigger venue or the rent was cheaper.

82. Field Notes, January 10, 1925, Robert Redfield Papers.

83. Unidentified resident quoted in Field Notes, January 10, 1925, Robert Redfield Papers. Another boxcar camp was reported along the Rock Island tracks further south at 123rd and Vincennes. Dr. Mary Gregg interview, March 30, 1925, Robert Redfield Papers.

84. Field Notes, April 1925, Robert Redfield Papers.

85. Field Notes, April 1925, Robert Redfield Papers.

86. Tamalina was the brand name of the *mixtamal* flour used in tamales, manufactured in México; *piloncillo* is a hard sugar confection made from unrefined cane sugar; *metates* are wide flat stones used primarily for grinding corn; *molcajetes* are much like a mortar and pestle made from volcanic stone used to grind spices.

87. *México* (Chicago), June 21, 1927. This newspaper was established January 18, 1924, and ran weekly or triweekly until December 18, 1930, when Sam Fraga, the editor, renamed it *El Nacional*. The paper folded sometime in 1935. Very few original copies or microfilmed editions survive.

88. Jones, "Mexican Colonies," 597.

89. As Louise Kerr points out, this had the ironic effect of concentrating Mexicans in a small area, which eventually gave them a solid power base after World War II. Kerr, "Chicano Experience," 69–115.

90. Max Guzmán interview.

91. Raymond Nelson, "The Mexican in South Chicago," box 1, folder "Mexican Life in Chicago," p. 14, Paul S. Taylor Papers.

92. Henry A. Matushek interview, by Raymond Nelson (1928), "The Mexican in South Chicago," box 1, folder "Mexican Life in Chicago," Paul S. Taylor Papers.

93. For more on "being Mexican," see chapter 5.

94. United Charities Case Notes, January 10, 1925, Robert Redfield Papers.

95. United Charities Case Notes, November 1924, Robert Redfield Papers. Dekoven Street runs east-west between the river on the east and Halsted on the west; 800 West is Halsted, and Dekoven is at about 1000 South (south of Taylor, north of Twelfth Street). The Great Chicago Fire of 1871 supposedly started at either 137 or 558 DeKoven (accounts vary) in Mrs. O'Leary's barn, just down the street from where this extended family was living.

96. Manuel and Alma Bravo interview.

97. United Charities Case of Placida and Severna Gonzáles, February 17, 1929, box 59, folder 2, Robert Redfield Papers.

98. George Edson, "Mexicans in Chicago" (1926), Bureau of Labor Statistics, U.S. Dept. of Labor, Paul S. Taylor Papers.

99. Grossman, *Land of Hope*; Trotter, *Great Migration*.

100. Pacyga, *Polish Immigrants*.

101. Field Notes for Hughes and Walcott, Dept. of Public Welfare Housing Survey, February 14, 1925, Robert Redfield Papers.

102. Clementina Rodríguez interview. "Prietito" refers to Blacks or people with very dark skin. In Mexico it can also refer to someone from Veracrúz, which has a notable population of Afro-Mexicans.

103. Journal, 1924–25, Robert Redfield Papers.

104. Unidentified desk sergeant interview, South Chicago Police Station, January 10, 1925, Robert Redfield Papers.

105. Mr. Parkin interview, January 21, 1925, Robert Redfield Papers. Parkin and O'Neil ministered to Mexicans at several churches in Chicago. This interview took place at the Methodist church at 9115 Houston Avenue in South Chicago.

106. *La Defensa* (Chicago), August 22, 1936, box 40 trans. WPA Foreign Language Press Survey Papers.

107. Cook County (Ill.) Coroner, *Race Riots,* 31–32; also quoted in *México* (Chicago), January 1924, Robert Redfield Papers. It is unclear from the reports if this was part of a more formal ganglike turf war. See also Near West Side, 1938, Chicago Area Project Papers.

108. Mary McDowell of the University of Chicago Settlement House and Jane Addams of Hull-House testified to the involvement of Ragen's Colts in the gang violence of the 1919 race riots. See the *Report of the Chicago Commission on Race Relations* (1922), City of Chicago, Special Collections, Regenstein Library, University of Chicago, 55. Ragen's Colts patrolled an area bounded by Cottage Grove on the West, Ashland on the East, Forty-third Street on the north, and Sixty-third Street on the south. On Ragen's Colts, see also Landisco, *Organized Crime,* 171.

109. *Report of the Chicago Commission on Race Relations* (1922), City of Chicago, Special Collections, Regenstein Library, University of Chicago. See also Tuttle, *Race Riot.*

110. *Report of the Chicago Commission on Race Relations* (1922), City of Chicago, Special Collections, Regenstein Library, University of Chicago, 15. Contemporary researchers, reformers, and social workers focused a great deal on youth gangs in Chicago. Foundational works emerged in Chicago School urban studies, including Thrasher, *The Gang.*

111. See *Report of the Chicago Commission on Race Relations* (1922), City of Chicago, Special Collections, Regenstein Library, University of Chicago, 28; and Thrasher, *The Gang.*

112. Daley later became a state senator and mayor of Chicago, in office from 1955–76. His son Richard also became mayor and still serves as mayor of Chicago.

113. Taylor, *Mexican Labor,* 222.

114. *La Lucha* (Chicago), April 28, 1934, box 40, WPA Foreign Language Press Survey Papers.

115. See Balderrama and Rodríguez, *Decade of Betrayal;* Hoffman, *Unwanted Mexicans.*

116. George Edson, "Mexicans in Chicago" (1926), Bureau of Labor Statistics, U.S. Dept. of Labor, p. 13, Paul S. Taylor Papers.

117. *México* (Chicago), January 23, 1927.

118. *La Noticia Mundial* (Chicago), August 29, 1927, box 1, folder: "Notes on Mexican Newspapers in Chicago," trans. Paul Taylor, Paul S. Taylor Papers.

119. Stern, "Buildings."

120. Quoted in ibid., 6–9.

121. Quoted in Taylor, *Mexican Labor,* 110.

122. Ibid., 113. On Mexicans "passing" for Spanish or white, see chapter 4.

123. An *enganchista* is a labor recruiter. The appellation has negative connotations similar to "unsavory." Spanish-language newspapers were filled with derisive accounts of the practices of these agents and often warned their readers against signing up with them.

124. Or even that they were American Blacks, for that matter. They could have been Afro-Mexicans or Afro-Cubans.

125. Taylor, *Mexican Labor,* 113.

126. See Balderrama and Rodríguez, *Decade of Betrayal;* Hoffman, *Unwanted Mexicans.*

127. Kerr, "Chicano Experience," chap. 3; Kiser and Kiser, *Mexican Workers,* chap. 2.

128. Benny Rodríguez interview.

129. This was in spite of a long tradition of Mexican labor activism in Mexico. On this and on those Mexicans who did join union efforts, see Vargas, *Labor Rights;* and Hernandez-Fujisaki, "Mexican Steelworkers"; also briefly noted in Halpern, *Down on the Killing Floor,* 82.

130. See Guzmán's testimony before the La Follette Senate subcommittee investigating the Memorial Day Massacre of 1937. U.S. Senate, "Resolution," 4944.

131. "Mexican Committee, 1937," box 6, folder 7, George Patterson Papers. The extent of Alcala's involvement with the SWOC remains undetermined, as the record is thin. His father, Pablo Alcala, became a U.S. citizen in 1941 (Petition for Naturalization No. 231579, NARA). Interestingly, Rubén Flores, the prominent figure in South Chicago who worked at the Tienda Colorada for many years, served as Pablo's witness in his application for citizenship.

132. Balderrama and Rodríguez, *Decade of Betrayal,* 216.

133. "Sunday Afternoon Discussion Group," August 5, 1936, Mary McDowell Papers.

134. Raymond Nelson, "The Mexican in South Chicago," box 1, Paul S. Taylor Papers.

135. Quoted in Taylor, *Mexican Labor,* 122.

136. Benny Rodríguez interview.

137. Lucio Franco interview.

138. As George Lipsitz points out, this kind of legislation, along with the Social Security Act, also passed in the 1930s, by excluding farm workers and domestics effectively denies protection to sectors of the workforce that are overwhelmingly minority, which deprives a disproportionate number of minorities protections and benefits that are routinely afforded to whites. See Lipsitz, *Possessive Investment,* 5.

139. On Blacks as strikebreakers in the meatpacking strikes of 1921–22, see Street, "'Best Union Members.'"

140. Taylor, *Mexican Labor,* 229.

141. Ibid.

142. Ibid., 46–47.

143. Enciso, "No cuenten conmigo."

144. Kiser and Kiser, *Mexican Workers,* 33. See also Enciso, "No cuenten conmigo."

145. Mexicans often had much less control over their work schedules than their European ethnic neighbors. See Necoachea, "Customs and Resistance."

146. Mexicans in the steel industry advanced into skilled work at a lower rate than Blacks. What little advance was evident was into semiskilled positions. Taylor, *Mexican Labor,* 157.

147. Quoted in ibid., 158.

148. Quoted in ibid., 159.

149. Quoted in ibid., 158.

150. Noted by several contemporary observers, including Paul S. Taylor, Manuel Gamio, and Robert Redfield.

151. I explore this point more fully in chapter 3. On the connections between whiteness and Americanness, see King, *Making Americans;* and Jacobson, *Whiteness,* esp. chaps. 2 and 7.

152. For an insightful discussion of how immigrant labor is tied to identity politics and whiteness, see Lipsitz, *Possessive Investment,* esp. chap. 3.

153. Quoted in Taylor, *Mexican Labor,* 101.

154. Journal, 21, box 59, Robert Redfield Papers.

155. Journal, 23, box 59, Robert Redfield Papers.

156. Quoted in Taylor, *Mexican Labor,* 101.

157. Quoted in ibid., 103.

158. Jones, "Conditions," 121.

159. Journal, 23, box 59, Robert Redfield Papers.

160. Quoted in Taylor, *Mexican Labor,* 110.

161. Quoted in ibid., 126.

162. Quoted in ibid., 152. Taylor quotes the account from the *(Berkeley, Calif.) Daily Gazette,* July 10, 1931. I could find no mention of this incident in the consulate records in Mexico City, though they are disorganized and incomplete for this period. On the interaction of Mexicans and U.S. judicial structures during this period, see Rosales, *¡Pobre Raza!* Gilbert González focuses on the interventions of the Mexican government, through the Mexican consulate, in the lives of Mexicans in the United States, specifically in California. See Gonzáles, *Mexican Consuls.*

163. Henry A. Matushek interview (1928), in Raymond Nelson, "The Mexican in South Chicago," box 1, folder "Mexican Life in Chicago," Paul S. Taylor Papers.

164. "Mexican Labor in Chicago, Calumet Area," box 1, Paul S. Taylor Papers.

165. Tuttle, *Race Riot.*

166. Journal, 1924, Robert Redfield Papers.

167. Rembis, "Breeding"; Rembis, "'Explaining Sexual Life.'" See also Willrich, *City of Courts,* on the psychopathic court and the influence of eugenics on judges like Harry Olson; and Rosen, *Preaching Eugenics.*

168. Journal, box 59, Robert Redfield Papers. The Marshall Field mattress factory was located at 711 West Harrison.

169. For an excellent monograph on similar practices in the Texas cotton industry, see Foley, *White Scourge.*

170. On criminal justice in Chicago, see Tanenhaus, *Juvenile Justice;* and Willrich, *City of Courts.*

171. The treatment of the Mexicans by the Irish and Polish police could be read also as symptomatic of assertions of manhood under (perceived) assault. Such behaviors and attitudes could be yet another manifestation of groups jostling for position and power in the American ethno-racial orders. It is important to note that African Americans also were discriminated against by the police and the courts—unlike the situation of Mexicans, however, this was recognized at the time. See Chicago Commission on Race Relations, *Negro in Chicago,* 327–56.

172. On the legal construction of "white" and particularly of immigrants' attempts to use legal means to establish their whiteness, see López, *White by Law.*

173. Chicago Commission on Race Relations, *Negro in Chicago,* 599.

174. Quoted in Taylor, *Mexican Labor,* 150.

175. Pacyga, "To Live amongst Others." On Irish and Poles in the 1919 race riots, see also Pacyga, "Chicago's 1919 Race Riot."

176. When it came to police dealings with organized labor, however, they seemed not to be as discriminating when choosing whom to beat up. See accounts of the Memorial Day Massacre of May 1937, especially the testimony of Guadalupe "Lupe" Marshall, a Mexican woman member of the Women's Auxiliary of SWOC, before the La Follette subcommittee, June 30, July 1 and 2, 1937. U.S. Senate, "Resolution," 4945–57. SWOC resolved later that year to demand the removal of Chicago Chief of Police Allman and Police Captain Mooney.

177. Ibid.

178. Quoted in Taylor, *Mexican Labor,* 151.

179. Quoted in ibid.

180. *La Noticia Mundial* (Chicago), August 21, 1927, box 1, folder: "Notes on Mexican Newspapers in Chicago," trans. Paul Taylor, Paul S. Taylor Papers.

181. Sidney Levin interview.

182. Escobar, *Race, Police,* 80; and Woods, "Progressives and the Police," esp. chaps. 3–9.

183. Schmidt, "William E. Dever."

184. Bukowski, *Big Bill Thompson,* 158.

185. Rafael Guardado Valadez interview.

186. *México* (Chicago), December 11, 1926.

187. *México* (Chicago), January 22, 1927, Paul S. Taylor Papers.

188. *México* (Chicago), October 16, 1926, Paul S. Taylor Papers.

189. Slayton, *Back of the Yards,* 181–82.

190. *El Nacional* (Chicago), January 7, 1931, box 40, trans. WPA Foreign Language Press Survey Papers.

191. "Informes Sobre Protección, Rendidos Durante el Año, Consulado en Chicago," Departamento de Asuntos Comerciales y Protección, 1935, Archivo Histórico de la Secretaria de Relaciónes Exteriores.

192. See their testimony in U.S. Senate, "Resolution," 4941–57.

193. Ibid., 4942.

194. Guzmán was a member of the SWOC, and Marshall was an occasional social worker at Hull-House. U.S. Senate, "Resolution," 4950.

195. Warnshuis, "Crime and Criminal Justice," 284.

196. Ibid.

197. Taylor, *Mexican Labor,* 144. After reviewing the 1930 manuscript census for Chicago, it appears that these numbers are very conservative. The official census count of Mexicans in Chicago was really twenty-one thousand in 1930 (U.S. Bureau of the Census, *Abstract,* 98), but my research indicates the population ranged from twenty-five to thirty thousand; thus Mexicans constituted closer to 1 percent of the population. See also Mary McDowell Papers, folder 9.

198. Rosales, *¡Pobre Raza!,* 4 and chaps. 4–5.

199. *Correo Mexicano,* September 30, 1926, quoted in Taylor, *Mexican Labor,* 151. "Pettyfogger" refers to an unscrupulous, deceitful lawyer or any person

who practices chicanery. The term appears only in Taylor's translation of the Spanish.

200. Mr. Parkin interview, January 21, 1925, Robert Redfield Papers. Parkin ministered at the Methodist Mission, 9115 Houston Avenue in South Chicago.

201. Taylor, "Crime," 230–31; Reisler, *By the Sweat,* 110.

202. *México* (Chicago), December 11, 1926 and November 25, 1926, quoted in Taylor, "Crime," 231 (Taylor's translation).

203. Ibid., 232.

204. *México* (Chicago), April 11, 1925, quoted in Taylor, "Crime," 232–33 (Taylor's translation).

205. *México* (Chicago), January 18, 1924, trans. Paul Taylor, box 1, Paul S. Taylor Papers.

206. Almaguer, "Chicano Men." On masculinity in Mexico, see for example Prieur, "Domination and Desire," and Irwin, *Mexican Masculinitites.*

207. Carlos López interview, June 27, 1926, box 2, folder 13, Manuel Gamio Papers.

208. Journal, 1924–25, Robert Redfield Papers.

209. Jones, "Mexican Colonies," 597.

210. Taylor, *Mexican Labor,* 193.

211. Ibid.

212. Jones and Wilson Pamphlet, Robert Jones Papers, box 25, Mary McDowell Papers.

213. "Departamento de Asuntos Comerciales y del Proteccion: informes, durante año," December 1935, Archivo Histórico de la Secretaria de Relaciónes Exteriores.

214. Taylor, *Mexican Labor,* 146. It should be noted that during this period Mexicans were convicted of misdemeanors at higher rates than "American whites." My calculations, based on Taylor's table 18, indicate that 22.9 percent of "American whites" were convicted of misdemeanors, while 38.5 percent of Mexicans were convicted.

215. Justino and Caroline Cordero interview. For a photograph of their wedding at the Church of the Virgen de Guadalupe, see Jirasek and Tortolero, *Images,* 29.

216. Andres Guadalupe Rios, Petition for Naturalization No. 202658, NARA.

217. Undated document from box 98, folder 10, Ernest W. Burgess Papers.

218. Taylor, *Mexican Labor,* 194.

219. Ibid., 195.

220. *México* (Chicago), February 26, 1927.

221. Interview with Dr. Ablaza and Dr. Doroteo Solis Kabayao, in George Edson, "Mexicans in Chicago," Bureau of Labor Statistics, U.S. Dept. of Labor, p. 13, Paul S. Taylor Papers. Interestingly, these two were Filipino doctors. Perhaps as expressed in their outrage, they too were caught up in jostling for whiteness. For more on Filipinos, including those in Chicago, see Posadas, *Filipino Americans,* and Posadas and Guyotte, "'Life's a Gamble.'"

222. Such accounts, however, are rare. Field Notes from United Charities case files, January 1925, Robert Redfield Papers.

223. Taylor, *Mexican Labor,* 247.

224. In this use of "single," I am not referring to their marital status but merely

to the fact that they were unaccompanied. The distinction is necessary because many of the Mexican men in Chicago who had wives (and families) did not necessarily have them in Chicago, so their "single" status was somewhat ambiguous to contemporary observers.

225. Manuel Bueno, "The Mexican in Chicago" (1924), Ernest W. Burgess Papers.

226. Quoted in Taylor, *Mexican Labor,* 238.

227. García, *World of Its Own,* 207.

228. He expressed this view during an interview he was conducting with Agapita Flores and Ruth Flores Rucoba in 1982.

229. Florence Lyon Gaddis, "Conflict between Mexicans and Poles Living Near Ashland and 47th Street, Autumn 1928," box 142, Ernest W. Burgess Papers.

230. *México* (Chicago), November 1, 1925, Paul S. Taylor Papers.

231. *La Noticia Mundial* (Chicago), November 20 1927, Paul S. Taylor Papers (Taylor's translation).

232. Quoted in Taylor, *Mexican Labor,* 144. On the tendency of Mexican men to control their wives and their wives less frequently tolerating such control, see chapter 4.

233. Bederman, *Manliness and Civilization.* See also Rotondo, *American Manhood,* and Peck, *Reinventing Labor.*

234. Lipsitz, *Possessive Investment;* Roediger, *Towards the Abolition;* Frankenberg, "Local Whitenesses"; Harris, "Whiteness as Property"; López, *White by Law.*

235. Bederman, *Manliness and Civilization.*

236. Manuel Bueno, "The Mexican in Chicago" (1924), Ernest W. Burgess Papers.

237. Carlos López interview, June 27, 1926, box 2, folder 13, Manuel Gamio Papers.

238. Manuel Bueno, "The Mexican in Chicago" (1924), p. 17, Ernest W. Burgess Papers.

239. Ibid., 18.

240. Interview with Miss Stanton, case worker with United Charities and in charge of Mexican work at the Mary McDowell Settlement House, Journal, October 20, 1924, pp. 15–16, Robert Redfield Papers. On the Italians and the Catholic church in Chicago, see D'Agostino, "Missionaries," chap. 3.

241. The bank was located at Grand and Halsted Streets.

242. *México* (Chicago), April 5, 1930. "Colonia" was used interchangeably to mean community, neighborhood, or colony. Its meaning as "colony" emerged particularly in discussions of unifying the Mexican peoples of Chicago.

243. Interview with Mrs. McAvoy, November 16, 1924, Robert Redfield Papers.

244. Field Notes for Hughes and Walcott Dept. of Public Welfare Housing Survey, February 14, 1925, Robert Redfield Papers.

245. Quoted in Taylor, *Mexican Labor,* 164.

246. Quoted in ibid., 165.

247. Quoted in ibid., 164.

248. Ibid., 165.

249. Quoted in ibid., 164.

250. Robert Jones, "The Religious Life of Mexicans in Chicago," n.d. (data from 1928), Robert Redfield Papers.

251. *La Defensa* (Chicago), August 22, 1936, box 40, trans. WPA Foreign Language Press Survey Papers.

252. "Mexican Labor in Chicago, Calumet Area," 17, box 1, Paul S. Taylor Papers.

253. *Chicago Defender*, August 2, 1919, 1. The *Defender* was the major Black newspaper in Chicago.

254. M. R. Ibañez, "Annual Report of the Mexican Work at the University of Chicago Settlement House for the Year 1930–1931," Mary McDowell Papers.

255. Quoted in Taylor, *Mexican Labor*, 221.

256. Mrs. McAvoy interview, November 16, 1924, Robert Redfield Papers.

257. John L. Brown, "Survey of Back-of-the-Yards, June 1938," p. 4, Chicago Area Project Papers.

258. On the ongoing construction of whiteness in relation to European groups, see Jacobsen, *Whiteness*.

259. Ehlalie Appelt wrote to the Mexican ambassador in Washington, D.C., who then forwarded the letter to the Foreign Relations office in Mexico City. That office translated the handwritten letter from German into Spanish and sent the translation to the Mexican consul in Chicago. The original letter is dated August 25, 1929, IV-75-28, Archivo Histórico de la Secretaria de Relaciónes Exteriores.

260. *México* (Chicago), January 9, 1929.

261. On "inbetweenness," see Barrett and Roediger, "Inbetween Peoples." I focus explicitly on the question of citizenship and "inbetweenness" in chapter 5.

Chapter 3: The Mexican Problem

1. "Americanismo," *México* (Chicago), June 5, 1926.

2. George Edson, "Mexicans in Chicago" (1926), Bureau of Labor Statistics, U.S. Dept. of Labor, Paul S. Taylor Papers.

3. This strategy of establishing belonging was mirrored nearly forty years later in the Chicano Movimiento's claims to Aztlán. The mythical land of Aztlán was reputed to be in what is now the U.S. Southwest. By locating their origin, their homeland, in Aztlán, Chicanos of the late 1960s and early 1970s forced a recognition of themselves as the original Americans. This strategy also worked to situate Chicanos as the original Mexicans, descendants of the Aztecs who supposedly emerged from Aztlán, conquering and settling most of what is now Mexico. By establishing their "true" Americanness in this way, Chicanos worked to claim rights of belonging, political representation, and power.

4. Including the writings of José Martí, Simón Bolívar, José Vasconcelos, and José Enrique Rodó. See chapter 5 for more on this subject.

5. Mier, *Cartas*, 84, 324. David Brading calls Mier "the first historian of the Mexican insurgency and its most original ideologue." Brading, *Origins*, 24. He later joined Nicolás Bravo and Vicente Guerrero in their revolt against the Spanish emperor. Mier's reference to the Indians also refers to early *indigenismo*. See chapter 5 for a more extensive discussion.

6. For a more extensive discussion of the concept of continental Americanness and its consequences for Mexican identity, see chapter 5.

7. Townsend, "Germans"; Horak, "Assimilation"; Zahrobsky, "Slovaks"; Wirth, *The Ghetto;* Abott, *Tenements;* Burgess and Newcomb, *Census Data, 1920;* Burgess and Newcomb, *Census Data, 1930.* See also Keating, *Building Chicago;* and Pacyga and Skerrett, *Chicago.*

8. McWilliams, *North,* 206–7.

9. The City of Chicago did allow noncitizens to vote in school-board elections during this era, but those rights did not extend to political races, namely aldermanic races, where the real power in the city lay. This is not to say that the occasional noncitizen Mexican did not exchange his "vote" for certain "protections," as the workings of the Chicago machine are legendary. I have been unable, however, to verify any accounts of this kind of activity.

10. Raymond Nelson, "The Mexican in South Chicago," box 1, folder "Mexican Life in Chicago," p. 21, Paul S. Taylor Papers.

11. Throughout the 1920s and 1930s, for example, reports generated by the University of Chicago Settlement House that pertained to the house's activities with Mexicans were all titled "Mexican Work." Box 21, Mary McDowell Papers. See also "History of the United Charities, 1857–1936," box 9, folder 2, United Charities Papers; Addams, *Twenty Years; The University of Chicago Settlement Handbook,* box 1, folder 4, Mary McDowell Papers; William Blackburn, "Brief Report of the Origin, Program, and Services of the University of Chicago Settlement House" (1928), box 2, folder 7, Mary McDowell Papers; Abbott, *Immigration;* Abbott, *Tenements;* Shaw, *Jack-Roller.*

12. For an account of similar moves by reformers in Los Angeles, see Sánchez, "Go After the Women."

13. Persons, *Ethnic Studies;* Willrich, *City of Courts.*

14. See, for example, Sklar, "Hull House"; and Sherrick, "Private Visions." On settlements generally, see Davis, *Spearheads;* and Kelley, "Early Days."

15. Park and Burgess, *Introduction.*

16. See Yu, *Thinking Orientals,* 41–42.

17. The notable exceptions to this were a handful of elite-trained social-science researchers like Manuel Gamio, who was working for (and was often paid by) the Mexican government in the hopes of equalizing relations between Mexico and the United States. See Enciso, "Manuel Gamio," esp. 1005–13; Weber, Melville, and Palerm, *Manuel Gamio,* esp. 33–39.

18. See, for example, the report of Gertrude Howe Britton and Kate Constable, "Our Mexican Patients at Central Free Dispensary," Rush Medical College Report, 1925, Paul S. Taylor Papers. On Mexicans at Houchen House, see Ruiz, *From Out of the Shadows,* 43–49.

19. *México* (Chicago), February 7, 1925, trans. Robert Redfield, Robert Redfield Papers.

20. For a more thorough discussion of "Anglo" views of Mexicans, see Weber, "Anglo Perceptions."

21. George Edson, "Mexicans in Chicago" (1926), Bureau of Labor Statistics, U.S. Dept. of Labor, p. 5, Paul S. Taylor Papers.

22. Gerstle, "Protean Character."

23. King, *Making Americans,* 87–89.

24. Ibid., 89.

25. Ruiz, Foreword to *Pots of Promise,* x.

26. McCarthy, "Which Christ."

27. Robert Jones, "The Religious Life of Mexicans in Chicago," n.d. (data from 1928), Robert Redfield Papers.

28. Gertrude Howe Britton and Kate Constable, "Our Mexican Patients at Central Free Dispensary," Rush Medical College Report, 1925, p. 6, Paul S. Taylor Papers.

29. Jones, "Mexican Colonies," 597.

30. For employers' expectations that Mexicans would rise economically "just as Germans and Poles have," see "Mexican Labor in Chicago, Calumet Area," p. 8, box 1, Paul S. Taylor Papers.

31. Raymond Nelson, "The Mexican in South Chicago," box 1, folder "Mexican Life in Chicago," p. 8, Paul S. Taylor Papers.

32. Mr. Belcher interview, November 19, 1924, Robert Redfield Papers.

33. See, for example, the pamphlet *Free Evening Schools, Americanization Classes, 1927*, box 1, folder "Mexican Labor in Chicago," pp. 11–14, Paul S. Taylor Papers. The pamphlet lists classes by industry and details days and times offered, and whether the classes are for men, women, or both.

34. Ibid.

35. It would be interesting to figure out the percentages of Mexican involvement in these classes to test whether Mexican men were channeled into particular job tracks. It is not clear why these subjects were lumped into Americanization, since they seem to be more about industrialization than Americanization (particularly curious, as industrialization was occurring in urban centers in Mexico as well).

36. *Circular of Information: Free Evening Schools: Elementary and High Americanization Classes*, Board of Education, City of Chicago, 1927, Paul S. Taylor Papers.

37. Ibid.

38. Ibid.

39. Nesbitt, *Chicago Standard* (1920), 10.

40. Nesbitt, *Chicago Standard* (1937), 7.

41. On ethnicity and food in the process of Americanization, see Gabaccia, *We Are What We Eat*, esp. chap. 5.

42. Ibid., 122–40.

43. Quoted in Taylor, *Mexican Labor*, 217.

44. Quoted in ibid.

45. Quoted in ibid., 131.

46. Gertrude Howe Britton and Kate Constable, "Our Mexican Patients at Central Free Dispensary," Rush Medical College Report, 1925, p. 2, Paul S. Taylor Papers.

47. Jones and Wilson, *Mexican in Chicago*, 28.

48. There were a reported 732 applicants for naturalization between December 1, 1924, and January 28, 1925, none of whom were Mexican. Journal, 1924–25, Robert Redfield Papers.

49. Abraham Bowers interview, October 5, 1924, Robert Redfield Papers.

50. This conflation of rights with U.S. citizenship—and therefore ability to vote—is at the heart of the criticism that William Flores, Rina Benmayor, and Renato Rosaldo have leveled at the notion of citizenship that has prevailed in this

country. See especially Flores, "Citizens vs. Citizenry"; and Rosaldo, "Cultural Citizenship."

51. Raymond Nelson, "The Mexican in South Chicago," box 1, folder "Mexican Life in Chicago," p. 9, Paul S. Taylor Papers. This is an idea that has emerged again in today's nativist, protectionist discourse following the events of September 11, 2001, and I thank Vicki Ruiz for sharing this insight with me.

52. Raymond Nelson, "The Mexican in South Chicago," box 1, folder "Mexican Life in Chicago," p. 10, Paul S. Taylor Papers.

53. Taylor, *Mexican Labor*, 162. Manuel Gamio devised a novel system of tracing money orders sent to Mexico to map Mexican mobility in the United States. See Gamio, *Mexican Immigration*.

54. Jones, "Conditions."

55. "Mexican Work, 1930–31," Mary McDowell Papers.

56. Based on examination of records from 1906 through 1941. Naturalization Petitions and Record Books, NARA.

57. Raymond Nelson, "The Mexican in South Chicago," box 1, folder "Mexican Life in Chicago," p. 31, Paul S. Taylor Papers.

58. Interview with Miss Stanton, University of Chicago Settlement House, October 20, 1924, Journal, Robert Redfield Papers.

59. Quoted in Taylor, *Mexican Labor*, 217.

60. Ibid.

61. Interview with Grabozo family narrated in a reprint of the article "An Experiment in Recreation," *The Family* (April–May 1930), by the Recreation Committee, United Charities of Chicago, United Charities Papers.

62. United Charities case of Plácida and Severna Gonzales, February 17, 1929, box 59, folder 2, Robert Redfield Papers.

63. It would be fascinating to explore the whole concept of "naturalizing" one's citizenship—as if a person were not in a natural state until they changed their citizenship to that of the United States.

64. Juan Martínez interview by Manuel Bueno, p. 24, box 187, folder 4, Ernest W. Burgess Papers.

65. Raymond Nelson, "The Mexican in South Chicago," box 1, folder "Mexican Life in Chicago," p. 31, Paul S. Taylor Papers.

66. Manuel Bueno interview, January 21, 1925, Journal 1924–25, pp. 78–79, Robert Redfield Papers.

67. Dorothy Anderson, "Notes from Sunday Afternoon Discussion Group February–August 1936," February 21, 1936, University of Chicago Settlement House Papers.

68. Foley, *White Scourge*; Montejano, *Anglos and Mexicans*.

69. Taylor, *Mexican Labor*, 218. Also quoted in Reisler, *By the Sweat*, 125.

70. *México* (Chicago), November 23, 1927.

71. Manuel Bueno interview, January 21, 1925, Field Notes, Robert Redfield Papers.

72. *El Heraldo* (Chicago), June 16, 1928, trans. Paul Taylor, Paul S. Taylor Papers. *El Heraldo de las Americas* was published in Chicago at 765 West Taylor, on the Near West Side. It was likely tied to other publications called *El Heraldo* in several major U.S. cities, including Los Angeles, and was sponsored by the Mexican consulate in each of the cities.

73. *El Nacional* (Chicago), August 13, 1932, box 41, folder IIIG, WPA Foreign Language Press Survey Papers.

74. *México* (Chicago), June 16 1928.

75. Ruth Camblón interview, November 1, 1924, Journal, Robert Redfield Papers. Among those few who did hire Mexicans were the Meinhardt Mop Company, Tuthill Spring Company, Barrett Company, Armour Packing Company, Swift Packing Company, the CB&Q Railroad, and the Illinois Central Railroad. As noted by Redfield, Ruth Camblón was an American who married an Argentian. She spent two months in Mexico learning Spanish and spoke enough "to get around."

76. Mr. Diaz interview, October 31, 1924, Robert Redfield Papers.

77. Clyde M. Brading interview, May 15, 1928, in Raymond Nelson, "The Mexican in South Chicago," box 1, folder "Mexican Life in Chicago," Paul S. Taylor Papers.

78. George Edson, "Mexicans in Chicago" (1926), Bureau of Labor Statistics, U.S. Dept. of Labor, box 1, folder "Reports and Correspondence," p. 3, Paul S. Taylor Papers.

79. Ibid.

80. Mr. Oberhart interview, November 8, 1924, Journal 1924, box 59, folder 2, Robert Redfield Papers.

81. Interview with an unidentified employer in George Edson, "Mexicans in Chicago" (1926), Bureau of Labor Statistics, Dept. of Labor, p. 3, Paul S. Taylor Papers.

82. Mr. A. Reed interview at YMCA in South Chicago, 1928, in Raymond Nelson, "The Mexican in South Chicago," box 1, folder "Mexican Life in Chicago," p. 31, Paul S. Taylor Papers.

83. Kerr, "Chicanas," 267.

84. Schools in the West Side reported 206 Mexicans. Stockyards: 126, North Side: 21, Northwest: 13. George Edson, "Mexicans in Chicago" (1926), Bureau of Labor Statistics, U.S. Dept. of Labor, p. 23, Paul S. Taylor Papers.

85. "Mexican Work Reports, November 1931," box 21, Mary McDowell Papers. A range of "Mexican Work Reports" exist for the late 1920s in which Mexicans increasingly were being provided separate classes, services, and clubs. There are nearly no reports filed from 1932 to 1936. Thereafter they resume fairly regularly.

86. Quoted in Taylor, *Mexican Labor*, 130.

87. Quoted in ibid.

88. See Weber, "Anglo Views."

89. "Minutes of Districts Committee Meeting, January 27, 1933," box 8, folder 4, United Charities Papers.

90. Balderrama and Rodríguez, *Decade of Betrayal*, 79; *Second Annual Report of the Illinois Emergency Relief Commission*, State of Illinois (June 1934).

91. Balderrama and Rodríguez, *Decade of Betrayal*, 53–54; Hoffman, *Unwanted Mexicans*, 120; Reisler. *By the Sweat*, 232.

92. McLean, "Mexican Return." See also Reisler, *By the Sweat*, 232.

93. Reisler, *By the Sweat*, 230.

94. Letter to Secretaria de Relaciónes Exteriores from Sra. H. Sahagún de la Mora, writing for the Immigrant Protective League, September 25, 1931, IV-350-15, Archivo Histórico de la Secretaria de Relaciónes Exteriores.

95. See the series of letters chronicling this exchange, IV-350-15 (1931) Archivo Histórico de la Secretaria de Relaciónes Exteriores.

96. In spite of not having work or land available once they got there. This practice continued into 1939, when the Mexican government reportedly helped repatriate eleven families from Houston to their homes in Mexico. "Mexicanos en Estados Unidos," Dept. Consular, 1939, III-240-8, Archivo Histórico de la Secretaria de Relaciónes Exteriores.

97. *El Nacional* (Chicago), May 28 1932, box 41, folder IIIG/IIIH, trans. WPA Foreign Language Press Survey Papers.

98. *El Nacional* (Chicago), May 14, 1932, box 41, folder IIIG/ID2c, trans. WPA Foreign Language Press Survey Papers.

99. Hoffman estimates "several thousand" (Hoffman, *Unwanted Mexicans,* 120). The U.S. Bureau of the Census estimates four thousand, but census figures are notoriously low. U.S. Bureau of the Census, *Abstract of the Fifteenth Census.*

100. Antonio L. Schmidt interview by Nicolás Hernández, May 19, 1937, box 41, folder IIIG, WPA Foreign Language Press Survey Papers.

101. Taylor, *Mexican Labor,* 28.

102. Ibid.

103. *El Nacional* (Chicago), May 28, 1932, box 41, folder IIIG/IIIH, trans. WPA Foreign Language Press Survey Papers.

104. Despite extensive research, I could not find any documents in the collections of the Secretaria de Relaciones Exteriores that listed consul assignments (names, cities, or dates). Francisco Pereda preceded Luis Lupián and served until at least 1921. Based on existing documents and letters, Lupián appeared to hold the consul position from about 1923 to about 1928. Apparently, Lupián went on to serve in Dallas, Texas, during the 1930s. Aveleyra served as consul from about 1930 to 1933, when the government of General Abelardo Rodríguez reportedly decided to move him out of Chicago. See *El Nacional* (Chicago), January 21, 1933, box 41, folder IIIH, trans. WPA Foreign Language Press Survey Papers. They must not have removed Aveleyra, because in 1935 he was still serving as Chicago's Mexican consul, as evidenced in his letters to the SRE. By May 1937 the consul was Antonio L. Schmidt.

105. *México* (Chicago), May 29, 1930, box 41, folder IIIG/IIIH, trans. WPA Foreign Language Press Survey Papers.

106. "Informes Sobre Protección Durante el Año 1935," Departamento de Asuntos Comerciales y de Protección, IV-706-3, Archivo Histórico de la Secretaria de Relaciónes Exteriores.

107. Enciso, "No Cuenten Conmigo."

108. According to a letter from 1935 (IV-706-3), the SRE apparently issued a memo (IV-67-126) in 1932 directing its consular offices to record repatriations. It is unclear whether the records for 1932–34 still survive.

109. "Informes Sobre Protección Durante el Año 1935," Departamento de Asuntos Comerciales y de Protección, IV-706-3, Archivo Histórico de la Secretaria de Relaciónes Exteriores.

110. Balderrama and Rodríguez, *Decade of Betrayal,* 209.

111. Taylor, *Mexican Labor,* 130.

112. See chapter 1.

113. Fernando Saúl Alanís Enciso, work in progress in the author's possession. See also Enciso, "El gobierno de México."

114. *El Nacional* (Chicago), September 5, 1931, box 41, folder IIIH/IIE2, trans. WPA Foreign Language Press Survey Papers.

115. "Informes Sobre Protección Durante el Año 1935," Departamento de Asuntos Comerciales y de Protección, IV-706-3, Archivo Histórico de la Secretaria de Relaciónes Exteriores.

116. Ibid.

117. Ibid. While "prejudicios" is technically correct, "prejuicios" is the more common usage of this word.

118. "Mexican Work," April 30, 1929, box 21, folder 1, University of Chicago Settlement House Papers.

119. Mexican consul records contain listings of deportation cases that were actually heard in court, but these likely would have been only a small sampling of deportations, since most deportees did not request formal hearings. See Balderrama and Rodríguez, *Decade of Betrayal*, 61–62.

120. *El Nacional* (Chicago), January 14, 1930.

121. Ibid.

122. "Repatriaciones," Dept. Consular, 1931, IV-354-4, Archivo Histórico de la Secretaria de Relaciónes Exteriores.

123. On the Flores Magón brothers and the Magonistas in exile, see Raat, *Revoltosos*, 13–39, 273–90.

124. *El Heraldo* (Chicago), 1928, trans. Paul Taylor, Paul S. Taylor Papers.

125. Ibid.

126. *México* (Chicago), June 16, 1928.

127. Unidentified Mexican male quoted in the "Mexican Work Report, 1930–31," box 21, University of Chicago Settlement House Papers.

128. *El Heraldo* (Chicago), 1928, trans. Paul Taylor, Paul S. Taylor Papers.

129. Robert Jones, "The Religious Life of Mexicans in Chicago," box 133, folder 4, Ernest W. Burgess Papers.

130. Folder 25, William E. Dever Papers.

131. The mayor's office revoked Skoden's license (for unclear reasons), and it had not been restored as of the date of Martínez's application.

132. Letter to Commanding Officer Thirteenth District, February 27, 1924, folder 25, William E. Dever Papers.

133. Quoted in Balderrama and Rodríguez, *Decade of Betrayal*, 84. They cite it as coming from Humphrey, "Mexican Repatriation from Michigan," but it is not there.

134. Green's imprisoning of the Mexican consul incident is discussed in chapter 2.

135. Max Guzmán interview.

136. Max Guzmán interview.

137. *México* (Chicago), June 30, 1928, trans. Paul Taylor, box 1, folder "Notes on Mexican Newspapers in Chicago," Paul S. Taylor Papers.

138. *México* (Chicago), November 23, 1927.

139. Ibid.

140. *México* (Chicago), September 4, 1926, box 1, folder: "Notes on Mexican Newspapers in Chicago," Paul S. Taylor Papers.

141. *México* (Chicago), November 23, 1927.

142. Ibid.

143. Maril, *Patrolling Chaos;* Dunn, "Immigration Enforcement."

144. "Registration of Aliens," Immigration Committee, U.S. Chamber of Commerce, 1926, p. 17, Paul S. Taylor Papers.

145. Ibid.

146. Stern, "Buildings."

147. Ignacio M. Valle interview, March 1925, Journal 1924–25, Robert Redfield Papers.

148. Departamento Consular, "Matriculas," 1929–30, IV-102-29, Archivo Histórico de la Secretaria de Relaciónes Exteriores.

149. Balderrama and Rodríguez, *Decade of Betrayal;* Hoffman, *Unwanted Mexicans.*

150. "Narrative Report on Mexican Neighbors, December 1931," Mexican Work Reports, box 21, Mary McDowell Papers.

151. Ibid.

152. Ibid.

153. "The First Six Months of 1939," folders 22–34, Mary McDowell Papers.

154. The Chicago Area Project was founded in 1939 by several researchers, including Clifford R. Shaw and Henry D. McKay. Their research focused on Chicago's neighborhoods to prevent and treat juvenile delinquency. The project also worked in conjunction with the Illinois Institute for Juvenile Research and the Illinois Youth Commission.

155. On the Italians, see Guglielmo, *White on Arrival.* See also Roediger, *Wages of Whiteness;* Jacobson, *Whiteness;* and Ignatiev, *How the Irish.*

156. I. Magaña, consul's representative, "Protecciones: Mexicanos en Estados Unidos," 1922, II-6-232, Archivo Histórico de la Secretaria de Relaciónes Exteriores.

157. Quoted in Taylor, *Mexican Labor,* 232. Notably, the equation of not being clean with being Mexican (for example, the derogatory and racializing phrase "dirty Mexicans") is familiar to the histories of Mexicans in the U.S. Southwest as a tool for discrimination.

158. Unnamed employee of the Chamber of Commerce, interviewed by Paul Taylor, Paul S. Taylor Papers.

159. *La Defensa* (Chicago), February 29, 1936, box 41, folder IIIG, trans. WPA Foreign Language Press Survey Papers.

160. Roosevelt, *Pan American Day.*

161. Robert C. Jones, "The Religious Life of the Mexican in Chicago," text for future publication, box 59, folder 2, p. 3, Robert Redfield Papers.

162. The phrasing and concept is borrowed from Foley, *White Scourge.* Foley makes a convincing case for Mexicans in Texas hovering in the ethno-racial borderlands between whiteness and blackness. See also Foley, "Partly Colored"; and Barrett and Roediger, "Inbetween Peoples."

Chapter 4: Striations Within

1. María Moreno Corona, Declaration of Intention No. 126276, Petition for Naturalization No. 196261, NARA.

2. On organized Americanization campaigns through the state and local institutions, see chapter 3. For a broader discussion on the national level over the course of the twentieth century, see King, *Making Americans,* esp. sections 2 and 3.

3. Manuel and Alma Bravo interview.

4. Delfina Navarro, Declaration of Intention No. 126807, Petition for Naturalization No. 195115, NARA.

5. Concepción Pérez, Declaration of Intention No. 193440, Petition for Naturalization No. 105378, NARA.

6. There is no indication what kind of machine she operated, but the witnesses on her petition for citizenship were workers in the garment industry, so it is likely that Concepción was also a laborer in a garment shop.

7. Celia Hernández, Declaration of Intention No. 119678, Petition for Naturalization No. 176592, NARA.

8. George L. Paz and Margaret Brennan, "The Spanish and Mexican Dance in Chicago," ca. 1937, p. 1, container A 741, WPA Federal Writers Project. Generously shared with me by Zaragosa Vargas.

9. Ibid., 3.

10. Ibid., 2.

11. *México* (Chicago), January 21, 1930.

12. *México* (Chicago), January 4, 1930.

13. George L. Paz and Margaret Brennan, "The Spanish and Mexican Dance in Chicago," ca. 1937, p. 5, container A 741, WPA Federal Writers Project.

14. Ibid., 4.

15. On Lupe Vélez (1908–44), see Corona, *Lupe Vélez;* Ramírez, *Lupe Vélez.* On Dolores del Rio (1905–83), see Hershfield, *Invention;* Taibo, *Dolores del Río;* and Reyes, *Dolores Del Rio.*

16. I discuss this point more fully in chapters 2 and 3.

17. Joseph Morales, Declaration of Intention No. 107763, Petition for Naturalization, No. 166903, NARA.

18. Unlike men's names, women's names often reflected their marital status. Eloisa Bermúdez was Eloisa Bermúdez de Barroso, indicating that she was the wife of Barroso. When he died in 1916, she became Eloisa Bermúdez Viuda (widow) de Barroso. See Declaration of Intention, No. 89324, Petition for Naturalization No. 171739, NARA.

19. Sofia Casso López, Declaration of Intention No. 128712, Petition for Naturalization No. 197731, NARA. While she and her deceased husband were both born in Mexico, they married in El Paso, Texas. Their three older children were born in El Paso.

20. María de los Angeles Navarro de Nuñez, Declaration of Intention No. 115751, Petition for Naturalization No. 179944, NARA.

21. Paz Fernández (Abundes), Declaration of Intention No. 113889, Petition for Naturalization No. 175231, NARA.

22. On desertion of other groups of poor women, especially white and Black women, see Willrich, "'Close That Place.'" Most of the women he discusses wrote to Dever beseeching him to prevent their husbands' access to alcohol, which they blamed for their desertion and lack of support (see esp. 568–69).

23. Those arguments generally take male activism among certain European ethnic groups against Prohibition to stand for group opposition to the prohibi-

tion of alcohol. Looking at the perspectives of ethnic European women, however, suggests that they favored temperance as a means of controlling men's alcohol-induced behaviors (from domestic violence to squandering the family rent on drink). Although Mayor Dever was "wet" (and many of his ethnic supporters were "wet"), he was committed to upholding the laws of Prohibition, which alienated him from his largely Democratic constituency. For more of this discussion, see Kantowicz, *Polish-American Politics*, 142–50; Nelli, *Italians*; 211–34; Green, "Irish Chicago," 438–39; and Cohen, *Making a New Deal.*

24. Stephen A. Higginson quoted Willrich, "'Close That Place,'" 563. See Higginson, "Short History."

25. Illinois ratified the Nineteenth Amendment on June 10, 1919. Illinois was one of a handful of states that allowed women to vote for president of the United States and in municipal elections beginning in 1913. For a narrative account of the struggle to obtain the rights of 1913, see Poplett and Porucznik, *Woman Who Never Fails.*

26. United Charities case notes, Robert Redfield Papers. Louise Kerr suggested that the growth of Chicago-born children began to impact the Mexican neighborhoods in distinctive ways by the early 1940s. Kerr, "Chicano Experience," 10. See also Baur, "Delinquency."

27. On Mexican masculinity, see Mirandé, *Hombres y Machos*; Melhuus and Stolen, *Machos*; Irwin, *Mexican Masculinities*; Román, "Tropical Fruit"; and Stavans, "Latin Phallus." On Mexican families in Mexico, see Arrom, "Perspectiva." On patriarchy in the household, see Dore, "Holy Family."

28. On gender, the body, and Mexican women, see Lamas, "Cuerpo."

29. United Charities case notes, Robert Redfield Papers.

30. Eva Guerrero, Petition for Naturalization No. 192395, NARA.

31. Raquel Chávez, Declaration of Intention No. 138251, Petition for Naturalization No. 214000, NARA. Raquel was only four feet, nine inches tall and weighed less than a hundred pounds!

32. Lasting nearly three years, the fever affected the villagers and the military encampments. By the time Raquel was divorced, the native peoples in her hometown, the Yaquis, were being dispersed and "Mexicanized" by the cultural campaigns President Cardenas waged throughout the countrysides of Mexico. Attempting to unify the country and to "make Mexicans" out of a diversity of peoples, Cárdenas's troops defeated Yaqui uprisings in the 1930s and ensured they went to newly opened schools.

33. Excerpt from mission statement in *The Eleanor Record: A Story of the Eleanor Association*, December 1933. The full statement reads: "The Eleanor Women's Foundation, which has provided Chicago women with safe spaces for growth and development since 1898, expands opportunities for women and girls to learn, collaborate, and serve each other and the greater community. The Foundation awards grants and sponsors education and services that enhance the ability of every woman and girl to care for herself and her community." See www.eleanorfoundation.org.

34. Jones, "Conditions," 81–82.

35. Ruiz, *From Out of the Shadows.*

36. Several excellent monographs trace the impact of mass culture on immigrant women: Peiss, *Cheap Amusements*; Meyerowitz, *Women Adrift*. Spe-

cifically on Mexican women, see Ruiz, *From Out of the Shadows*; Ruiz, "'Star Struck'"; and Kerr, "Chicanas."

37. Jones, "Conditions."

38. *México* (Chicago), May 15, 1926.

39. Louise Kerr explores the reification of traditional gender roles among Mexicans in Chicago during the Depression in "Chicanas."

40. For a useful, if dated, historiographic survey of this topic, see Kerber, "Separate Spheres."

41. Rodríguez, "Roman Catholicism."

42. For an in-depth discussion of the practices of *curanderas*, see Trotter and Chavira, *Curanderismo*.

43. *México* (Chicago), January 9, 1929.

44. Exerpted from Mary McDowell Settlement House records, 1924, Robert Redfield Papers.

45. Of the fifty-eight industries and businesses in Chicago that employed Mexicans during this period, twenty-five employed women. Jones, "Conditions," 121. See also Peiss, *Cheap Amusements*; and Meyerowitz, *Women Adrift*.

46. Christine Stansell finds similar practices in the nineteenth century. Stansell, *City of Women*.

47. Immigrant Protective League Papers.

48. Journal 1924, Robert Redfield Papers.

49. Reisler, *By the Sweat*, 99–100.

50. Taylor, *Mexican Labor*, 77–79, 95–98; Reisler, *By the Sweat*, 104.

51. Ruiz, *From Out of the Shadows*, 76.

52. Herlinda de la Vega, Declaration of Intention No. 110919, Petition for Naturalization No. 171129, NARA.

53. Meyerowitz, *Women Adrift*; Cohen, *Making a New Deal*; Ruiz, *From Out of the Shadows*.

54. See Meyerowitz, *Women Adrift*, esp. chaps. 1 and 4. On Mexican women, family economy, and division of household labor, see Zavella, *Women's Work*, esp. chaps. 3 and 5; Ruiz, *Cannery Women*, esp. chap. 1; and Williams, *Mexican American Family*.

55. Horowitz, *"Negro and White,"* 61.

56. Slayton, *Back of the Yards*, 67–76; Reisler, *By the Sweat*. See also Reisler, "Mexican Immigrant."

57. Jones, "Conditions," 59. Only some of the camps had families living in them; many exclusively housed men, like one in West Pullman, where nineteen Mexican men lived alongside two Irish men, one Bulgarian, and two men whose nationality was unknown (58).

58. Quoted in Taylor, *Mexican Labor*, 200.

59. Quoted in ibid., 198.

60. Reprint from *The Family*, April–May 1930, "An Experiment in Recreation: Recreation Committee, United Charities of Chicago, Part I: Material and Method of Experiment," Family Welfare Association of America, box 8, United Charities Papers.

61. Quoted in Taylor, *Mexican Labor*, 198.

62. Sidney Levin interview.

63. Stansell, *City of Women*. See also Ruiz, *Cannery Women*.

64. Manuel Bueno, "The Mexican in Chicago" (1924), box 187, folder 4, Ernest W. Burgess Papers.

65. Raul DuBois Interview, n.d. [ca. 1927], Manuel Gamio Field Notes, box 2, folder 5, Manuel Gamio Papers.

66. Quoted in Taylor, *Mexican Labor*, 200.

67. Quoted in ibid.

68. *México* (Chicago), May 9, 1928, box 1, folder 2, Paul S. Taylor Papers.

69. Interview with unnamed Mexican man, n.d. [ca. 1927], Manuel Gamio Field Notes, box 2, folder 5, Manuel Gamio Papers.

70. Taylor, *Mexican Labor*, 247.

71. If these women were U.S.–born and their husbands were not U.S. citizens, they lost their citizenship. They retained the citizenship of their new husbands. This law was revised in 1922, when U.S.–born women then were allowed to petition the federal government to regain their citizenship of birth using a slightly expedited naturalization process.

72. Manuel and Alma Bravo interview, p. 18.

73. Ibid.

74. Ibid., p. 19.

75. Ida Flake, Declaration of Intention No. 97454, Petition for Naturalization No. 165866, NARA.

76. José Flores, Declaration of Intention No. 114499, Petition for Naturalization No. 171814, NARA.

77. Enrique Aguirre, Declaration of Intention No. 95554, Petition for Naturalization No. 189180, NARA.

78. Foley, "Partly Colored," 125.

79. Interview with Ignacio Sandoval, male about thirty years old, box 2, folder 5, Manuel Gamio Papers.

80. Madeline Kneberg, "An Informal Study of Broken Homes and Delinquency among Mexicans in the City," 1933, box 133, folder 4, Ernest W. Burgess Papers.

81. One method of monitoring teenage behavior was to have a chaperone, usually an older relative, accompany the girls wherever they went. Although there was no mention of this practice in this incident nor in oral histories of Mexican women in Chicago, this does not rule out its possible existence.

82. Ruiz, *From Out of the Shadows*, 65.

83. Raymond Nelson, "The Mexican in South Chicago," box 1, folder "Mexican Life in Chicago," pp. 14, 33, Paul S. Taylor Papers.

84. *México* (Chicago), March 10, 1928.

85. Agapita Flores and Ruth Flores Rucoba interview. Further information from Agapita's husband's citizenship papers, Declaration of Intention No. 106655, Petition for Naturalization No. 163549, NARA.

86. George Edson, "Mexicans in Chicago" (1926), Bureau of Labor Statistics, U.S. Dept. of Labor, p. 7, Paul S. Taylor Papers.

87. Ibid. "Sheik" was the title Valentino held since about 1923. He died shortly after the 1926 release of his film, *The Son of the Sheik*. See photos from the film in *México* (Chicago), September 11, 1926, 4. Valerie Matsumoto found similar references in her work on Japanese Americans in California. See Matsumoto, *Farming*.

88. Jack García interview, p. 13.

89. Sidney Levin interview, p. 12.

90. For more coverage of conflicts between parents and children generally, and delinquent children specifically, see Breckenridge and Abbott, *Delinquent Child*. On children shoplifting, see John L. Brown, Back of Yards report (1938), p. 12, Chicago Area Project Papers.

91. Quoted in Taylor, *Mexican Labor*, 200.

92. D'Emilio and Freedman, *Intimate Matters*, chap. 10.

93. *El Nacional* (Chicago), August 13, 1932.

94. Chicago Police Department Homicide Reports, vol. 4, p. 30 A, November 8, 1925, Illinois Regional Archives Depository.

95. Dr. Mandel Sherman, "The Unmarried Mother," 1938, box 8, folder 3, pp. 10–11, United Charities Papers.

96. "Minutes, Meeting of Districts Committee" March 22, 1935, p. 2, folder 6, box 8, United Charities Papers.

97. Quoted in Jones, "Conditions," 85.

98. I thank Kevin Gaines for this insightful question, posed in 1998 in Austin, Texas.

99. Heap, "'Slumming.'" See also Heap, *Homosexuality*.

100. "Yearbook, 1939," Hull-House Reports, folder 443, p. 46, Hull-House Papers.

101. For a powerful analysis of how racism is embedded in the ideology of freedom, see Holt, *Problem of Freedom*.

102. Manuel Gamio Field Notes, box 2, folder 8, Manuel Gamio Papers. Gamio did not use this interview in his published work.

103. *México* (Chicago), November 10, 1928, box 40, folder IC/IA, 1a, trans. WPA Foreign Language Press Survey Papers.

104. Gutiérrez, *When Jesus Came*.

105. Gertrude Britton to Anne Blair, December 10, 1925, box 133, folder 4, Ernest W. Burgess Papers.

106. Raymond Nelson, "The Mexican in South Chicago," box 1, folder "Mexican Life in Chicago," p. 17, Paul S. Taylor Papers.

107. *México* (Chicago), June 23, 1928, box 1, folder 2, Paul S. Taylor Papers.

108. Interview with Mr. and Mrs. LaBetts, n.d. [ca. 1925–26], box 98, folder 10, Ernest W. Burgess Papers.

109. Ibid.

110. Manuel Gamio Field Notes, June 27, 1926, box 2, folder 13, Manuel Gamio Papers. Paul Taylor also interviewed López and discovered he was a roving reporter for *México* and a clerk in a men's clothing store.

111. The Mexican Catholic chapel in South Chicago (on Mackinaw Avenue between Ninetieth and Ninety-first Streets) was originally built by Illinois Steel to serve their Mexican workers who were prohibited from joining neighboring Polish parishes. In 1924, Father James Tort, the Spanish, Claretian priest, began working there at the request of Cardinal Mundelein. Attendance was so high that by 1928 an eighty-thousand-dollar church was completed nearby (at Ninety-first Street and Brandon Avenue) and named Our Lady of Guadalupe. This was the first permanent Spanish-language church established in Chicago. Louise Kerr suggests that the internal cohesion of each Mexican settlement can be measured by its recognition by the Archdiocese. See Kerr, "Chicano Settlements."

112. Sidney Levin interview.

113. "Those Who Deny Their Country," *México* (Chicago), February 1925, trans. Robert Redfield, box 59, folder 2, Robert Redfield Papers.

114. Their fears were not unfounded, as the parade was jointly sponsored by Chicago's Communist Unemployed Councils and Socialist Workers' Committee on Unemployment. Cohen, *Making a New Deal*, 251.

115. "Monthly Report on Mexican Work, November 1932," box 21, University of Chicago Settlement House Papers. In the early 1930s, threats of deportation for any Mexican, regardless of citizenship, were very real.

116. The rally was held in the coliseum at Fifteenth and Wabash, December 4, 1936.

117. "Annual Report, 1935," box 25, University of Chicago Settlement House Papers.

118. Kerr, "Chicano Experience," 85.

119. *La Defensa* (Chicago), January 25, 1935, trans. WPA Foreign Language Press Survey Papers.

120. *La Defensa* (Chicago), April 11, 1936; June 20, 1936; and October 10, 1936, trans. WPA Foreign Language Press Survey Papers.

121. "Annual Report, 1935," box 25, University of Chicago Settlement House Papers.

122. Kerr, "Chicano Experience," 85–89; "Mexicans in PWOC." See also Cohen, *Making a New Deal*, 338. Cohen neglects to consider the role of allegiances to Mexico or even that of El Frente Popular in motivating these workers. Especially notable was their suggestive club name, obviously sympathetic to Lázaro Cárdenas and his support of labor.

123. Ruiz, *From Out of the Shadows*, 95–97. See also Ruiz, *Cannery Women*.

124. Ruiz, *From Out of the Shadows*, 95. See also Gutiérrez, *Walls and Mirrors*, 1, 12–15; and Sánchez, *Becomong*, 246–49.

125. Denning, *Cultural Front*, xviii.

126. "Mexican Adult Group Sunday Afternoon Discussions," box 25, University of Chicago Settlement House Papers.

127. Kerr, "Chicano Experience," 88; *El Ideal Catolico Mexicano* (Chicago), November 3, 1936, trans. WPA Foreign Language Press Survey Papers.

128. More research needs to be done on whether these Spaniards were fleeing the turmoil in Spain that eventually brought Franco into power.

129. Petition for Naturalization No. 109105; Petition for Naturalization No. 115706, NARA.

130. Petition for Naturalization No. 10944; Petition for Naturalization No. 909120, NARA.

131. George L. Paz, "The Spanish and Mexican Clubs in Chicago," ca. 1937, container A741, WPA Federal Writers Project. Generously shared with me by Zaragosa Vargas.

132. Gutiérrez, *Corn Mothers.*

133. Interview with Carlos Pérez López, South Chicago, 1926, box 2, folder 5, Manuel Gamio Papers.

134. Interview with Señor Galindo, South Chicago, 1924, box 2, folder 5, Manuel Gamio Papers.

135. John Benjamin Galindo, Petition for Naturalization No. 138473, NARA. He was sworn in as a U.S. citizen in 1936.

136. *México* (Chicago), June 23, 1928, Paul S. Taylor Papers.

137. Meyer and Sherman, *Course of Mexican History*, 584.

138. García, *Rise*; García, *Mexican Americans*. Significantly, political mobilization on any scale did not occur in Chicago until the early 1950s, well over a decade after LULAC chapters were formed in the Southwest. The first LULAC chapter in Chicago was accepted into the national association in 1956. Benson Latin American Collection, University of Texas at Austin. See also Sánchez, *Becoming*.

139. García, *Rise*. See also Marquez, *LULAC*; Orozco, "Origins."

140. *La Prensa*, founded in 1913, lasted until 1963, with significant decline in its later years. Lozano founded *La Opinión* in 1926 and eventually moved from Texas to Los Angeles to oversee its publication.

141. Interview with Dr. Medina, June 21, 1926, box 3, folder 11, Manuel Gamio Papers. Dr. Medina was a dentist and advertised widely throughout several areas of Mexican settlement in the Chicago area.

142. At the age of thirty-seven in January 1929, Dr. Meixueiro registered with the Mexican consulate in Chicago. Relaciones de matriculas, IV-102-29, Archivo Histórico de la Secretaria de Relaciónes Exteriores.

143. *El Heraldo de las Americas*, November 1, 1924, trans. Robert Redfield, box 59, folder 2, p. 1, Robert Redfield Papers.

144. Interview with Dr. Medina, June 21, 1926, box 3, folder 11, Manuel Gamio Papers.

145. "Mexican Work 1929–1930," box 21, Mary McDowell Papers. In 1909, the Chicago Bureau of Charities and the Chicago Relief and Aid Society consolidated, forming the United Charities of Chicago. Joel Hunter was director from 1919–47. In 1935, the Family Service Bureau of United Charities was established to focus on family problems with an increasing emphasis on preventative counseling. In 1938, the United Charities assumed responsibility for the Referral Center for Unmarried Mothers, which in 1944 grew into the Women's Service Division. See United Charities Papers.

146. Raymond Nelson, "The Mexican in South Chicago," box 1, folder "Mexican Life in Chicago," p. 18, Paul S. Taylor Papers.

147. Ibid.

148. Field notes on Hull-House area, June 24, 1926, box 3, folder 11, Manuel Gamio Papers.

149. *México* (Chicago), November 10, 1928, box 40, WPA Foreign Language Press Survey Papers.

150. Ibid.

151. Markers of class in the United States were different than those in Mexico. See Pablo Vila, *Border Identifications: Narratives of Religion, Gender, and Class on the U.S.-Mexico Border* (Austin: University of Texas Press, 2005). See also William French, *A Peaceful and Working People: Manners, Morals, and Class Formation in Northern Mexico* (Albuquerque: University of New Mexico Press, 1996); Lourdes Benería, *The Crossroads of Class and Gender: Industrial Homework Subcontracting and Household Dynamics in Mexico City* (Chicago: University of Chicago Press, 1987); and Woodrow Wilson Borah, *Race and Class in Mexico* (Berkeley: University of California Press, 1954).

152. Interview with Mr. Belcher, November 19, 1924, Robert Redfield Papers.

153. Interview with I. M. Valle, February 14, 1925, Robert Redfield Papers.
154. United Charities case notes, Journal 1924–25, Robert Redfield Papers.
155. Ibid.
156. "Entertainment for Mexican Adult Groups, 15 July 1933," box 21, p. 2, University of Chicago Settlement House Papers..
157. Sidney Levin interview. As boys, "Minnie" and "Boots" were inseparable in high school, according to Jesse Escalante (interview, January 16, 2004).
158. Field Notes, box 2, folder 9, Manuel Gamio Papers.
159. Taylor, *Mexican Labor*, 93.
160. See discussion in chapter 3.
161. Lucio Franco interview.
162. Ignacio Elizalde interview, February 14, 1925, Robert Redfield Papers.

Chapter 5: Mexicans Emergent

1. *El Heraldo de las Americas* (Chicago), November 1, 1924, trans. Robert Redfield, box 59, folder 2, Robert Redfield Papers. A year earlier, the famous Mexican Police Band had come from Mexico to play the fiesta at the behest of the Mexican consul, Luis Lupian. Inclusion of the Mexican people of Chicago and of the mutual-aid society was new. "Bandas de Musica: Informes sobre la Actuacion de la Banda de Policia," Departamento Consular, 38-11-104, Archivo Histórico de la Secretaria de Relaciónes Exteriores.
2. *El Heraldo de las Americas* (Chicago), November 1, 1924, trans. Robert Redfield, box 59, folder 2, Robert Redfield Papers.
3. For another discussion of Mexico Lindo, see Rosales, *¡Pobre Raza!*
4. For work on a more recent period in Chicago's history that views Chicago as part of Latin America, see De Genova, "Race."
5. As coined by Brading, *Origins*, 1.
6. Gutmann, *Meanings*, chap. 9, esp. 225–32, 241–48.
7. Sáenz, *Indian Citizen*, 8. This is a reprint of the article that first appeared ca. 1939 in "an obscure little worker's paper" (as noted in the preface by Concha Romero James, chief of the Division of Intellectual Cooperation, Pan American Union). James, Preface, 7. See also Sáenz, *Mexico;* and Sáenz, *Mexico Integro.* During his career, Sáenz served as the director of the Mexican National Preparatory School, assistant secretary of education, minister to Ecuador and Denmark, ambassador to Peru, and director of the Inter-American Indian Institute.
8. Brading, *Origins*, 1.
9. In the Battle of Chapúltepec in 1847, the cadets—the Niños Heroes—were the last line of defense against the invading U.S. army. Many of these children died in defense of their country. Benito Juárez was the first Indian president of Mexico, serving from 1855–72 as head of the liberal government during the French intervention.
10. Brading, *Origins*, 55.
11. Ibid., 83–84.
12. Neo-Aztec nationalism reemerged in the late 1960s as an aspect of cultural nationalism in the Chicano Movement. In their claims to authenticity as original Americans, Chicanos valorized their indigenous roots, learned Aztec dances, discovered Nahuatl, and reclaimed this identity for themselves. See Chávez, "*Mi*

Raza Primero!"; and Muñoz, *Sixties Chicano*. On identity and political strategy, see Márquez, *Constructing*.

13. There was a counterstrain of *indigenismo* that saw nothing about the *indio* to valorize. See Becker, *Setting*; and Lomnitz-Adler, *Exits*.

14. Sáenz, *Mexico*, 14.

15. Vigorous historiographic debates exist over this general understanding of *indigenismo*. Scholars like Marjorie Becker, Claudio Lomnitz-Adler, and Mary Kay Vaughn have argued that postrevolutionary *indigenistas* believed the Indian to be degenerate and irredeemable and thus looked to the *mestizo* as the true ideal national figure. See also the convincing work of Alexander Dawson that shows a competing image of the *indio* in *indigenismo* that positioned the *indio* as the model for the emerging nation-state. Dawson, "From Models"; Becker, *Setting*; Lomnitz-Adler, *Exits*; and Vaughan, *Cultural Politics*.

16. For an excellent elaboration of this discussion, see Dawson, "From Models."

17. For a more in-depth and insightful discussion, see Stern, "From Mestizophilia."

18. Dawson, "From Models," 307. See also Dawson, *Indian and Nation*.

19. Dawson, "From Models," 307–8.

20. Brading, *Origins*, 98.

21. For a clear example of the idealized Indian body, see Oliveros, *Valores*. Early in his thinking, as undersecretary of education under President Obregon, Moisés Sáenz also emphasized the physical power of the *indio* and its desirability. See Sáenz, *Mexico*, 8–9.

22. Dawson, "From Models," 290.

23. Sáenz, *Indian Citizen*, 3. This shift in perspective can also be seen as feeding into his eventual pluralist vision as articulated in *México Integro*. As Dawson points out, Sáenz "was clearly transformed by his experience among the Indians of Carapan [Peru]." Dawson, "From Models," 300 n.100. Claudio Lomnitz-Adler has suggested that this apparent shift actually indicated the extent to which the ideal racial type within *indigenismo* was the *mestizo*. Dawson, however, has convincingly argued that the slippage is inherent because *indio* and *mestizo* were used as fluid, de-essentialized categories. Alexandra Minna Stern has argued that this mestizophilia fractured under the failure of homogenization, and by the late 1930s, the turn was more toward identifying the particularlities of specific indigenous groups as cultural-biological units that needed to be assessed for their place on the barbarism-civilization scale. See Lomnitz-Adler, *Exits*; Dawson, "From Models"; and Stern, "From Mestizophilia."

24. Jones and Wilson, *Mexican in Chicago*, 28.

25. Another interesting aspect to explore would be the effects/impacts of Wilsonian idealism and its pan-Americanist rhetoric.

26. Bolívar (1783–1830) fought for the political unification of the former colonies of Spain during the early decades of the nineteenth century. Focusing primarily on South America (including what is now Bolivia, Ecuador, Venezuela, Peru, Colombia, and Panama), he underscored their common history with Spain as a central tenet of republican unity in Latin America. His ideas spread throughout all countries of Latin America. On his life and thought, see Vitale, *La larga marcha*; and Benitez, *Bolívar y Martí*.

27. Rodó (1872–1917) was a prominent Uruguayan philosopher, essayist, and critic.

28. Martí, *Antología*. This collection contains selections from his years of exile in New York (1881–95), including his views on the race situation in the United States and commentary on the efforts of labor unionists in the United States. See also Martí, *Obras completas*.

29. Roosevelt delivered his corollary to Congress in his annual address on December 6, 1904.

30. Darío, "To Roosevelt."

31. See also Carey McWilliams on the "Spanish fantasy" of those coming from Mexico to the United States. McWilliams, *North*.

32. Sáenz, "Foreign Investments and Mexican Nationalism," in Sáenz and Priestley, *Some Mexican*, 6–7.

33. Ibid., 7.

34. Ibid.

35. Vaughan, *State*, 239–66.

36. Vasconcelos, *La raza cósmica*.

37. This also tied in with Vasconcelos and Obregón's attempts to honor Article 3 of the 1917 Constitution, which mandated the establishment of a free and secular educational system.

38. Vasconcelos, *Mexican Ulysses*, 152.

39. James, Preface.

40. Taylor, *Mexican Labor*, 133.

41. Ibid., 218.

42. Jones, "Conditions," 116. The organization was based at 828 Sholte Street in Chicago.

43. Quoted in Taylor, *Mexican Labor*, 218.

44. Gamio, *Mexican Immigrant*.

45. Quoted in Taylor, *Mexican Chicago*, 218.

46. The Harris Foundation Lectures began in 1923 to improve knowledge of world affairs and promote better understanding of the world's peoples by Americans. In 1926 the subject was Mexico, and Herbert Ingram Priestley, José Vasconcelos, Manuel Gamio, and Moíses Sáenz each delivered lectures relevant to contemporary conditions in Mexico. Priestly: "Basic Features of Mexican Problems" (June 19, 1926); "The United States and Mexico" (July 14, 1926). Vasconcelos: "Mexican Civilization as Compared with the Civilizations of the United States and Other Latin-American Countries" (June 30, 1926); "Democracy in Latin America" (July 7, 1926); "The Race Problem in Latin America" (July 13, 1926). Gamio: "Some Sociological Aspects of American-Mexican Relations" (July 1, 1926); "The Indian Population in Mexico" (July 12, 1926). Sáenz: "Foreign Investments and Nationalism in Mexico" (July 6, 1926); "Humanism and the Mexican Laborer" (July 8, 1926). The lectures were subsequently published as two bound volumes: Sáenz and Priestley in *Some Mexican Problems*, and Vasconcelos and Gamio in *Aspects of Mexican Civilization*.

47. *México* (Chicago), May 15, 1926. Martí lived as a Cuban political refugee in New York from 1881–95, during which time he developed and disseminated the ideas in "Nuestra America." He was instrumental in forming the Cuban Revolutionary party and worked alongside Puerto Ricans in New York to free

Cuba and Puerto Rico from Spanish colonialism. He was killed upon his return to Cuba in 1896.

48. De la Campa, *Latin Americanism.*

49. Petition for Naturalization No. 94258 (October 1930); Petition for Naturalization No. 83414 (February 1930), NARA.

50. Petition for Naturalization No. 98254 (May 1931), NARA. The petition is that of the wife, Gladys Leavens Bunner Acosta, who had to go through the formal process of attaining U.S. citizenship despite having married someone who was technically (since the Citizenship Act of March 1917) a citizen. The irony here is that those women who were born U.S. citizens and married noncitizens lost their citizenship and had to formally petition to reclaim it after marriage.

51. Petition for Naturalization No. 96011 (March 1931), NARA.

52. Petition for Naturalization No. 95992 (March 1931), NARA.

53. Petition for Naturalization No. 129625 (May 1935); Petition for Naturalization No. 97327 (May 1931), NARA.

54. Petition for Naturalization No. 81510 (January 1930); Petition for Naturalization No. 81487 (November 1929), NARA.

55. Information drawn from survey of 1930 manuscript census for Packingtown, the Near West Side, and South Chicago.

56. Julio I. Puente interview by Robert Redfield, Winter 1925, Redfield Journal, 1924–25, pp. 80–81, Robert Redfield Papers. Puente's status in the community would have been complicated by gaining U.S. citizenship—after 1917, Puerto Ricans were granted U.S. citizenship.

57. The newspaper was likely related to other papers of the same name sponsored by other Mexican consulates in the United States. For a reference to the paper in Los Angeles during this period, see Sánchez, "'New Nationalism,'" 237. It would be interesting to compare the two papers and see how similar they were and whether or not the Latin Americanist bent was particular to Chicago.

58. *La Noticia Mundial* (Chicago), August 7, 1927, trans. Paul Taylor, box 1, folder: "Notes on Mexican Newspapers in Chicago," Paul S. Taylor Papers.

59. As in the claims to Latin Americanism raised by the founders of LULAC. Ironically, this organization appeared to be nearly nonexistent in Chicago during the 1930s. Perhaps this was due to the lack of second- and third-generation Chicago Mexicans.

60. *La Noticia Mundial* (Chicago), January 28, 1928, trans. Paul Taylor, box 1, folder: "Notes on Mexican Newspapers in Chicago," Paul S. Taylor Papers.

61. Robert Jones, "The Religious Life of the Mexican in Chicago," draft text for future publication based on data gathered in 1928, in box 59, folder 2, p. 3, Robert Redfield Papers.

62. Alonzo's first name was written as Marcio, but given the rarity of such a name amongst Mexicans, it was more likely Mauricio (perhaps "Marcio" was how Edson heard the name). He was a Texas-born Mexican of Mexican parents and married to a Norwegian woman. George Edson, "Mexicans in Saginaw, Michigan" (1926), Bureau of Labor Statistics, U.S. Dept. of Labor, box 1, Correspondence: "Reports Regarding Mexican Labor in the Midwest," p. 2, Paul S. Taylor Papers.

63. Manuel Bueno interview, January 21, 1925, Robert Redfield Papers.

64. *México* (Chicago), December 5, 1928, trans. Paul Taylor, box 1, Folder "Notes on Mexican Newspapers in Chicago," Paul S. Taylor Papers.

65. *México* (Chicago), March 7, 1928, trans. Paul Taylor, box 1, Folder "Notes on Mexican Newspapers in Chicago," Paul S. Taylor Papers.

66. *México* (Chicago), April 11, 1925, p. 1.

67. The organization included nine groups. From Chicago: the Benito Juárez Mutual Aid Society, Club Anáhuac, Obreros Libres, and the Sociedad Hispano Americana; from Joliet: Comisión Honorífica and the Sociedad Mutualista Montezuma; from Waukegan: Club Atlas Mexicano; and from Indiana Harbor: the Benito Juárez Mutual Aid Society of Indiana Harbor.

68. See *México* (Chicago), August 21, 1926.

69. Taylor, *Mexican Chicago*, 140.

70. Meeting of the Association for the Unification and Defense of the Mexican Colony, April 13, 1934, "Adult dept. activities 4/7/34 to 4/14/34," box 20, p. 2, University of Chicago Settlement House Papers. Apparently the group held regular meetings and joined with the Mexican Settlement Benefit Committee to sponsor programs to help Mexicans in the area (see also p. 4).

71. See *ABC*, April 1943, pp. 1 and 3, box 89, folder 1, Chicago Area Project Papers.

72. Ibid.

73. Manuel and Alma Bravo interview, p. 14.

74. It is important to remember that there was a vibrant and active labor movement in Mexico starting in the late nineteenth century, and many Mexicans who came to the United States had experience working near or with organized labor. See Vargas, *Labor Rights.*

75. Quoted in Taylor, *Mexican Labor*, 120.

76. There were few Mexicans in skilled trade unions like the Chicago Machinists local (even though they had no citizenship requirement). The building trades (carpenters, painters, sheet-metal workers) did require U.S. citizenship and also had few Mexican members. Ibid., 121.

77. Sidney Levin interview, p. 17.

78. See Cohen, *Making a New Deal*, 166–67.

79. I refer here to the labor monographs of historians like Lizabeth Cohen, Roger Horowitz, and Rick Halpern. See ibid.; Horowitz, *"Negro and White"*; Halpern, *Down on the Killing Floor.*

80. Sidney Levin interview, p. 16.

81. I agree with Lizabeth Cohen, for instance, that Mexicans joined CIO unions, but my research contradicts her view that these Mexican union members "came to share CIO leaders' commitment to ethnic unity." Cohen, *Making a New Deal*, 339.

82. Jack García interview, p. 17.

83. Max Guzmán interview, p. 9.

84. *México* (Chicago), June 30, 1928, trans. Paul Taylor, box 1, Folder "Notes on Mexican Newspapers in Chicago," Paul S. Taylor Papers.

85. On collective national identities among other ethnic groups in Chicago, see Pacyga, *Polish Immigrants*; Guglielmo, *White on Arrival*; and Nelli, *Italians.* For Mexican ethnic identity in Chicago after World War II, see Padilla, *Latino.*

86. Rosales, *¡Pobre Raza!*, 24.

87. *El Heraldo de las Americas*, November 1, 1924, trans. Robert Redfield, box 59, folder 2, Robert Redfield Papers.

88. Ibid.

89. Ibid.

90. *México* (Chicago), September 16, 1926.

91. Ibid.

92. Calles (1924–28) maintained government control back-stage through the weak presidencies of Emilio Portes Gil (1928–30), Pascual Ortiz Rubio (1930–32), and Abelardo L. Rodríguez (1932–34). During this period, he also presided over the establishment and consolidation of the principal political party that came to be known as the PRI.

93. Secular Mexican constitutional articles included Article 3 (establishing secular education in schools); Article 5 (outlawing religious orders); Article 24 (outlawing public worship except in churches); Article 27 (limiting religious organizations from owning property); and Article 130 (preventing clergy from voting or from wearing religious clothing). The Calles Law in 1926 explicitly allowed priests to be fined for wearing religious dress or imprisoned for criticizing the government.

94. Bailey, *¡Viva Cristo Rey!*

95. Taylor, *Mexican Labor*, 133.

96. Raymond Nelson, "The Mexican in South Chicago," box 1, folder "Mexican Life in Chicago," p. 26, Paul S. Taylor Papers.

97. Ibid., 27.

98. For an extended institutional analysis of the strategies of the Catholic church and various Protestant groups employed with regard to Mexicans (and in which Mexicans are treated largely as pawns in institutional struggles), see McCarthy, "Which Christ." See also Jones, "Conditions," 89–93.

99. *Corréo Mexicano*, October 15 and December 4, 1926, trans. Paul Taylor, *Mexican Labor*, 137.

100. Taylor, *Mexican Labor*, 132–33.

101. *El Heraldo Juvenil* (Chicago), May 1928. I suspect that this is the youth version of *El Heraldo de las Americas*, the newspapers sponsored by Mexican consulates in various U.S. cities.

102. Club Anáhuac was based in Packingtown and averaged about thirty-five members in 1928. Club Atlético Cuauhtémoc was in the Hull-House neighborhood (Near West Side) and averaged thirty members in 1928. See Jones, "Conditions," 115.

103. *México* (Chicago), January 30, 1929. Quetzalcóatl was the most powerful of the Aztec gods.

104. *La Alianza* (Chicago), May 1936, trans. WPA Foreign Language Press Survey Papers.

105. *El Nacional* (Chicago), July 15, 1933, trans. WPA Foreign Language Press Survey Papers. Benito Juárez was president of Mexico from 1855–58. His *indioness* and humble roots were glorified, particularly in the postrevolutionary years. Guelateo (more common spelling) is the town in the Mexican state of Oaxaca where Juárez was born.

106. Departamento Consular, 1934, IV-487-16, Archivo Histórico de la Secretaria de Relaciónes Exteriores.

107. *La Esperanza* (Chicago), December 13, 1931, trans. WPA Foreign Language Press Survey Papers.

108. Globe Theater, 1145 Blue Island at Roosevelt Road, April 6, 7, and 8, 1943;

Theater Joy, 9223 Commercial Avenue, April 10 and 11, 1943. See advertisements in *ABC*, box 89, folder 1, p. 9, Chicago Area Project Papers.

109. Today the site is the most visited of all sacred sites in the Western Hemisphere.

110. "Informes sobre protección, rendidos durante el año, Consulado de Chicago," Departamento de asuntos comerciales y de protección, 1935, IV-706-3, Archivó Histórico de la Secretaria de Relaciónes Exteriores.

111. Eugenio Prequeira, Consul of Mexico in Chicago, "Informe sobre Comite Pro-Mexico de Chicago," April 5, 1935, IV-709-21, Archivó Histórico de la Secretaria de Relaciónes Exteriores.

112. Deutsch, *Women and the City*, 40.

113. Ibid.

114. Interview with Manuel Bravo by Robert Redfield, January 21, 1925, Journal, 1924–25, pp. 78–79, Robert Redfield Papers.

115. Taylor, *Mexican Labor*, 219. The visit had to be after November 17, 1929, the date that Ortíz Rubio won the election over José Vasconcelos (he won with tremendous backing from Calles behind the scenes).

116. Ibid. Mexicans in Chicago kept up with political news in Mexico, following, for instance, the assassination plot against Ortíz Rubio and Portes Gil (*México* [Chicago], January 28, 1930); or earlier, the rumors of General Calles's affair with Leanor Llorente—"will they get married in secret?"—accompanied by photos of the couple returning from Paris (*México* [Chicago], January 4, 1929).

117. *México* (Chicago), January 26, 1929. The play was called *Mexico: Glorioso y Tragico* (Mexico: glorious and tragic).

118. There were seven presidents of Mexico from 1915 to 1940: Venustiano Carranza (1915–20); Alvaro Obregón (1920–24); Plutarco Elías Calles (1924–28); Emilio Portes Gil (1928–30); Pascual Ortiz Rubio (1930–32); Abelardo L. Rodríguez (1932–34); and Lázaro Cárdenas (1934–40). See also chapter 1.

119. *Guía Diplomatica y Consular* (1902), pp. 77–79, Archivo Histórico de la Secretaria de Relaciónes Exteriores.

120. Luis Lupián (consul from about 1924 to 1926) and Rafael Aveleyra (consul from 1929 to about 1933), for example, filed many more reports relating their efforts on behalf of Mexicans in Chicago than any other consuls to Chicago during the revolutionary period until 1940.

121. See chapter 3 for a more in-depth presentation of the stages of repatriation drives in Chicago and the accompanying immigration legislation.

122. Story pieced together from documents of Mexican consulate in Chicago at Archivo Histórico de la Secretaria de Relaciónes Exteriores, "Protección," Departamento Consular, 1931, IV-190-8.

123. Rafael Guardado Valadez interview, p. 10.

124. *El Heraldo de las Americas*, November 1, 1924, trans. Robert Redfield, box 59, folder 2, Robert Redfield Papers.

125. Ignacio Elizalde interview, March 30, 1925, Journal, pp. 100–103, Robert Redfield Papers.

126. George Edson, "Mexicans in Gary, Indiana," Bureau of Labor Statistics, U.S. Dept. of Labor, box "Correspondence", folder "Summary of Mexicans in the North Central States," p. 8, Paul S. Taylor Papers.

127. Quoted in Taylor, *Mexican Labor*, 271.

128. Quoted in ibid.

129. Quoted in ibid., 215.

130. The editors of *México* included J. Xavier Mondragon (director) and F. P. Miranda (editor).

131. *México* (Chicago), October 20, 1928, trans. WPA Foreign Language Press Survey Papers.

132. The term is used in *México* (Chicago), March 7, 1928, trans. Paul Taylor box 1, folder: "Notes on Mexican Newspapers in Chicago," Paul S. Taylor Papers.

133. Reprint from *The Family*, April and May 1930, Family Welfare Association of America, "An Experiment in Recreation: Recreation Committee, United Charities of Chicago, Part I: Material and Method of Experiment," General Files, box 8, folder 1930–31, United Charities Papers.

134. Mrs. McAvoy interview, November 16, 1924, Robert Redfield Papers.

135. *México* (Chicago), March 7, 1928, box 1, folder: "Notes on Mexican Newspapers in Chicago," trans. Paul Taylor, Paul S. Taylor Papers.

136. Notice printed in *El Nacional* (Chicago), April 29, 1933, trans. WPA Foreign Language Press Survey Papers. It is not evident where the group obtained these children: Chicago? Other parts of the United States? Or Mexico?

137. *México* (Chicago), March 7, 1928, trans. Taylor, *Mexican Labor*, 176.

138. *El Heraldo de las Americas*, November 15, 1924, trans. Robert Redfield, box 59, folder 2, Robert Redfield Papers.

139. Quoted in Taylor, *Mexican Labor*, 270.

140. Quoted in ibid.

141. El Chapultepec: 3231 Ninety-first Street, South Chicago, and 742 Blue Island and 4320 Ashland, Chicago. Bello Jalisco, a restaurant: 4318 Ashland Avenue, Chicago; El Azteca: 10732 Torrence Ave., South Chicago; El Cinco de Mayo: 914 South Halsted, Chicago.

142. "In order to obtain separate figures for Mexicans, it was decided that all persons born in Mexico, or having parents born in Mexico, who were not definitely White, Negro, Indian, Chinese or Japanese, would be returned as Mexicans." U.S. Bureau of the Census, *Two Hundred Years*. Ironically, the impetus for creating such a category had come largely from newly formed Mexican American civil-rights groups like LULAC in Texas. In the 1930 manuscript census for Chicago, it is clear the category was inconsistently applied. I found examples of Mexicans born in the United States who were enumerated as "Mexican," Mexicans born in Mexico enumerated as "white," and Mexican-born parents who were counted as "white" while their Mexican-born children were enumerated as "Mexican." On racialization, I draw from the original work of Omi and Winant, *Racial Formation*, and several scholars who have built on this, including Lipsitz, *Possessive Investment*, and Foley, *White Scourge*.

143. Numbers calculated from 1920 and 1930 census figures by Louise Kerr. For more discussions of the repatriations in Chicago, see chapter 1. Also see Kerr, "Chicano Experience." To date, there are only two significant studies of Mexican repatriations in the 1930s, both of which deal with much larger regions than Chicago. See Balderrama and Rodríguez, *Decade of Betrayal*; and Hoffman, *Unwanted Mexicans*.

144. *México* (Chicago), June 17, 1928.

145. *The Crown* (Chicago), June 7, 1946, Chicago Historical Society.

BIBLIOGRAPHY

Archival and Manuscript Collections Consulted

Archivo Histórico de la Secretaria de Relaciónes Exteriores, Mexico City.

Back-of-the-Yards Collection, Chicago Public Library Archives.

Chicago Area Project Papers, Chicago Historical Society.

Chicago Commons Settlement House Papers, Chicago Historical Society.

Chicago Police Department Homicide Records, Illinois Regional Archives Depository, Chicago.

Chicago Polonia, Oral History Archives, Chicago Historical Society.

Colored Big Brothers Papers, Chicago Area Projects Papers, Chicago Historical Society.

Cook County Coroner's Inquest Records, Illinois Regional Archives Depository, Chicago.

Cook County Medical Examiner Papers, County Building, Chicago.

Ernest W. Burgess Papers, Special Collections, Joseph Regenstein Library, University of Chicago.

Fideicomiso Archivos de Plutarco Elías Calles y Fernando Torreblanca, Mexico City.

George Patterson Papers, Chicago Historical Society.

Hull-House Papers, Jane Addams Memorial Collection, University of Illinois at Chicago.

Illinois Historical Society Archives, Springfield.

Illinois Regional Archives Depository, Springfield.

Immigrant Protective League Papers, Chicago Historical Society.

Immigration and Naturalization Service Papers, Washington, D.C.

Juvenile Welfare Association, Chicago Public Library Archives.

Life Histories, WPA Federal Writers Project, Chicago, http://lcweb2.loc.gov/wpaintro/wpahome.html

Lower West Side Community Collection, Chicago Public Library Archives.

Manuel Gamio Papers, Bancroft Library, University of California at Berkeley.

Mary McDowell Papers, Chicago Historical Society.

Municipal Reference Collection, Chicago Public Library Archives.

National Archives and Records Administration, Great Lakes Region, Chicago. Records of the District Courts of the United States, Record Group 21, Northern District of Illinois, Eastern Division (Chicago), Naturalization Petition and Record Books, 1906–75.

Paul S. Taylor Papers, Bancroft Library, University of California at Berkeley.

Robert E. Park Papers, Special Collections, Joseph Regenstein Library, University of Chicago.
Robert Redfield Papers, Special Collections, Joseph Regenstein Library, University of Chicago.
South Chicago Community Collection, Chicago Public Library Archives.
United Charities Papers, Chicago Historical Society.
United Packinghouse Workers of America Interviews, 1917–83, Illinois Labor History Society, Chicago.
United Packinghouse Workers of America Oral History Project Interviews, 1985–86, Wisconsin Historical Society, Madison.
United Packinghouse Workers of America Papers, Wisconsin Historical Society, Madison.
U.S. National Archives, Department of State, Washington, D.C.
United Steelworkers Papers, District 31, Chicago Historical Society.
University of Chicago Settlement House Papers, Chicago Historical Society.
West Side Community Collection, Chicago Public Library Archives.
William E. Dever Papers, Chicago Historical Society.
WPA Federal Writers Project, Manuscript Division, Library of Congress, Washington, D.C.
WPA Foreign Language Press Survey Papers, Special Collections, Joseph Regenstein Library, University of Chicago.
Young Men's Christian Association Papers, Chicago Historical Society.

Newspapers

La Alianza (Chicago)
Chicago Daily Tribune
Chicago Herald Examiner
Chicago Sun-Times
Cleveland Advocate
Daily Calumet (South Chicago)
La Defensa (Chicago)

El Heraldo de las Americas (Chicago)
El Indicador (Chicago)
La Lucha (Chicago)
México (Chicago)
El Nacional (Chicago)
La Noticia Mundial (Chicago)
La Raza (Chicago)

Oral Histories

Agapita Flores interview, by Gabriela F. Arredondo, November 30, 2003, Chicago.
Agapita Flores and Ruth Flores Rucoba interview, 1982, transcription by Gabriela F. Arredondo and Emma Estrada Lukin, Chicago Historical Society.
Anthony Romo interview, by Jesse Escalante, December 28, 1981, transcription by Gabriela F. Arredondo and Emma Estrada Lukin, Chicago Historical Society.
Benny Rodríguez interview, by Jesse Escalante, January 21, 1980, transcription by Gabriela F. Arredondo and Emma Estrada Lukin, Chicago Historical Society.
Clementina Rodríguez interview, by Jesse Escalante, January 21, 1980, transcription by Jesse Escalante, Chicago Historical Society.
Gilbert "Chato" Martínez interview, by Jesse Escalante, n.d. (ca. 1980), transcribed by Gabriela F. Arredondo and Adrián Flores, Chicago Historical Society.

Jack García interview, by Jesse Escalante, n.d. (ca. 1979), transcription by Gabriela F. Arredondo and Adrián Flores, Chicago Historical Society.

Jesse Escalante interview, by Gabriela F. Arredondo, December 2, 2003, and January 16, 2004, Chicago.

José Cruz Díaz interview, by Jesse Escalante, October 12, 1979, transcription by Gabriela F. Arredondo and Adrián Flores, Chicago Historical Society.

Justino and Caroline Cordero interview, by Jesse Escalante, October 22, 1979, transcription by Gabriela F. Arredondo and Emma Estrada Lukin, Chicago Historical Society.

Lucio Franco interview, by Jesse Escalante, November 30, 1981, transcription by Gabriela F. Arredondo and Emma Estrada Lukin, Chicago Historical Society.

Manuel and Alma Bravo interview, by Jesse Escalante, n.d. (ca. 1980), transcription by Gabriela F. Arredondo and Emma Estrada Lukin, Chicago Historical Society.

Max Guzmán interview, by Jesse Escalante, February 7, 1980, transcribed by Gabriela F. Arredondo and Emma Estrada Lukin, Chicago Historical Society.

Mercedes Rios (Radica) interview, by Jesse Escalante, n.d. (ca. 1980), transcribed by Gabriela F. Arredondo and Adrián Flores, Chicago Historical Society.

Mr. and Mrs. Pete Martínez interview, by Jesse Escalante, n.d. (ca. 1980), transcribed by Gabriela F. Arredondo and Adrián Flores, Chicago Historical Society.

Nick Svalina interview, by Jesse Escalante, December 7, 1979, transcription by Gabriela F. Arredondo and Emma Estrada Lukin, Chicago Historical Society.

Rafael Guardado Valadez interview, by Jesse Escalante, n.d. (ca. 1980), transcribed by Gabriela F. Arredondo and Emma Estrada Lukin, Chicago Historical Society.

Ruth Rucoba and Agapita Flores interview, by Jesse Escalante, 1982, transcription by Gabriela F. Arredondo and Emma Estrada Lukin, Chicago Historical Society.

Sidney Levin interview, by Jesse Escalante, May 29, 1980, transcription by Jesse Escalante, Chicago Historical Society.

Secondary Sources

Abbott, Edith. *Immigration: Select Documents and Case Records.* Chicago: University of Chicago Press, 1924.

———. *The Tenements of Chicago, 1908–1935.* Chicago: University of Chicago Press, 1936.

Addams, Jane. *The Second Twenty Years at Hull-House, September 1909 to September 1929, with a Record of a Growing World Consciousness.* New York: Macmillan, 1930.

———. *Twenty Years at Hull-House, with Autobiographical Notes.* New York: Macmillan, 1910.

Alejandre, Jesús Arroyo. *Migración Rural Hacia Estados Unidos: Un Estudio Regional en Jalisco.* Mexico City: Consejo Nacional Para la Cultura y las Artes, 1991.

Almaguer, Tomás. "Chicano Men: A Cartography of Homosexual Identity and Behavior." *Differences* 3.2 (Summer 1991): 75–100.

———. *Racial Fault Lines: The Historical Origins of White Supremacy in California*. Berkeley: University of California Press, 1994.

Alonso, Ana María. "Conforming Disconformity: 'Mestizaje,' Hybridity, and the Aesthetics of Mexican Nationalism." *Cultural Anthropology* 19.4 (November 2004): 459–90.

Applebaum, Nancy, Anne MacPherson, and Karin Rosemblatt, eds. *Race and Nation in Modern Latin America*. Chapel Hill: University of North Carolina Press, 2003.

Arias, Patricia, and Claudia Rivas. *Estadística Agrícola de Jalisco*. Guadalajara: Universidad de Guadalajara, Dirección General Académica, 1994.

Armentrout, Walter W., Sara A. Brown, and Charles E. Gibbon. *Child Labor in the Beet Fields of Michigan*. New York: National Child Labor Committee, 1923.

Arredondo, Gabriela F. "Cartographies of Americanisms: Possibilities for Transnational Identities, Chicago, 1916–1939." In *Geographies of Latinidad: Mapping Latina/o Studies into the Twenty-first Century*. Ed. Matt García, Marie Leger, and Angarad Valdívia. Durham, N.C.: Duke University Press, forthcoming.

Arredondo, Gabriela F., Aída Hurtado, Norma Klahn, Olga Nájera-Ramírez, and Patricia Zavella, eds. *Chicana Feminisms: A Critical Reader*. Durham, N.C.: Duke University Press, 2003.

Arrom, Silvia. "Perspectivas Sobre Historia de la Familia en México." In *Familias Novohispanas: Siglos XVI al XIX*. Ed. Pilar Gonzalbo Aizpuru. Mexico City, D.F., El Centro: El Colegio de México, 1991. 389–99.

Badillo, David A. "Los Immigrantes Mexicanos y el Barrio de Hull-House: Integración de Reforma y Religion." In *La Communidad Mexicana en Estados Unidos: Aspectos de su Historia*. Ed. Fernando Saúl Alanís Enciso. Conaculta: El Colegio de San Luis, 2004. 127–54.

Bailey, David C. *¡Viva Cristo Rey! The Cristero Rebellion and the Church-State Conflict in Mexico*. Austin: University of Texas Press, 1974.

Balderrama, Francisco E., and Raymond Rodríguez, *Decade of Betrayal: Mexican Repatriation in the 1930s*. Albuquerque: University of New Mexico Press, 1995.

Barrett, James R. *Work and Community in the Jungle: Chicago's Packinghouse Workers, 1894–1922*. Urbana: University of Illinois Press, 1987.

Barrett, James R., and David Roediger. "Inbetween Peoples: Race, Nationality, and the 'New Immigrant' Working Class." *Journal of American Ethnic History* 16.3 (Spring 1997): 3–45.

Baur, Edward Jackson. "Delinquency among Mexican Boys in South Chicago." M.A. thesis, University of Chicago, 1938.

Becker, Marjorie. *Setting the Virgin on Fire: Lázaro Cárdenas, Michoacán Peasants, and the Redemption of the Mexican Revolution*. Berkeley: University of California Press, 1995.

Bederman, Gail. *Manliness and Civilization: A Cultural History of Gender and Race in the United States, 1880–1917*. Chicago: University of Chicago Press, 1995.

Belnap, Jeffrey, and Raúl Fernández, eds. *José Martí's "Our America": From National to Hemispheric Cultural Studies*. Durham, N.C.: Duke University Press, 1998.

Benitez, José Antonio. *Bolívar y Martí en la Integración de América Latina*. Vedado, La Havana: Prensa de la Torriente Editorial, 2002.

Betten, Neil, and Raymond A. Mohl. "From Discrimination to Repatriation: Mexican Life in Gary, Indiana, during the Great Depression." *Pacific Historical Review* 42 (August 1973): 370–88.

Biggott, Joseph C. *From Cottage to Bungalow: Houses and the Working Class in Metropolitan Chicago, 1869–1929.* Chicago: University of Chicago Press, 2001.

Blanco, Mónica. *Revolución y Contienda Política en Guanajuato, 1908–1913.* Mexico City: El Colegio de México, 1995.

Bogardus, Emory. "Mexican Repatriates." *Sociology and Social Research* 18 (November–December 1933): 169–76.

Brading, D. A. *The Origins of Mexican Nationalism.* Cambridge: Center of Latin American Studies, 1985.

Breckenridge, Sophonisba Preston, and Grace Abbott. *The Delinquent Child and the Home.* New York: Russell Sage Foundation, 1912.

Bukowski, Douglas. *Big Bill Thompson, Chicago, and the Politics of Image.* Urbana: University of Illinois Press, 1998.

Burgess, Ernest W., and Charles S. Newcomb, eds. *Census Data of the City of Chicago, 1920.* Chicago: University of Chicago Press, 1931.

———. *Census Data of the City of Chicago: 1930.* Chicago: University of Chicago Press, 1933.

Camarillo, Albert. *Chicanos in a Changing Society: From Mexican Pueblos to American Barrios in Santa Barbara and Southern California, 1848–1930.* Cambridge, Mass.: Harvard University Press, 1979.

Cárdenas, Gilbert. "Los Desarraigados: Chicanos in the Midwestern Region of the United States." *Aztlán: International Journal of Chicano Studies Research* 7 (Summer 1976): 153–86.

Cardoso, Lawrence A. *Mexican Emigration to the United States, 1897–1931.* Tucson: University of Arizona Press, 1980.

Castro, José Rivera. *En la Presidencia de Plutarco Calles, 1924–1928.* Mexico City: Instituto de Investigaciones Sociales de la Universidad Nacional Autónoma de México, 1983.

Chabram-Dernersesian, Angie. "On the Social Construction of Whiteness within Selected Chicano Discourses." In *Displacing Whiteness: Essays in Social and Cultural Criticism.* Ed. Ruth Frankenberg. Durham, N.C.: Duke University Press, 1997. 107–64.

Chávez, Ernesto. *"Mi Raza Primero!" (My People First!): Nationalism, Identity, and Insurgency in the Chicano Movement in Los Angeles, 1966–1978.* Berkeley: University of California Press, 2002.

Chicago Commission on Race Relations. *The Negro in Chicago: A Study of Race Relations and a Race Riot.* Chicago: University of Chicago Press, 1922.

Cohen, Lizabeth. *Making a New Deal: Industrial Workers in Chicago, 1919–1939.* New York: Cambridge University Press, 1990.

Conzen, Kathleen Neils, David A. Gerber, Ewa Morawska, George E. Pozzetta, and Rudolph J. Vecoli. "The Invention of Ethnicity: A Perspective from the U.S.A." *Journal of American Ethnic History* 12 (Fall 1992): 3–41.

Cook County (Ill.) Coroner. *The Race Riots: Biennial Report, 1918–1919, and Official Record of Inquests on the Victims of the Race Riots of July and August, 1919, Whereby Fifteen White Men and Twenty-three Colored Men Lost Their Lives and Several Hundred Were Injured.* Chicago: City of Chicago, 1920.

Corona, Moisés Vázquez. *Lupe Vélez: A Medio Siglo de Ausencia.* Mexico City, D.F.: EDAMEX, 1996.

Correa, José Carmen Soto. *Movimientos Campesinos de Derecha en el Oriente Michoácano: Comuneros, Campesinos, Caudillos, y Partidos.* Mexico City: Hoja Casa Editorial, 1996.

Currell, Susan, and Christina Cogdell, eds. *Popular Eugenics: National Efficiency and American Mass Culture in the 1920s.* Athens: Ohio University Press, 2006.

D'Agostino, Peter. "Missionaries in Babylon: The Adaptation of Italian Priests to Chicago's Church, 1870–1940." Ph.D. dissertation, University of Chicago, 1993.

Darío, Rubén. "To Roosevelt." In *Selected Poems by Rubén Darío.* Trans. Lysander Kemp. Austin: University of Texas Press, 1988. 125.

Dawson, Alexander S. "From Models for the Nation to Model Citizens: Indigenismo and the 'Revindication' of the Mexican Indian, 1920–1940." *Journal of Latin American Studies* 30 (1998): 279–308.

Dawson, Alexander S. *Indian and Nation in Revolutionary Mexico.* Albuquerque: University of New Mexico Press, 2003.

Davis, Allen F. *Spearheads for Reform: The Social Settlements and the Progressive Movement, 1890–1914.* New York: Oxford University Press, 1967.

De Genova, Nicholas. "Race, Space, and the Reinvention of Latin America in Mexican Chicago." *Latin American Perspectives* 25.5 (September 1998): 87–116.

———. "Working the Boundaries, Making the Difference: Race and Space in Mexican Chicago." Ph.D. dissertation, University of Chicago, 1999.

De la Campa, Román. *Latin Americanism.* Minneapolis: University of Minnesota Press, 1999.

De León, Arnoldo. *Ethnicity in the Sunbelt: Mexican Americans in Houston.* College Station: Texas A&M University Press, 2001.

D'Emilio, John, and Estelle B. Freedman. *Intimate Matters: A History of Sexuality in America.* New York: Harper and Row, 1988.

Denning, Michael. *The Cultural Front: The Laboring of American Culture in the Twentieth Century.* New York: Verso, 1997.

Deutsch, Sarah. *Women and the City: Gender, Space, and Power in Boston, 1870–1940.* New York: Oxford University Press, 2000.

Dore, Elizabeth. "The Holy Family: Imagined Households in Latin American History." In *Gender Politics in Latin America: Debates in Theory and Practice.* Ed. Elizabeth Dore. New York: Monthly Review Press, 1997. 101–17.

Dunn, Timothy J. "Immigration Enforcement in the U.S.–Mexico Border Region, the El Paso Case: Bureaucratic Power, Human Rights, and Civic Activism." Ph.D. dissertation, University of Texas at Austin, 1999.

Enciso, Fernando Saúl Alanis. "El gobierno de México y la repatriación de mexicanos de Estados Unidos 1934–1940." Ph.D. dissertation, El Colegio de México, 2000.

———. *La Communidad Mexicana en Estados Unidos: Aspectas de su Historia.* Conaculta: El Colegio de San Luis, 2004.

———. "Manuel Gamio: El Inicio de las Investigaciones sobre la Inmigración Mexicana a Estados Unidos." *Hmex* 52.4 (2003): 979–1020.

———. "No Cuenten Conmigo: La Pólitica de Repatriación del Govierno Mexicano y Sus Nacionales en Estados Unidos, 1910–1928." *Mexican Studies/Estudios Mexicanos* 19.2 (Summer 2003): 401–61.

Erdmans, Mary Patrice. *Opposite Poles: Immigrants and Ethnics in Polish Chicago, 1976–1990.* University Park: Pennsylvania State University Press, 1998.

Escobar, Edward J. *Race, Police, and the Making of a Political Identity: Mexican Americans and the Los Angeles Police Department, 1900–1945.* Berkeley: University of California Press, 1999.

Fields, Barbara. "Whiteness, Racism, and Identity." *International Labor and Working Class History* 60 (Fall 2001): 48–56.

Flores, William. "Citizens vs. Citizenry: Undocumented Immigrants and Latino Cultural Citizenship." In *Latino Cultural Citizenship: Claiming Identity, Space, and Rights.* Ed. William Flores and Rina Benmayor. Boston: Beacon Press, 1997. 255–77.

Foley, Neil. "Partly Colored or Other White: Mexican Americans and Their Problem with the Color Line." In *Beyond Black and White: Race, Ethnicity, and Gender in the U.S. South and Southwest.* Ed. Stephanie Cole and Alison M. Parker. Arlington: University of Texas Press, 2004. 123–44.

———. *The White Scourge: Mexicans, Blacks, and Poor Whites in Texas Cotton Culture.* Berkeley: University of California Press, 1997.

Frankenberg, Ruth. "Local Whitenesses, Localizing Whiteness." In *Displacing Whiteness: Essays in Social and Cultural Criticism.* Ed. Ruth Frankenberg. Durham, N.C.: Duke University Press, 1997. 1–33.

Funchion, Michael F. "Irish Chicago: Church, Homeland, Politics, and Class—the Shaping of an Ethnic Group, 1870–1900." In *Ethnic Chicago: A Multicultural Portrait.* Ed. Melvin G. Holli and Peter d'A. Jones. Grand Rapids, Mich.: W. B. Eerdmans, 1995.

Gabaccia, Donna R. "Liberty, Coercion, and the Making of Immigration Historians." *Journal of American History* 84.2 (September 1997): 570–75.

———. *We Are What We Eat: Ethnic Food and the Making of Americans.* Cambridge, Mass.: Harvard University Press, 1998.

Gamio, Manuel. *Forjando Patria (pro Nacionalismo).* Mexico City: Porrúa Hermanos, 1916.

———. *The Mexican Immigrant.* New York: Arno Press, 1969.

———. *Mexican Immigration to the United States: A Study of Human Migration and Adjustment.* Chicago: University of Chicago Press, 1930.

Ganz, Cheryl R., and Margaret Strobel, eds. *Pots of Promise: Mexicans and Pottery at Hull-House, 1920–1940.* Urbana: University of Illinois Press, 2004.

García, Juan R. "History of Chicanos in Chicago Heights." *Aztlán: International Journal of Chicano Studies Research* 7 (Summer 1976): 291–306.

———. *Mexicans in the Midwest, 1900–1932.* Tucson: University of Arizona Press, 1996.

———. "Midwest Mexicanos in the 1920s: Issues, Questions, and Directions." *Social Science Journal* 19 (April 1982): 88–99.

García, Mario T. *Mexican Americans: Leadership, Ideology, and Identity, 1930–1960.* New Haven, Conn.: Yale University Press, 1989.

García, Matt. *A World of Its Own: Race, Labor, and Citrus in the Making of Greater Los Angeles, 1900–1970.* Chapel Hill: University of North Carolina Press, 2001.

García, Matt, Marie Leger, and Angarad Valdivia, eds. *Geographies of Latinidad:*

Mapping Latina/o Studies into the Twenty-first Century. Durham, N.C.: Duke University Press, forthcoming.

García, Richard A. "The Making of the Mexican-American Mind, San Antonio, 1929–1941: A Social and Intellectual History of an Ethnic Community." Ph.D. dissertation, University of California at Irvine, 1980.

———. *Rise of the Mexican American Middle Class, San Antonio, 1929–1941.* College Station: Texas A&M University Press, 1991.

Garcilazo, Jeffrey M. "*Traqueros*: Mexican Railroad Workers in the United States, 1870–1930." Ph.D. dissertation, University of California at Santa Barbara, 1995.

Gerstle, Gary. "The Protean Character of American Liberalism." *American Historical Review* 99 (1994): 1043–73.

Girón, Victor Manuel Castillo. *Sólo Dios y el Norte: Migración a Estados Unidos y Desarrollo en una Región de Jalisco.* Guadalajara: Universidad de Guadalajara, 1995.

González, Gilbert G. *Mexican Consuls and Labor Organizing: Imperial Politics in the American Southwest.* Austin: University of Texas Press, 1999.

Graham, Richard, ed. *The Idea of Race in Latin America, 1870–1940.* Austin: University of Texas Press, 1990.

Green, Paul Michael, and Melvin G. Holli, eds. *The Mayors: The Chicago Political Tradition.* Carbondale: Southern Illinois University Press, 2005.

Grossman, James R. *Land of Hope: Chicago, Black Southerners, and the Great Migration.* Chicago: University of Chicago Press, 1991.

Guerin-González, Camille. *Mexican Workers and American Dreams: Immigration, Repatriation, and California Farm Labor, 1900–1939.* New Brunswick, N.J.: Rutgers University Press, 1994.

Guglielmo, Thomas Angelo. *White on Arrival: Italians, Race, Color, and Power in Chicago, 1890–1945.* New York: Oxford University Press, 2003.

Gutiérrez, David. *Walls and Mirrors: Mexican Americans, Mexican Immigrants, and the Politics of Ethnicity.* Berkeley: University of California Press, 1995.

Gutiérrez, Ramón. *When Jesus Came, the Corn Mothers Went Away: Marriage, Sexuality, and Power in New Mexico, 1500–1846.* Stanford, Calif.: Stanford University Press, 1991.

Gutmann, Matthew C. *The Meanings of Macho: Being a Man in Mexico City.* Berkeley: University of California Press, 1996.

Hall, Linda B. "Alvaro Obregón and the Politics of Mexican Land Reform." *Hispanic American Historical Review* 60 (1980): 213–38.

Hall, Linda B., and Don M. Coerver. *Revolution on the Border: The United States and Mexico, 1910–1920.* Albuquerque: University of New Mexico Press, 1988.

Hall, Stuart. "Cultural Identity and Diaspora." In *Identity: Community, Culture, Difference.* Ed. Jon Rutherford. London: Lawrence and Wishart, 1990. 220–34.

———. "Signification, Representation, Ideology: Althusser and the Post-Structuralist Debates." *Critical Studies in Mass Communication* 2.2 (June 1985): 91–114.

Halpern, Rick. *Down on the Killing Floor: Black and White Workers in Chicago's Packinghouses, 1904–1954.* Urbana: University of Illinois Press, 1997.

Handlin, Oscar. *The Uprooted: The Epic Story of the Great Migrations that Made the American People.* Boston: Little Brown, 1951.

Harris, Cheryl I. "Whiteness as Property." *Harvard Law Review* 106.8 (June 1993): 1707–91

Hart, John Mason. *Border Crossings: Mexican and Mexican-American Workers.* Wilmington, Del.: Scholarly Resources Books, 1998.

Heap, Chad. *Homosexuality in the City: A Century of Research at the University of Chicago.* Chicago: University of Chicago Press, 1998.

———. "'Slumming': Sexuality, Race, and Urban Commercial Leisure, 1900–1940." Ph.D. dissertation, University of Chicago, 2000.

Hernández-Fujigaki, Jorge. "Mexican Steelworkers and the United Steelworkers of America in the Midwest: The Inland Steel Experience, 1936–1976." Ph.D. dissertation, University of Chicago, 1991.

Hershfield, Joanne. *The Invention of Dolores del Rio.* Minneapolis: University of Minnesota Press, 2000.

Higginson, Stephen A. "A Short History of the Right to Petition Government for the Redress of Grievances." *Yale Law Journal* 96 (November 1986): 142–66.

Higham, John. *Strangers in the Land: Patterns of American Nativism, 1860–1925.* New Brunswick, N.J.: Rutgers University Press, 1988.

Hodes, Martha. "The Mercurial Nature and Abiding Power of Race: A Transnational Family Story." *American Historical Review* 108.1 (February 2003): 84–118.

Hoffman, Abraham. *Unwanted Mexicans in the Great Depression: Repatriation Pressures, 1929–1939.* Tucson: University of Arizona Press, 1974.

Holli, Melvin G., and Peter d'A. Jones, eds. *Ethnic Chicago.* Grand Rapids, Mich.: W. B. Eerdmans, 1981.

———. *Ethnic Chicago: A Multicultural Portrait.* Grand Rapids, Mich.: W. B. Eerdmans, 1995.

———. *The Ethnic Frontier: Essays in the History of Group Survival in Chicago and the Midwest.* Grand Rapids, Mich.: W. B. Eerdmans, 1977.

Holt, Thomas C. "Explaining Racism in American History." In *Imagined Histories: American Historians Interpret the Past.* Ed. Anthony Molho and Gordon S. Wood. Princeton, N.J.: Princeton University Press, 1998. 117–18.

———. "Marking: Race, Race-Making, and the Writing of History." AHA Presidential Address. *American Historical Review* 100.1 (February 1995): 1–20.

———. *The Problem of Freedom: Race, Labor, and Politics in Jamaica and Britain, 1832–1938.* Baltimore: Johns Hopkins University Press, 1992.

Horak, Jacob. "Assimilation of Czechs in Chicago." Ph.D. dissertation, University of Chicago, 1920.

Horowitz, Roger. *"Negro and White, Unite and Fight": A Social History of Industrial Unionism in Meatpacking, 1930–1990.* Urbana: University of Illinois Press, 1997.

Horsman, Reginald. *Race and Manifest Destiny: The Origins of American Racial Anglo-Saxonism.* Cambridge, Mass.: Harvard University Press, 1981.

Houghteling, Leila. *The Income and Standard of Living of Unskilled Laborers in Chicago.* Chicago: University of Chicago Press, 1927.

Hughes, Elizabeth Ann. *Illinois Persons on Relief in 1935.* WPA Project No. 165-54-6018. Chicago: Works Progress Administration, 1937.

Humphrey, Norman D. "Mexican Repatriation from Michigan: Public Assistance in Historical Perspective." *Social Service Review* 15 (September 1941): 497–513.

Ignatiev, Noel. *How the Irish Became White*. New York: Routledge, 1995.

Irwin, Robert McKee. *Mexican Masculinities*. Minneapolis: University of Minnesota Press, 2003.

James, Concha Romera. Preface to *The Indian Citizen of America*, by Moíses Sáenz. *Points of View* 9 (September 1946): 1–3.

Jirasek, Rita Arias, and Carlos Tortolero. *Images of America Series: Mexican Chicago*. Chicago: Arcadia Publishing, 2001.

Johnson, Elizabeth S. "Wages, Employment Conditions, and Welfare of Sugar Beet Laborers." *Monthly Labor Review* 46 (February 1938): 332–40.

Jones, Anita Edgar. "Conditions Surrounding Mexicans in Chicago." Ph.D. dissertation, University of Chicago, 1928.

———. "Mexican Colonies in Chicago." *Social Service Review* 2.4 (December 1928): 579–97.

Jones, Richard C. *Ambivalent Journey: U.S. Migration and Economic Mobility in North-Central Mexico*. Tucson: University of Arizona Press, 1995.

Jones, Robert C., and Louis R. Wilson. *The Mexican in Chicago*. Chicago: Comity Commission of the Chicago Church Federation, 1931.

Joseph, G. M., and Daniel Nugent, eds. *Everyday Forms of State Formation: Revolution and the Negotiation of Rule in Modern Mexico*. Durham, N.C.: Duke University Press, 1994.

Kantowicz, Edward R. *Polish-American Politics in Chicago, 1888–1940*. Chicago: University of Chicago Press, 1975.

Kaplan, Caren, Norma Alarcón, and Minno Moallem, eds. *Between Woman and Nation: Nationalisms, Transnational Feminisms, and the State*. Durham, N.C.: Duke University Press, 1999.

Katz, Friedrich. *Riot, Rebellion, and Revolution: Rural Social Conflict in Mexico*. Princeton, N.J.: Princeton University Press, 1988.

———. *The Secret War in Mexico: Europe, the United States, and the Mexican Revolution*. Chicago: University of Chicago Press, 1981.

Katzew, Ilona, and Susan Deans Smith, eds. *Race and Classification: The Case of Mexican America*. Stanford, Calif.: Stanford University Press, 2008.

Kazal, Russel A. "Revisiting Assimilation: The Rise, Fall, and Reappraisal of a Concept in American Ethnic History." *American Historical Review* 100 (April 1995): 437–71.

Keating, Ann Durkin. *Building Chicago: Suburban Developers and the Creation of a Divided Metropolis*. Columbus: Ohio State University Press, 1988.

Kelley, Nicholas. "Early Days at Hull House." *Social Service Review* 28.4 (December 1954): 424–29.

Kerber, Linda. "Separate Spheres, Female Worlds, Woman's Place: The Rhetoric of Women's History." *Journal of American History* 75 (1988): 9–39.

Kerr, Louise Año Nuevo. "Chicanas in the Great Depression." In *Between Borders: Essays On Mexicana/Chicana History*. Ed. Adelaida R. Del Castillo. Encino, Calif.: Floricanto Press, 1990. 257–68.

———. "The Chicano Experience in Chicago: 1920–1970." Ph.D. dissertation, University of Illinois at Chicago, 1976.

———. "Chicano Settlements in Chicago." *Journal of Ethnic Studies* 2.4 (Winter 1975): 22–32.

King, Desmond. *Making Americans: Immigration, Race, and the Origins of the Diverse Democracy.* Cambridge, Mass.: Harvard University Press, 2000.

Kiser, George C., and Martha W. Kiser, eds. *Mexican Workers in the United States: Historical and Political Perspectives.* Albuquerque: University of New Mexico Press, 1979.

Knight, Alan. "Racism, Revolution, and Indigenismo: Mexico, 1910–1940." In *The Idea of Race in Latin America, 1870–1940.* Ed. Richard Graham. Austin: University of Texas Press, 1990. 71–107.

Laird, Judith F. "Argentine, Kansas: The Evolution of a Mexican American Community, 1905–1940." Ph.D. dissertation, University of Kansas, 1975.

Lamas, Marta. "Cuerpo: Diferencia Sexual y Género." *Debate Feminista* 5.10 (September 1994): 3–31.

Landisco, John. *Organized Crime in Chicago.* Chicago: University of Chicago Press, 1929.

Lecuona, Guillermo Raúl Zepeda. *Constitucionalistas, Iglesia Católica, y Derecho del Trabajo en Jalisco, 1913–1919.* Mexico City: Instituto Naciónal de Estudios Históricos de la Revolución Mexicana, 1997.

Leftwich, Max H. "The Migratory Harvest Labor Market: An Illinois Case Study." Ph.D. dissertation, University of Illinois at Urbana-Champaign, 1975.

Lipsitz, George. *The Possessive Investment in Whiteness: How White People Profit from Identity Politics.* Philadelphia: Temple University Press, 1998.

Lomnitz-Adler, Claudio. *Exits from the Labyrinth: Culture and Ideology in the Mexican National Space.* Berkeley: University of California Press, 1992.

———. "Modes of Citizenship in Mexico." Paper presented at the Social History Workshop, University of Chicago, 1998.

López, Ian Haney. *White by Law: The Legal Construction of Race.* New York: New York University Press, 1998.

Lowe, Lisa. *Immigrant Acts: On Asian American Cultural Politics.* Durham, N.C.: Duke University Press, 1996.

Macias, Ana. *Against All Odds: The Feminist Movement in Mexico to 1940.* Westport, Conn.: Greenwood Press, 1982.

Maril, Robert Lee. *Patrolling Chaos: The U.S. Border Patrol in Deep South Texas.* Lubbock: Texas Tech University Press, 2004.

Márquez, Benjamin. *Constructing Identities in Mexican-American Political Organizations: Choosing Issues, Taking Sides.* Austin: University of Texas Press, 2003.

———. *LULAC: The Evolution of a Mexican American Political Organization.* Austin: University of Texas Press, 1993.

Martí, José. *Antología/Martí.* Ed. Susana Cella. Buenos Aires: Ediciones Instituto Movilizador de Fondos Cooperativos, 2003.

———. *Obras Completas.* La Havana: Editorial Nacional de Cuba, 1965.

Martínez, Anne M. "Bordering on the Sacred: Religion, Nation, and U.S.–Mexican Relations, 1910–1929." Ph.D. dissertation, University of Minnesota, 2003.

Martínez-Echazábal, Lourdes. "Mestizaje and the Discourse of National/Cultural Identity in Latin America, 1845–1959." *Latin American Perspectives* 25.3 (1998): 21–42.

Matsumoto, Valerie. *Farming the Home Place: A Japanese American Community in California, 1919–1982.* Ithaca, N.Y.: Cornell University Press, 1993.

McCaffrey, Lawrence S., Ellen Skerrett, Michael F. Funchion, and Charles Fanning. *The Irish in Chicago.* Urbana: University of Illinois Press, 1997.

McCarthy, Br. Malachy Richard. "Which Christ Came to Chicago: Catholic and Protestant Programs to Evangelize, Socialize, and Americanize the Mexican Immigrant, 1900–1940." Ph.D. dissertation, Loyola University of Chicago, 2002.

McLean, Robert N. "The Mexican Return." *The Nation,* August 24, 1932, 135–37.

McWilliams, Carey. *Factories in the Field: The Story of Migratory Farm Labor in California.* Berkeley: University of California Press, 1935.

———. *North from Mexico: The Spanish-Speaking People of the United States.* 1949; reprint, New York: Greenwood Press, 1968.

Melhuus, Marit, and Kristi Anne Stolen, eds. *Machos, Mistresses, Madonnas: Contesting the Power of the Latin American Gender Imagery.* New York: Verso, 1996.

Menchaca, Martha. *Recovering History, Constructing Race: The Indian, Black, and White Roots of Mexican Americans.* Austin: University of Texas Press, 2001.

"Mexicans in PWOC." *CIO News—Packinghouse Workers' Organizing Committee (PWOC) Edition,* June 12, 1939.

Mendoza, Valerie M. "The Creation of a Mexican Immigrant Community in Kansas City, 1890–1930." Ph.D. dissertation, University of California at Berkeley, 1997.

Meyer, Jean. *The Cristero Rebellion: The Mexican People between Church and State, 1926–1929.* New York: Cambridge University Press, 1976.

Meyer, Michael C., and William L. Sherman. *The Course of Mexican History.* 4th ed. New York: Oxford University Press, 1991.

Meyerowitz, Joanne J. *Women Adrift: Independent Wage Earners in Chicago, 1880–1930.* Chicago: University of Chicago Press, 1988.

Mier, Fray Servando Teresa de. *The Memoirs of Fray Servando Teresa de Mier.* Ed. Susan Rotker. Trans. Helen Lane. New York: Oxford University Press, 1998.

Mignolo, Walter D. *Local Histories/Global Designs: Coloniality, Subaltern Knowledges, and Border Thinking.* Princeton, N.J.: Princeton University Press, 2000.

Miller, Marilyn Grace. *Rise and Fall of the Cosmic Race: The Cult of Mestisaje in Latin America.* Austin: University of Texas Press, 2004.

Mirandé, Alfredo. *Hombres y Machos: Masculinity and Latino Culture.* Boulder, Colo.: Westview Press, 1997.

Mohl, Raymond A., and Neil Betten. *Steel City: Urban and Ethnic Patterns in Gary, Indiana, 1906–1950.* New York: Holmes and Meier, 1986.

Montejano, David. *Anglos and Mexicans in the Making of Texas.* Berkeley: University of California Press, 1990.

Montoya, María E. *Translating Property: The Maxwell Land Grant and the Conflict over Land in the American West, 1840–1900.* Berkeley: University of California Press, 2002.

Muñoz, Carlos. *The Sixties Chicano Movement: Youth, Identity, Power.* London: Verso, 1989.

Murphy, Arthur D., and Alex Stepick. *Social Inequality in Oaxaca, a History of Resistance and Change: Conflicts in Urban and Regional Development.* Philadelphia: Temple University Press, 1993.

Necoachea, Gerardo Gracia. "Customs and Resistance: Mexican Immigrants to Chicago, 1910–1930." In *Border Crossings: Mexican and Mexican-American Workers*. Ed. John M. Hart. Wilmington, Del.: Scholarly Resources, 1998. 185–207.

Nelli, Humbert S. *From Immigrants to Ethnics: The Italian Americans*. New York: Oxford University Press, 1983.

———. *Italians in Chicago, 1880–1930: A Study in Ethnic Mobility*. New York: Oxford University Press, 1970.

Nesbitt, Florence. *The Chicago Standard Budget for Dependent Families*. Chicago: Chicago Council of Social Agencies, 1920.

———. *The Chicago Standard Budget for Dependent Families*. Chicago: Council of Social Agencies of Chicago, Division on Family and Child Welfare, 1937.

Ngai, Mae M. "The Architecture of Race in American Immigration Law: A Reexamination of the Immigration Act of 1924." *Journal of American History* 86.1 (1999): 67–92.

———. *Impossible Subjects: Illegal Aliens and the Making of Modern America*. Princeton, N.J.: Princeton University Press, 2004.

Oboler, Suzanne. *Ethnic Labels, Latino Lives: Identity and the Politics of (Re)presentation in the United States*. Minneapolis: University of Minnesota Press, 1995.

Oliveros, Antonio Gutiérrez y. *Valores Espirituales de la Raza Indigena: Su Educacion desde los Tiempos Precortesianos hasta Nuestra Dias*. Mexico: Talleres Graficos de la Nacion, 1929.

Omi, Michael, and Howard Winant. *Racial Formation in the United States: From the 1960s to the 1980s*. New York: Routledge, 1986.

Orozco, Cynthia. "The Origins of the League of United Latin American Citizens (LULAC) and the Mexican American Civil Rights Movement in Texas with an Analysis of Women's Political Participation in a Gendered Context, 1910–1929." Ph.D. dissertation, University of Texas, 1992.

Pacyga, Dominic A. "Chicago's 1919 Race Riot: Ethnicity, Class, and Urban Violence." In *The Making of Urban America*. Ed. Raymond A. Mohl. 2d ed. Wilmington, Del.: Scholarly Resources, 1997. 187–207.

———. *Polish Immigrants and Industrial Chicago: Workers on the South Side, 1880–1922*. Columbus: Ohio State University Press, 1991.

———. "To Live amongst Others: Poles and Their Neighbors in Industrial Chicago, 1865–1930." *Journal of American Ethnic History* 16.1 (Fall 1996): 55–74.

Pacyga, Dominic A., and Ellen Skerrett. *Chicago: City of Neighborhoods: Histories and Tours*. Chicago: Loyola University Press, 1986.

Padilla, Felix. *Latino Ethnic Consciousness: The Case of Mexican Americans and Puerto Ricans in Chicago*. South Bend, Ind.: University of Notre Dame Press, 1985.

Padua, Jorge N. *Educación, Industrialización, y Progreso Técnico en México: Un Estudio de Caso en la Zona Conurbada de la Desembocadura del Río Balsas*. Mexico City: El Colegio de México, 1984.

Palmer, Susan L. "Building Ethnic Communities in a Small City: Romanians and Mexicans in Aurora, Illinois, 1900–1940." Ph.D. dissertation, Northern Illinois University, 1986.

Park, Robert E., and Ernest W. Burgess. *Introduction to the Science of Sociology*. Chicago: University of Chicago Press, 1921.

Peck, Gunther. *Reinventing Free Labor: Padrones and Immigrant Workers in the North American West, 1880–1930.* New York: Cambridge University Press, 2000.

Peiss, Kathy. *Cheap Amusements: Working Women and Leisure in Turn-of-the-Century New York.* Philadelphia: Temple University Press, 1986.

Pérez, Emma. *The Decolonial Imaginary: Writing Chicanas into History.* Bloomington: Indiana University Press, 1999.

Persons, Stow. *Ethnic Studies at Chicago, 1905–1945.* Urbana: University of Illinois Press, 1987.

Pessar, Patricia R., and Sarah J. Mahler. "Gendered Geographies of Power: Analyzing Gender across Transnational Spaces." *Identities* 7.4 (2001): 441–59.

Pierson, Ruth Roach, and Nupur Chaudhuri, eds. *Nation, Empire, Colony: Historicizing Gender and Race.* Bloomington: Indiana University Press, 1998.

Poplett, Carolyn O., and Mary Ann Porucznik. *The Woman Who Never Fails: Grace Wilbur Trout and Illinois Suffrage.* Oak Park, Ill.: Historical Society of Oak Park and River Forest, 2000.

Portes, Alejandro, and John W. Curtis. "Changing Flags: Naturalization and Its Determinants among Mexican Immigrants." *International Migration Review* 27 (1987): 352–71.

Posadas, Barbara M. *The Filipino Americans.* Westport, Conn.: Greenwood Press, 1999.

Posadas, Barbara M., and Roland L. Guyotte. "'Life's a Gamble': State Politics, Gender, and the Global Context of Filipino Migration to the United States." In *Remapping Asian American History.* Ed. Sucheng Chan. Walnut Creek, Calif.: Altamira Press, 2003.

Potter, Claire. *War on Crime: Bandits, G-Men, and the Politics of Mass Culture.* New Brunswick, N.J.: Rutgers University Press, 1998.

Prieur, Annick. "Domination and Desire: Male Homosexuality and the Construction of Masculinity in Mexico." In *Machos, Mistresses, Madonnas: Contesting the Power of Latin American Gender Imagery.* Ed. Marit Melhuus and Kristi Anne Stolen. New York: Verso, 1996. 83–107.

Purnell, Jennie. *Popular Movements and State Formation in Revolutionary Mexico: The Agraristas and Cristeros of Michoacán.* Durham, N.C.: Duke University Press, 1999.

Raat, W. Dirk. *Revoltosos: Mexico's Rebels in the United States, 1903–1923.* College Station: Texas A&M University Press, 1981.

Rabinovitz, Lauren. *For the Love of Pleasure: Women, Movies, and Culture in Turn-of-the-Century Chicago.* New Brunswick, N.J.: Rutgers University Press, 1998.

Ramírez, Gabriel. *Lupe Vélez: La Mexicana que Escupía Fuego.* Mexico City: Cineteca Nacional, 1986.

Reich, Peter L. *Mexico's Hidden Revolution: The Catholic Church in Law and Politics since 1929.* South Bend, Ind.: University of Notre Dame Press, 1996.

Reisler, Mark. *By the Sweat of Their Brow: Mexican Immigrant Labor in the United States, 1900–1940.* Westport, Conn.: Greenwood Press, 1976.

———. "The Mexican Immigrant in the Chicago Area during the 1920s." *Journal of the Illinois State Historical Society* 66.2 (Summer 1973): 144–58.

Rembis, Michael. "Breeding Up the Human Herd: Gender, Power, and Eugenics in Illinois, 1890–1940." Ph.D. dissertation, University of Arizona, 2003.

Rénique, Gerardo. "Race, Region, and Nation: Sonora's Anti-Chinese Racism and Mexico's Postrevolutionary Nationalism, 1920s-1930s." In *Race and Nation in Modern Latin America*. Ed. Nancy P. Applebaum, Anne S. MacPherson, and Karin Alejandra Rosemblatt. Chapel Hill: University of North Carolina Press, 2003. 211–36.

Reyes, Aurelio de los, and García Rojas. *Dolores Del Rio*. Prologue by Carlos Monsiváis. Mexico City: Grupo Condumex, Fernández Cueto Editores, 1996.

Richard, Carlos Macías. *Vida y Temperamento: Plutarco Elías Calles*. Sonora, Mexico: Instituto Sonorense de Cultura, Gobierno del Estado de Sonora, fondo de Cultura Económica, 1995.

Rodríguez, Jaime E., ed. *The Revolutionary Process in Mexico: Essays on Political and Social Change, 1880–1940*. Los Angeles: University of California at Los Angeles, 1990.

Rodríguez, Maria Elena. "Mary Dilley, Curandera: A Modern South Texas Folk Healer." Ph.D. dissertation, Texas A&M University, 1993.

Roediger, David R. *Colored White: Transcending the Racial Past*. Berkeley: University of California Press, 2000.

———. *Towards the Abolition of Whiteness: Essays on Race, Politics, and Working-Class History*. London: Verso, 1994.

———. *Wages of Whiteness: Race and the Making of the American Working Class*. New York: Verso, 1991.

Román, David. "Tropical Fruit." In *Tropicalizations: Transcultural Representations of Latinidad*. Ed. Frances Aparicio and Susana Chávez-Silverman. Hanover, N.H.: Dartmouth College Press, 1997. 199–35.

Romo, Ricardo. *East Los Angeles: History of a Barrio*. Austin: University of Texas Press, 1983.

Roosevelt, Franklin Delano. *Pan American Day Address of President Franklin D. Roosevelt* [Delivered at the Governing Board of the Pan American Union, Washington, D.C., April 12, 1933]. Washington, D.C.: Pan American Union, 1933.

Rosaldo, Renato. "Cultural Citizenship, Inequality, and Multiculturalism." In *Latino Cultural Citizenship: Claiming Identity, Space, and Rights*. Ed. William V. Flores and Rina Benmayor. Boston: Beacon Press, 1998. 27–38.

Rosales, F. Arturo. *¡Pobre Raza! Violence, Justice, and Mobilization among México Lindo Immigrants, 1900–1936*. Austin: University of Texas Press, 1999.

Rosales, Francisco A. "Mexican Immigration to the Urban Midwest during the 1920s." Ph.D. dissertation, Indiana University, 1978.

———. "Regional Origins of Mexicano Immigrants to Chicago during the 1920s." *Aztlán: International Journal of Chicano Studies Research* 7 (Summer 1976): 187–201.

Rosen, Christine. *Preaching Eugenics: Religious Leaders and the American Eugenics Movement*. New York: Oxford University Press, 2004.

Rotondo, Anthony. *American Manhood: Transformation in Masculinity from the Revolution to the Modern Era*. New York: Basic Books, 1993.

Rouse, Roger. "Questions of Identity: Personhood and Collectivity in Transnational Migration to the U.S." *Critique of Anthropology* 15.4 (1995): 351–80.

Ruíz, Ramón García. *Breve Historia de la Educación en Jalisco.* Mexico City: Secretaría de Educación Pública, 1958.

Ruiz, Vicki L. *Cannery Women, Cannery Lives: Mexican Women, Unionization, and the California Food Processing Industry, 1930–1950.* Albuquerque: University of New Mexico Press, 1987.

———. Foreword to *Pots of Promise: Mexicans and Pottery at Hull-House, 1920– 1940.* Ed. Cheryl R. Ganz and Margaret Strobel. Urbana: University of Illinois Press, 2004. ix–xii.

———. *From Out of the Shadows: Mexican Women in Twentieth-Century America.* New York: Oxford University Press, 1998.

———. "'Star Struck': Acculturation, Adolescence, and the Mexican American Woman, 1920–1950." *Building with Our Hands: New Directions in Chicana Studies.* Ed. Adela de la Torre and Beatriz Pesquera. Berkeley: University of California Press, 1993. 109–29.

Ruiz, Vicki L., and Virginia Sánchez Korrol, eds. *Latina Legacies: Identity, Biography, and Community.* New York: Oxford University Press, 2005.

Sáenz, Moisés. *The Indian Citizen of America* (Pamphlet). *Points of View* 9 (September 1946): 1–8.

———. *Mexico: An Appraisal and a Forecast.* New York: Committee on Cultural Relations with Latin America, 1929.

———. *Mexico Integro.* Lima: Imprenta Torres Aguirre, 1939.

Sáenz, Moisés, and Herbert Ingram Priestley. *Some Mexican Problems.* Chicago: University of Chicago Press, 1926.

Salas, Elizabeth. *Soldaderas in the Mexican Military: Myth and History.* Austin: University of Texas Press, 1990.

Sánchez, George J. *Becoming Mexican American: Ethnicity, Culture, and Identity in Chicano Los Angeles, 1900–1945.* New York: Oxford University Press, 1993.

———. "'Go after the Women': Americanization and the Mexican Immigrant Woman, 1915–1929." In *Unequal Sisters: A Multicultural Reader in U.S. Women's History.* Ed. Ellen Carol DuBois and Vicki L. Ruiz. Routledge: New York, 1990. 250–63.

———. "The 'New Nationalism,' Mexican Style: Race and Progressivism in Chicano Political Development during the 1920s." In *California Progressivism Revisited.* Ed. William Deverell and Tom Sutton. Berkeley: University of California Press, 1994. 229–44.

Sandoval, Chela, *Methodology of the Oppressed: Theory out of Bounds.* Minneapolis: University of Minnesota Press, 2000.

Saxton, Alexander. *The Rise and Fall of the White Republic: Class Politics and Mass Culture in Nineteenth-Century America.* London: Verso, 1990.

Schmidt, John R. "William E. Dever: A Chicago Political Fable." In *The Mayors: The Chicago Political Tradition.* Ed. Paul M. Green and Melvin G. Holli. Carbondale: Southern Illinois University Press, 1995. 82–98.

Shaw, Clifford. *The Jack-Roller.* Chicago: University of Chicago Press, 1930.

Sherrick, Rebecca. "Private Visions, Public Lives: The Hull-House Women in the Progressive Era." Ph.D. dissertation, Northwestern University, 1980.

Simon, Daniel T. "Mexican Repatriation in East Chicago, Indiana." *Journal of Ethnic Studies* 2 (Summer 1974): 11–23.

Simpson, Tyler N. *The Ejido: Mexico's Way Out.* Chapel Hill: University of North Carolina Press, 1937.

Sklar, Kathryn Kish. "Hull House in the 1890s: A Community of Women Reformers." In *Unequal Sisters: A Multi-Cultural Reader in U.S. Women's History.* Ed. Ellen Carol DuBois and Vicki L. Ruiz. New York: Routledge, 1990. 109–22.

Slayton, Robert L. *Back of the Yards: The Making of a Local Democracy.* Chicago: University of Chicago Press, 1986.

Sollors, Werner, ed. *Interracialism: Black-White Intermarriage in American History, Literature, and Law.* New York: Oxford University Press, 2000.

Soto, Shirlene. *Emergence of the Modern Mexican Woman: Her Participation in Revolution and Struggle for Equality, 1910–1940.* Denver: Arden Press, 1990.

Spinney, Robert G. *City of Big Shoulders: A History of Chicago.* DeKalb: Northern Illinois University Press, 2000.

Stansell, Christine. *City of Women: Sex and Class in New York, 1789–1860.* Urbana: University of Illinois Press, 1987.

Stavans, Ilán. "The Latin Phallus." In *The Latino Studies Reader: Culture, Economy, and Society.* Ed. Antonia Darder and Rodolpho D. Torres. Malden, Mass.: Blackwell, 1998. 228–39.

Stepan, Nancy Leys. *"The Hour of Eugenics": Race, Gender, and Nation in Latin America.* Ithaca, N.Y.: Cornell University Press, 1991.

Stern, Alexandra Minna. "Buildings, Boundaries, and Blood: Medicalization and Nation-Building on the U.S.–Mexico Border, 1910–1930." *Hispanic American Historical Review* 79.1 (1999): 41–81.

———. *Eugenic Nation: Faults and Frontiers of Better Breeding in Modern America.* Berkeley: University of California Press, 2005.

———. "Eugenics and Racial Classification in Modern Mexican America." In *Race and Classification: The Case of Mexican America.* Ed. Ilona Katzew and Susan Deans Smith. Stanford, Calif.: Stanford University Press, 2008.

———. "From Mestizophilia to Biotypology: Eugenics, Race, and Nationalism in Mexico, 1910–1950." In *Race and Nation in Modern Latin America.* Ed. Nancy Applebaum, Anne MacPherson, and Karin Rosemblatt. Chapel Hill: University of North Carolina Press, 2003. 187–210.

Stoler, Ann Laura. "Racial Histories and Their Regimes of Truth." *Political Power and Social Theory* 11 (1997): 183–206.

Stout, Joseph Allen. *Border Conflict: Villistas, Carrancistas, and the Punitive Expedition, 1915–1920.* Fort Worth: Texas Christian University Press, 1999.

Street, Paul. "The 'Best Union Members': Class, Race, Culture, and Black Worker Militancy in Chicago's Stockyards during the 1930s." *Journal of American Ethnic History* 20.1 (Fall 2000): 18.

Stutzman, Ronald. "El Mestizaje: An All-Inclusive Ideology of Exclusion." In *Cultural Transformations and Ethnicity in Modern Equador.* Ed. Norman E. Whitten Jr. Urbana: University of Illinois Press, 1981. 45–94.

Taibo, Paco Ignacio. *Dolores del Río, Mujer en el Volcán: Biografía.* Mexico City, D.F.: Planeta, 1999.

Tanenhaus, David S. *Juvenile Justice in the Making.* New York: Oxford University Press, 2004.

———. "Policing the Child: Juvenile Justice in Chicago, 1870–1925." Ph.D. dissertation, University of Chicago, 1997.

Taylor, Paul S. "Crime and the Foreign-Born." In *The Mexican Immigrant and the Problem of Crime and Criminal Justice.* Wickersham Commission. Washington, D.C.: Government Printing Office, 1931. 12–26.

———. *Mexican Labor in the United States: Chicago and the Calumet Region.* Vol. 7, no. 2. Berkeley: University of California Publications in Economics, 1932.

Thrasher, Frederic M. *The Gang: A Study of 1,313 Gangs in Chicago.* Chicago: University of Chicago Press, 1927.

Tillotson's Pocket Map and Street Guide of Chicago and Suburbs. Chicago: Winters Publishing Co., 1914.

Townsend, Andrew. "The Germans of Chicago." Ph.D. dissertation, University of Chicago, 1910.

Trotter, Joe William Jr., ed. *The Great Migration in Historical Perspective: New Dimensions of Race, Class, and Gender.* Bloomington: Indiana University Press, 1991.

Trotter, Robert T., and Juan Antonio Chavira. *Curanderismo.* Athens: University of Georgia Press, 1991.

Tuck, Jim. *The Holy War in Los Altos: A Regional Analysis of Mexico's Cristero Rebellion.* Tucson: University of Arizona Press, 1982.

Turner, John Kenneth. *Barbarous Mexico: An Indictment of a Cruel and Corrupt System.* 2d ed. New York: Cassell, 1912.

Tutino, John. *From Insurrection to Revolution in Mexico: Social Bases of Agrarian Violence, 1750–1940.* Princeton, N.J.: Princeton University Press, 1986.

Tuttle, William. *Race Riots: Chicago in the Red Summer of 1919.* Urbana: University of Illinois Press, 1970.

U.S. Bureau of the Census. *Abstract of the Fifteenth Census of the United States Taken in the Year 1930.* Washington, D.C.: Government Printing Office, 1933.

———. *Population Abstract of the United States.* McClean, Va.: Documents Index Incorporated, 1993.

———. *Two Hundred Years of United States Census Taking: Population and Housing Questions, 1790–1990.* Washington, D.C.: Government Printing Office, 1993.

U.S. Senate, 75th Congress, 1st session, pursuant to S. Res. 266 (74th Congress). "A Resolution to Investigate Violations of Free Speech and Assembly and Interference with the Right of Labor to Organize and Bargain Collectively." Part 14: The Chicago Memorial Day Incident, June 30, July 1–2, 1937. Washington, D.C.: Government Printing Office, 1937. 4944.

Valdés, Dennis Nodín. *Al Norte: Agricultural Workers in the Great Lakes Region, 1917–1970.* Austin: University of Texas Press, 1991.

———. *Barrios Norteños: St. Paul and Midwestern Mexican Communities in the Twentieth Century.* Austin: University of Texas Press, 2000.

———. "Betabeleros: The Formation of an Agricultural Proletariat in the Midwest, 1897–1930." *Labor History* 30 (Fall 1989): 536–62.

———. "Mexican Revolutionary Nationalism and Repatriation during the Great Depression." *Mexican Studies/Estudios Mexicanos* 4 (Winter 1988): 1–23.

Vargas, Zaragosa. *Labor Rights Are Civil Rights: Mexican American Workers in the Twentieth Century.* Princeton, N.J.: Princeton University Press, 2005.

———. *Proletarians of the North: A History of Mexican Industrial Workers in*

Detroit and the Midwest, 1917–1933. Berkeley: University of California Press, 1993.

Vasconcelos, José. *A Mexican Ulysses: An Autobiography.* Trans. Bloomington: Indiana University Press, 1963.

———. *La Raza Cósmica: Misión de la Raza Iberoamericana.* Paris: Agencia Mundial de Librería, 1925.

Vasconcelos, José, and Manuel Gamio. *Aspects of Mexican Civilization.* Chicago: University of Chicago Press, 1926.

Vaughan, Mary Kay. *Cultural Politics in Revolution: Teachers, Peasants, and Schools in Mexico, 1930–1940.* Tucson: University of Arizona Press, 1997.

———. *The State, Education, and Social Class in Mexico, 1880–1928.* DeKalb: Northern Illinois University Press, 1982.

Vitale, Luis. *La Larga Marcha por la Unidad y la Identidad Latinoamericana: De Bolívar al Che Guevara, Recuperando la Memoria Histórica.* Buenos Aires: Cucaña Ediciones, 2002.

Wade, Peter. *Blackness and Race Mixture: The Dynamics of Racial Identity in Colombia.* Baltimore: Johns Hopkins University Press, 1993.

———. *Race and Ethnicity in Latin America.* Serling, Va.: Pluto Press, 1997.

———. "Race and Nation in Latin America: An Anthropological View." In *Race and Nation in Modern Latin America.* Ed. Nancy Applebaum, Anne MacPherson, and Karin Rosemblatt. Chapel Hill: University of North Carolina Press, 2003. 263–82.

Warnshuis, Paul L. "Crime and Criminal Justice among the Mexicans of Illinois." In *The Mexican Immigrant and the Problem of Crime and Criminal Justice.* Wickersham Commission. Washington, D.C.: Government Printing Office, 1931. 284.

Weber, David S. "Anglo Views of Mexican Immigrants: Popular Perceptions and Neighborhood Realities in Chicago, 1900–1940." Ph.D. dissertation, Ohio State University, 1982.

Weber, Devra. *Dark Sweat, White Gold: California Farm Workers, Cotton, and the New Deal.* Berkeley: University of California Press, 1994.

Weber, Devra, Roberto Melville, and Juan Vicente Palerm, eds. *Manuel Gamio: El Inmigrante Mexicano; La Historia de Su Vida, Entrevistas Completas, 1926–1927.* México: Secretaría de Governación, 2002.

Weeks, John R., and Joseph Spielberg Benítez. "The Cultural Demography of Midwestern Chicano Communities." In *The Chicano Experience.* Ed. Stanley West and June Macklin. Boulder, Colo.: Westview Press, 1979. 229–51.

West, Stanley, and June Macklin, eds. *The Chicano Experience.* Boulder. Colo.: Westview Press, 1979.

Williams, Norma. *The Mexican American Family: Tradition and Change.* Dix Hills, N.Y.: General Hall, 1990.

Willrich, Michael. *City of Courts: Socializing Justice in Progressive Era Chicago.* New York: Cambridge University Press, 2003.

———. "'Close That Place of Hell': Poor Women and the Cultural Politics of Prohibition." *Journal of Urban History* 29.5 (July 2003): 555–74.

Wilson, Kay Diekman. "The Historical Development of Migrant Labor in Michigan Agriculture." M.A. thesis, Michigan State University, 1977.

Wirth, Louis. *The Ghetto.* Chicago: University of Chicago Press, 1928.

Woods, James G. "The Progressives and the Police: Urban Reform and the Professionalization of the Los Angeles Police." Ph.D. dissertation, University of California at Los Angeles, 1973.

Yu, Henry. *Thinking Orientals: Migration, Contact, and Exoticism in Modern America.* New York: Oxford University Press, 2001.

Zahrobsky, Mary. "The Slovaks in Chicago." M.A. Thesis, University of Chicago, 1924.

Zavella, Patricia. *Women's Work and Chicano Families: Cannery Workers of the Santa Clara Valley.* Ithaca, N.Y.: Cornell University Press, 1987.

INDEX

Page references in italics refer to illustrations

Ablaza, Dr., 193n221
Acculturation. *See* Americanization
Acosta, Antonio, 153
Acosta, Gladys Leavens Bunner, 153, 213n50
Activism: and deportation, 135; ethnic European, 203n23; of Mexican immigrants, 135–37, 158, 209n138; of Mexican women, 164; Polish, 142
Addams, Jane, 39, 189n108
Adventure, as motive for migration, 26, 27, 116
Agricultural workers, Mexican, 36; in beet-sugar industry, 23, 24–25; families, 34; prejudice against, 59
Aguirre, Enrique, 127, *127*
Aguirre, Zephyr, 127
Alanis, Fernando, 98
Alcala, José, 60, 190n131
Alcala, Pablo, 190n131
Alcántara, Camilo, 139
Alonzo, Aurelio, 99
Alonzo, Mauricio, 213n62
Alvarez, Francisca, 98
Amador, Armando C., 80, *152*; on citizenship, 92
Americanism: Chicago Mexicans and, 6, 12, 80–82, 105, 111, 129; continental, 80–81; exceptionalist, 81; freedom in, 124; hemispheric, 156; markers of, 6; of Mexican women, 6
Americanization, 83–90; Chicago venues for, 90; in churches, 85;

classes in, 86–87; cleanliness in, 87; dietary standards for, 87–88; education in, 84, 85; Eurocentric, 83, 172; food in, 87, 89, 197n41; gendered responses to, 88; institutional campaigns for, 203n2; of Mexican immigrants, 8, 80, 82, 83–90, 105, 107, 143; Mexican immigrants' response to, 88; of Mexican women, 83, 88, 90; nationalist model of, 101; organizations for, 84–85; Protestantism in, 85; and racialization, 110; steps toward, 6, 83; technical courses in, 87, 197n35; and upward mobility, 6; during World War II, 14
Americanness: of Chicanos, 195n3; and Mexican identity, 195n6; whiteness and, 82–83, 176n28, 191n151
Anticlericalism, Mexican, 161–62; of Mexican Revolution, 20–21
Arielism, 149; male bias in, 150
Armour Square Area (Chicago), Mexican population of, 48
Arredaro, Salvador, 58
Asian immigrants, 103; heterogeneity of, 175n12
Assimilationism, 2, 84
Association for the Unification and Defense of the Mexican Colony (Chicago), 158, 214n70
Aveleyra, Rafael, 78, 97–98, 99, 200n104; advocacy work of, 167, 216n120
Aviña, Enstolio, 66
El Azteca restaurant (South Chicago), 171

239

GABRIELA F. ARREDONDO is associate professor of Latin American and Latina/o studies at the University of California at Santa Cruz. She received her Ph.D. in history from the University of Chicago and is a fellow at the Center for the Comparative Study of Race and Ethnicity at Stanford University.

The University of Illinois Press
is a founding member of the
Association of American University Presses.

Composed in 9.5/12.5 Trump Mediaeval
by Celia Shapland
at the University of Illinois Press
Manufactured by Sheridan Books, Inc.

University of Illinois Press
1325 South Oak Street
Champaign, IL 61820-6903
www.press.uillinois.edu